Immanence and Micropolitics

Sartre, Merleau-Ponty, Foucault and Deleuze

Christian Gilliam

EDINBURGH
University Press

Edinburgh University Press is one of the leading university presses in the UK. We publish academic books and journals in our selected subject areas across the humanities and social sciences, combining cutting-edge scholarship with high editorial and production values to produce academic works of lasting importance. For more information visit our website: edinburghuniversitypress.com

© Christian Gilliam, 2017

Edinburgh University Press Ltd
The Tun – Holyrood Road
12(2f) Jackson's Entry
Edinburgh EH8 8PJ

Typeset in 10.5/13 pt Sabon by
Servis Filmsetting Ltd, Stockport, Cheshire

A CIP record for this book is available from the British Library

ISBN 978 1 4744 1788 4 (hardback)
ISBN 978 1 4744 1789 1 (webready PDF)
ISBN 978 1 4744 1790 7 (epub)

The right of Christian Gilliam to be identified as the author of this work has been asserted in accordance with the Copyright, Designs and Patents Act 1988, and the Copyright and Related Rights Regulations 2003 (SI No. 2498).

Immanence and Micropolitics

Series Editors: Alex Thomson, Benjamin Arditi, Andrew Schaap
International Advisory Editors: Michael Dillon, Michael J. Shapiro, Jeremy Valentine

Offering new perspectives on contemporary political theory, books in this series 'take on' the political in accordance with the ambivalent colloquial sense of the phrase – as both an acceptance and a challenge. They interrogate received accounts of the relationship between political thought and political practice, criticise and engage with the contemporary political imagination, and reflect on the ongoing transformations of politics. Concise and polemical, the texts are oriented towards critique, developments in Continental thought, and the crossing of disciplinary borders.

Titles in the *Taking on the Political* series include:

Polemicization: The Contingency of the Commonplace
Benjamin Arditi and Jeremy Valentine

Cinematic Political Thought
Michael Shapiro

Untimely Politics
Samuel A. Chambers

Speaking Against Number: Heidegger, Language and the Politics of Calculation
Stuart Elden

Post-Marxism versus Cultural Studies
Paul Bowman

Post-Foundational Political Thought: Political Difference in Nancy, Lefort, Badiou and Laclau
Oliver Marchart

Democratic Piety: Complexity, Conflict and Violence
Adrian Little

Gillian Rose: A Good Enough Justice
Kate Schick

Ethics and Politics after Poststructuralism: Levinas, Derrida and Nancy
Madeleine Fagan

Space, Politics and Aesthetics
Mustafa Dikeç

History and Event: From Marxism to Contemporary French Theory
Nathan Coombs

www.edinburghuniversitypress.com/series/totp

Contents

Preface and Acknowledgements	vii
Introduction	1
Ontology and Desire in Contemporary Thought	4
Chapter Outlines	14
1. Sartre and the Instigation of Immanence	21
The First Stage: Phenomenology and the Transcendental Ego	24
The Second Stage: the Body and Lived Experience	34
The Third Stage: the *Critique* and Sartre's Micropolitics	44
Existential Ethics and Immanent Freedom	49
Conceptual Limits	52
2. Merleau-Ponty and the Fold of the Flesh	56
The Crisis of Modern Thought	57
Phenomenology Reconsidered via the Body	62
Existential Ethics and Authenticity Revisited	69
Merleau-Ponty's Self-Criticism and Immanent Critique	76
Folded Flesh as n-dimensional Depth	79
Tender is the Flesh	89
3. Foucault and the Force of Power-Knowledge	95
The Order of Things and Foucault's Relation to Phenomenology	97
Archaeology and the Logic of Dispersion as Fold	101
From Archaeology to Genealogy	105
Power as Force Relation, Knowledge as Segment	107

	Double-Conditioning	114
	The Subject and Ethics	118
	From Pleasure to Desire	124
4.	Deleuze and the Micropolitics of Desire	131
	Transcendental Empiricism	133
	The Will to Power as Disjunctive Fold	137
	The Double-Axiom of Thought and Immanent Ethics	146
	Desiring-Production (*Micro*political)	152
	Social Production (*Macro*political)	154
	How to Become a Body without Organs/What Can a Body Do?	162
	Conclusion: From Immanence to Micropolitics	169
	The Three Disjunctions of Micropolitics	172
	The Three Disjunctions of Resistance	179
	A Dangerous Opportunity	183
Bibliography		188
Index		203

Preface and Acknowledgements

This book arises from the acknowledgment that in spite of numerous proclamations concerning the 'death of the subject', it lives on. Although one can locate several divergences in conceptual and normative orientation within contemporary political theory, the subject – including the identities by which it is coordinated and the institutions through which it travels – is still retained as the indispensable precondition of thought, meaning and action. It has thus become the *sine quo non* of politics. It is my view that such a vision of the political serves to obscure the genuine site of political transformation *and*, with its emphasis on a subject-identity-institution triad, assists the very power relations and macropolitical structures (bio-power, governmentality) that forestall genuine emancipatory work. The genuine site I have in mind is that of the 'micropolitical'. At its most basic, this can be understood in terms of the unconscious and affective self, the life of desire and libidinal attachment, which conditions our subjective experience of reality, preceding and determining the self in the guise of an ego and the identities by which it coordinates itself and thereby underpinning and directing our conscious deliberations and actions. Though such a life conditions reality it is simultaneously conditioned by the experience itself, typically in the form of macropolitical structures. There is as such no truly public-private distinction to be had, or nothing truly beyond that which we live in ultimate flux that can be relied upon as a pre-socio-political or extra-socio-political ground.

I arrived at this understanding of the micropolitical primarily through the works of Michel Foucault and Giles Deleuze, though it was significantly enhanced and shaped by my encounters with various other philosophers, especially Jean-Paul Sartre and Maurice Merleau-Ponty. The aforementioned develop extremely similar themes to Deleuze and Foucault, specifically in that they all employ an ontology of 'pure' immanence as a means of locating a pre-personal and pre-individual zone of political subjectivity and transformation, and insofar as they all place great emphasis on existential practices of the self as a form of authentic resistance to relations of power. What truly struck me in my readings, however, was the lack of coincidence in such similarity and the veritable fact that this has yet to be truly identified and discussed within the context of political philosophy.

The existentialism of Sartre and Merleau-Ponty – an existentialism continually viewed as antithetical to the 'poststructuralist' micropolitics of Foucault and Deleuze – inspires, underpins, shapes and makes sense of micropolitics. Thus, unlike previous works on micropolitics, which may be considered philosophically light or at least neglectful of the importance of ontology, this book provides its true philosophical context. This context, I hold, is *essential* to fully understanding the pertinence and efficacy of micropolitics as a politics without a subject. Indeed, it is precisely through neglecting the philosophical context of micropolitics, or rather the genealogy of the ontology of 'pure' immanence underpinning it, that even those writing within the micropolitical milieu have tended to retain some version of the subject-identity-institutional triad.

This book is clearly philosophical in tenor, inasmuch as it is conceptually concerned with our human 'being' (immanence) and the relation this has to socio-economic and political life. Yet, the book is also contemporary and concrete inasmuch as it situates this philosophical endeavour within the context of Westernised post-industrial societies. The macropolitical structures that condition the micropolitical and are conditioned by it are themselves shaped and underpinned by the axiomatic of capital. There is a real, enduring and inescapable materialism to this philosophy. In this sense, I envision a strong connection between my project and Marxism. Indeed, in addition to Nietzsche, Marx is to this book what the spectre is to the feast. He is the haunting shadow, the background figure that casts itself over the work. And though rarely mentioned directly, he shapes much of the book's meaning and significance. We can venture to say, in fact, that my project is an emancipatory one, for it seeks to provide the conceptual basis for overturning the destructiveness of Westernised post-industrial capitalism. But what makes this project different from *dialectical* materialism, is that it does not emphasise contradiction and negation. It emphasises instead 'folded' or 'disjunctive' relations. This entails an entirely different understanding of the nature of power and resistance. Power is not negative or anti-energy, but a productive force relation operating on, with and through desire, or our virtual self. Resistance, then, is not a mere question of negating powers of government through social movement, democratic endeavour and so forth. Though such activity can and has no doubt proven efficacious, it is not primary. True resistance concerns engaging with practices of the self, working through power relations via desire, so as to bring about a fundamental change to the very self that such relations of power are reliant upon. That is to say, we must change ourselves before we can hope to change our politics.

The justification, if you will, for such a politics is also different from traditional Marxism. It is one consistent with the epistemological element of immanence that dictates there is no transcendent vantage point or metaphysical crunch upon which we could build a reliable moral code or system. Though this may imply nihilism, immanence invites us to consider the value of life-affirmation, which entails the affirmation of the creative becoming that, as I will come to argue, defines our 'virtual unconscious' self, i.e. desire. That is, to affirm life as it is out there and for us, beyond existential reproach and *ressentiment*. To ask life to justify itself under the auspices of reason—what greater nihilism could there be? To respect and even celebrate the radical, fundamental difference, the creative becoming it entails and effuses, is the true mark of affirmation and the true antidote to nihilism. And yet, it is this creative becoming that is most at stake in post-industrial capitalism. The creative becoming of the self is continually supressed and manipulated in the interests of sustaining economic growth and stability. In less opulent parts of the world, humans are deprived even of the most basic material and opportunities for life. Then of course there is its unrelenting destruction of the environment. Capitalism is inherently life-negating. It is an existential threat, and thus its overturning far exceeds the concerns of contemporary ethics. It is not a question of right and wrong, but a simple question of life itself, of the survival of its productive, abundant and creative capacities. My view, to put it more directly, is that capitalism threatens precisely that which is the precondition of bio-social evolution and, related to it, a more open, sustainable and affirming society and world.

Affirming life entails affirming those with whom we share it and who fill out our own. We are all multiple selves, after all; a multiplicity of a multiplicity. This work, and its author, is no exception. There are a myriad of people and encounters, some direct and easily recognisable, others indirect and discreet, that have influenced every utterance found inside the pages of this book. With regards to the direct and recognisable, I must profess how truly grateful I am to my family, especially my mother, father and brother. Aside from always inspiring and encouraging me, they provided love and support in true abundance and to the best of their ability. Indeed, they taught me in both practice and deed how to affirm life, holistically and without inquisitive nihilism. My friends, in a seemingly though unintentionally Epicurean manner, have also been instrumental in this regard. Chief among them: Alex, Dan, Gunseli, Iz, John, Kostas, Miles, Nick, Sana, Steph and my PhD friends from Royal Holloway.

I would like to thank Dr Alex Thompson for giving me the opportunity to contribute to the *Taking on the Political* series with Edinburgh University Press and for his invaluable input in this project. I would also like to express my sincere gratitude to Professor Nathan Widder. He proved himself both a wonderful mentor and an honourable friend. I am particularly thankful for the amount of time and effort he put into the manuscript in its PhD form, meticulously reading and considering every word, line and thought, and for the respect and patience he showed to my ever-changing and progressing ideas. In addition to Nathan, I would like to thank members of the Royal Holloway Cotemporary Political Theory Research Group, particularly regarding their input throughout the *Anti-Oedipus* sessions, as well as Dr Michael Bacon, Professor William Connolly, Dr Iain MacKenzie, Professor Paul Patton, Dr Jonathan Seglow and Dr Henry Somers-Hall. All those mentioned have aided my understanding of contemporary political theory and philosophy, namely by way of conversation, feedback and inspiration. Finally, I would like to thank Palgrave Macmillan, who kindly gave me permission to reproduce sections of the following article: 'Sartre as a Thinker of (Deleuzian) Immanence: Prefiguring and Complementing the Micropolitical', in *Contemporary Political Theory*, doi:10.1057/cpt.2016.2 (1 March 2016).

Introduction

It is often supposed that politics operates by way of conscious deliberation and the rational pursuit of an interest of some kind. There are innumerable instances, historical and contemporary, that immediately put this view into doubt. Instances that warrant a closer examination of the nature of the human subject at the centre of such deliberation. It is apparent that in the Westernised world, the working class seldom vote for political parties or pursue political matters representative of their real interests. Indeed, this touches on one of the most pertinent questions of our time: how has capitalism managed to live on and thrive despite the rapid acceleration of its exploitative and destructive tendencies following the 2008 financial crash; despite causing intense techno-scientific transformations that threaten great ecological disequilibrium; despite having caused a deterioration of individual and collective human modes of life; despite prompting a regressive infantilisation of all social relations; despite pushing the world into a new, dangerous form of global apartheid; and despite nullifying creative endeavours by forcing us into a prison of financially expedient cultural codification and standardised mediocrity? My primary and overriding ambition in this book, is to offer a conceptual – that is to say philosophical – answer to this question. In so doing, I challenge the terms by which we have come to understand 'the political', political power and political praxis. I push forward a *post*-capitalist (note: not 'anti-') emancipatory project that is a-subjective as opposed to subject-centred; a-systematic as opposed to anti-system; and post-identity as opposed to identity-centred. This is a politics that locates and demands the transformation of our selves *within* and *through* capitalist relations of power and the material and social excesses it conjures – below the level of subject positions, identities and

2 Immanence and Micropolitics

institutions – as a prerequisite to the transformation of our 'politics', in its more traditional, grander sense.

My ambition is preceded and shaped by Marxist thinking on the one hand, and philosophical matters relating to human ontology on the other. Marx conceptualised the continuation of capitalism in the face of its exploits, in terms of 'ideology', i.e. the political manipulation of definitive forms of social consciousness, or quite simply our 'ideas' and thus our intersubjective understandings of our material world, by which the economic and political interests of a *particular* class – typically the bourgeoisie as owners of the means of production – are presented and accepted as *universal*, natural and eternal. This relates to Marx's infamous topology: *base-superstructure*. The economic base of which the bourgeoisie are key benefactors and representatives determines the legal and political superstructure which corresponds to and is supported by ideology. Despite the seemingly deterministic nature of this conceptualisation, however, Marx and classical Marxist scholars argued that the contradictions and exploitation inherent to industrial capitalism (e.g. alienation, anarchy in production/overproduction, monopolisation, and dead labour) would become so extreme as to lead to a fundamental questioning and thus disruption of the dominant ideology. When combined with the proletariatisation of the middle classes and the peasantry and the mass urbanisation of the proletariat, the subjugated workers would be led away from a false state of social consciousness towards an organised, identifiable and homogenous *class consciousness*. The proletariat revolution would begin in earnest.

The revolutions Marx had predicted (in England, in Germany), however, never truly materialised. Only in pre-industrialised, pre-urbanised and mostly agricultural nations, such as Russia, and more bizarrely China, did the 'revolution' occur. The immediate question, then, was this: how did the revolution fail to materialise in the industrialised West, as prophesised? Neo-Marxist scholars, as exemplified and influenced by Antonio Gramsci, turned to an argument that, though surprisingly simple, changed the face of twentieth-century thought. It was maintained that ideology, as propagated in civil society and exercised primarily through cultural means, is far more efficacious in its ability to normalise and justify exploitation among the exploited than Marx had reckoned. For Gramsci, ideology so defined had turned the alien interests and ideas of the capitalists into the 'common sense' or the commonly held assumptions concerning the nature of the material world, thereby garnering active 'consent' for the valuative basis of its functioning. As a number of sociologists (e.g. Mannhein) and critical theorists (e.g. Ardono and Horkheimer) added, ideology is the primary instrument of social reproduction. Mid-twentieth-century French Structuralists, specifically Louis Althusser, expanded heavily on these themes and played up their anti-humanist undertones. Specifically, Althusser maintained that ideology exists in material practices that serve to produce, or rather *constitute*, subjects.[1] In turn, ideology becomes the product of those practices, inasmuch as it produces subjects who, while always already inculcated, *misrecognise* themselves as volitional and act within the confines of and comply with institutional and disciplinary rules on that illusory basis. Ideology, in this case, is not just simply the power of ideas, but also and chiefly the unconscious power of subjectification.[2]

This turn to the question of subjectivity itself, or rather the political determination of our being and its relation to global capitalism, signifies a more resolute and profound connection between political theory and human ontology: the study of the fundamental aspects of *being* human, or, as Heidegger put it, our 'being-in-the-world' and the relation this has to politics. This concern with being has remained and grown exponentially and primarily through the post-*Marxist*[3] ambition to rescue crucial aspects of Marxist thought from the collapse of Marxism as a global cultural and political force, and reimagine such aspects so as to encompass democratic anxieties and new intellectual movements. Specifically, where neo-Marxists indebted to Grasmci focus on pre-conscious interests, post-Marxists incorporate elements of psychoanalytic theory, such as the 'unconscious libidinal investments' of desire, into an analysis of the formation and role of political identity and subjectivity as related to ideology and discourse; where structuralists emphasise processes of signification of desire, identity and subjectivity in terms of structural determination beyond agentic or volitional rupture, post-Marxists incorporate elements of poststructuralism that emphasise the excess inherent within the signifying and subjectificating process; and where Marx's topology and historical materialism had arguably reduced all struggles and therefore questions of subjectivity to that of class, post-Marxists incorporate elements of democratic theory and Nietzschean genealogy to favour a more pluralistic and asynchronistic take on historical struggle.

The central point here, as far as I am concerned, is that there exists an agentic-affective dimension to political subjectivity, situated within historically and socially contingent relations of power-knowledge and lying behind and often constituting pre-conscious interests, ideas and of course conscious thought. This dimension, or layer, denotes the primary site of constitution *and* transformation of political subjectivity and thus politics more generally. Indeed, we not only hold ideas and discourses alien to our interests, we *desire* those ideas and discourses. And even when we do not desire such ideas, such discourses, or even when our pre-conscious interests and self-professed political identification is, say, antithetical to capitalism, we can still desire and thus operate in a manner that is conducive to its functioning. That is also to say, we can and do come to desire our own repression. Such an image of the self simultaneously challenges the Kantian apodictic experience of morality as law, as that which flows from the noumenal to the phenomenal real, as well as the Rawlsian models of procedural justice, insofar as both rely on the supposed self-transparency and pre-social rationality of conscious thought. Even that which we take to be morally intuitive and procedurally rational, and even our most private and intimate sense of self, reflects a socially configured, politically charged and thus produced desire or unconscious layer of thinking. Unconscious desire, then, is primary in terms of understanding contemporary politics, political transformation and emancipation – which signifies how the question of the self is central to my opening question and overriding aim. There are two very different ways to conceptualise such unconscious libidinal investments, and thus two different ways to construe the political significance of desire, which arise from two quite different ontologies, i.e. ontologies of transcendence on the one hand and ontologies of immanence on the other. The starting point of our emancipatory project, then, touches on an ontological divergence.

Ontology and Desire in Contemporary Thought

The post-Marxist tradition, as I have defined it, intersects with and simultaneously influences what has come to be known in Anglo-American contemporary political theory, as the 'ontological turn'. Ontology, in its broadest sense, refers to the 'science of being', as in the study of the basic categories of existence. The ontological turn I refer to, concerns human ontology, as in the study of our human *being*. An ontological turn may sound rather odd to those well versed in the Continental tradition of political philosophy, for human ontology has long been at the forefront of it, specifically since Martin Heidegger's seminal *Being and Time*. But the same is not true of Anglo-American academia, where, in the immediate aftermath of the Second World War, there was a flagrant turn to a brute form of 'ontological minimalism' in the guise of 'anti-metaphysics'; or rather, a rejection of ontology as conflated with what Isaiah Berlin (2002: 190) called 'metaphysical rationalism'.[4] Only in the 1980s did Anglo-American thought begin to consider ontological matters, and even then only to a limited degree.[5] Recent theoretical debates in Anglo-American academia have since expanded on this foray into human ontology, namely by drawing on, and contributing to, the post-Marxist concern with desire. In so doing, these debates have changed completely the terms by which we come to understand political subjectivity as primarily related to matters of hegemony, democracy and pluralism; known as 'theories of radical democracy', or alternatively the 'third element' of contemporary political theory (the first being liberalism, the second communitarianism).[6] Indeed, I would argue that 'post-Marxism' as a signifying label is now synonymous with this 'third element'. This element, and so post-Marxism, is often subdivided into theories of lack and theories of abundance, though both relate to and hinge on the aforementioned ontological divide between transcendence and immanence.

Transcendence refers to that which is external or other, as opposed to internal, and thus to that which conditions from above, beyond or outside. This is a tradition central to Continental philosophy, starting with Plato in antiquity. But unlike previous 'positive' understandings of transcendence as it figures in Plato's ideal Form of the Good, Judeo-Christian perfect divinity, and to a certain extent Cartesianism and fragments of German idealism, the contemporary notion of transcendence as personified by what has already been identified as post-Marxist or radical theories of 'lack' utilises instead a *negative* conception. It is maintained that an unnameable and unrepresentable 'beyond' stands as the groundless ground for subjectivity, constituting a subject as responsible before some law. Thus, the *form* of transcendence is retained even while positive figures of transcendence are rejected.

In reading Lacan with Hegel, for instance, Slavoj Žižek's basic contention is that subjectivity emerges from contradiction or a withdrawal from reality. Connecting this position more generally with Kant and German idealism, Žižek argues that the All of reality, which exists in itself, has to be rejected as a paralogism – what is viewed as an epistemological limitation is in fact the ontological condition of reality itself. But where Kantian transcendentalism envisions a gap or split between the phenomenal and noumenal, Žižek envisions a split between a symbolic identity and the noumenal-like force of desire constituted by lack. That is, while the process of identification with a signifier in language is indispensable to the foundation of the individual and political subject (i.e. Althusserian ideology), a *lack* inherent to language itself or a gap between identification and identity ensures the continual failure of identity to achieve complete determination, and thus for social objectivity to be fully constituted.

Ideology (particularly ideologies of capitalism) offers the impossible (and thus the fantasy of) concealment of this irrevocable inconsistency, out of which the very desire for the concealment is born. That is, following the Lacanian formula, *desire is desire for that which we lack* in the signifying process, attached to an unattainable and imaginary object of fullness or the something missing (the *objet petit a*), as forbidden to the social by *that* authority or group.[7] This means, in turn, that emancipation from ideology requires identifying oneself with the gap and thus engaging with a *death drive* or will for something different. On an institutional level, emancipation requires that democratic politics continues to keep open, extend and radicalise the gap, and thereby forestall and impede any ideological impulse or promise to fill it— what Lefort calls the *empty place of power*. Indeed, it is through the ceaseless tussle to temporarily occupy this place that antagonists can achieve temporary constructions of efficacious collective political subjectivity. As Laclau is famed for arguing, a *particular* group can invert the hegemonic ideology (an ideology that may very well prevent the institutionalisation of lack) by establishing a 'chain of equivalence' with differing political interests and identities, via the entirely negative instance of an identified mutual interlocutor, the big Other, as an alternative forbidder responsible for the impossibility of social fullness.

The point is that there is still a need for some form of a temporarily centred *subject* with a sense of its identity and an appropriate institution to bolster its capacity to act.[8] Or rather, this is a politics that requires circumnavigating the paradox of the partial and incomplete nature of identity (lack) and the indispensability of identity (fullness) and the subject to which it relates, for political action and emancipatory practices that seek to institutionalise such lack. Privileging this level of 'politics', however, seems to me partial, abstract and ultimately counter-productive. It is my contention that an ontology of 'pure' immanence develops an alternative, enduring and necessary post-identity and a-subjective conceptualisation of political resistance and emancipation, a conceptualisation that reveals formations of identity and the subject to which such formations correspond as precisely that which – when taken as the *sine qua non* of political resistance – forestalls authentic resistance. We must change ourselves, change our desire and thus our mode of thinking, before we can hope to change our politics and thus before we can hope to overturn capitalism. Of course, democratic and hegemonic politics premised on negotiations of identity can and do yield results. But this level of politics is not primary in terms of the formation of subjectivity upon which it relies and thus it is not completely efficacious in terms of understanding power and articulating genuine resistance to it. The politics of immanence is.

Rooted in the thought of Spinoza and the ancient Stoics on the nature of divinity, immanence refers to a state of being internal or remaining within, in which the condition (e.g. God) does not transcend but rather is in the conditioned (e.g. existence). Thus immanence presents a philosophy in which existence is not dependent on a higher power external to it. Remaining at the level of this broad definition, Hegel's dialectic of identity, the Lacanian notion of desire that it is premised on, and thus theories of lack, may be said to develop an *ontological* immanence, according to which the difference between for-itself and in-itself is itself 'for us'; that is, the distinction between the noumenal and phenomenal is experienced in the immanence of our thought.[9] What separates contemporary philosophies of immanence from contemporary philosophies of transcendence is the conceptual application of immanence to the formal structure and conditioning of subjectivity. This results in a notion of subjectivity without a subject – 'a life' as Giles Deleuze (2001: 27), our chief protagonist, puts it – in which the (pre)conditions[10] of experience are derived from experience itself, as opposed to the paralogic inconsistency, the second-order difference that arises from their relation. The conditions of experience remain within experience, without negative rupture. In more technical terms, this means that the apparently *a priori* transcendental conditions that allow us to make sense of experience in a meaningful and cogent manner are construed in terms of unconscious and thus pre-personal and pre-individual form-generating resources, which are derived from experience itself; an experience of a material Outside world that provokes such resources and through which they are expressed. Deleuze comes to conceptualise this immanent and unconscious life in terms of a 'virtual multiplicity', for it speaks, to put it simply, to a series of differential psychic relations that are real, though prior to expression, i.e. not actual.

In his works with Guattari, Deleuze maintains that the 'virtual multiplicity' of subjectivity is one of *desire* or vital affectivity. Desire, once again, returns to the fore. And in continuing to hold that the virtual multiplicity, now the virtual-affective (desire) conditions of experience, is derived from experience itself, Deleuze and Guattari go on to construe it as a force that is open to and thus always already assembled by a series of complex experiential relations pertaining to an *immanent* Outside or *actual* multiplicity. What is more, this Outside is a material, political and socio-economic one, which means *desire is always already political*. Through micro-desire, then, the self can be shaped, below and constituting conscious awareness and segmented identities, in the interests of, though often affecting in turn, a broad variety of political strategies. *This, to be sure, is what micropolitics is*. The microscopic, hidden, virtual constitutive factor of the self upon which political relations of power and formations act and rely. And though still maintaining that we may come to desire our own repression, it is through this immanent concept of micro-desire, that Deleuze and Guattari come to reject Lacan's understanding of desire in terms of lack, in favour of abundance. Desire does not lack anything. In fact, it is abundant in its productive energy. It produces our experience of reality, and in accordance with social production, or relations of power-knowledge, as Michel Foucault would put it. It is productive and produced. Lack certainly exists, but it is not ontologically primary or constitutive. Lack is manufactured, or developed in desire, often for the purpose of serving post-industrial economies that are reliant on the unnecessary and excessively frivolous consumption of goods.

Contemporary thinkers of transcendence/lack, primarily Slavoj Žižek (2012a: 28), argue that the distinction, and producer-produced relationship between the virtual life of desire and the actual socio-political Outside, amounts to an ontological deadlock. Either the virtual is the *cause* of material effects, of the actual (the idealist pole); or it is the *effect* of material causes (the materialist pole). It cannot logically be both. In the first case, the virtual Life is elevated to a new name of the pure flux of Becoming as the only true encompassing Whole, the One-ness of Being itself, i.e. what Deleuze, following Duns Scotus, refers to as Univocity. That is, the virtual is conceptualised as the original, primary constitutive site of everything and thus as prior to and the determining factor of the actual world of reified distinct entities and differences, i.e. beings. As with Plato's intelligible Good, it is taken as a self-contained unity, with nothing above it, and nothing outside of it that can affect it. Indeed, in the vein of Badiou's infamous critique of Deleuze, Žižek (ibid.: 25) claims Deleuze returns to a kind of 'Plotinian process of emanation'. Sense is relegated to that of a *shadowy effect* of the immanent production of the One. Thus, although a transcendent One, univocal Being is still immanent unto itself, which is also to say it has no real Outside or Other. We are provided with a domain of complete inclusivity of differences, a pipedream of harmony, wherein all substantial identities through which the political and political subjectivity is constituted, coordinated and (re)articulated, are dissolved it into a network of non-substantial, differential relations.[11] In the second case, the Sense-Event, the flow of pure Becoming, is the immaterial effect of the intrication of bodily-material causes. The positive bodily entities are themselves the product of the pure flow of Becoming. This is held to be utterly *apolitical* inasmuch as it evokes structuralism in its inability to account for the production of the new, or the very dialectical rupture or void that accounts for the Event, i.e. where an effect can exceed its cause, so that although an act emerges through power (and is as such inherent to it), it can outgrow and explode it, such that it can be ontologically 'higher' than its cause.

Aside from presenting an inconsistency, both poles eschews the very 'gap in immanence', as personified by the negative subject of lack and the inexplicable Other, through which we can conceptualise the paralogism of reality, the impossibility of society and, in turn, the possibility of 'the political' (ibid.). Deleuze and Guattari's *Anti-Oedipus* – where the virtual is first transformed into desire – is held to signify a misguided attempt to bypass the ontological deadlock and subsequent apoliticism of Deleuze's metaphysics, through an accelerated embrace of the idealist pole via desire as a pre-linguistic libidinal flux, as the new pure flow of Becoming of a productive monistic one. This is said to generate, quite ironically, a dualism which 'bears witness to the fact that his [Deleuze's] process of Becoming is itself secretly anchored in a unified Subject' (ibid.:

64). Deleuze and Guattari's resistive ethic of becoming a *Body without Organs*, is read in terms of returning to the One of desire, as if to return to Plato's Good, and thus opposing all dualisms that seek to obscure it by divvying it up and separating it from itself.[12] In this way, *Anti-Oedipus* is seen to overdetermine the Hegelian 'void' in/of immanence (the interstice out of which the subject emerges) as a purely virtual entity, reducing the subject to (just another) substance and designating the re-emergence of the virtual within the order of actuality (ibid.: 61–2). The subject is related to Becoming and substance to Being. And although guised in a language that evokes 'the old Leftist radicalism linked to a philosophical idealist subjectivism' (ibid.: 28) – as in the resistance to a structure that represses the primordial essentialist entity (desire) – the related emphasis on aesthetic 'micro' experiments of desire as a means of becoming a BwO (a Body without Organs), is charged with bringing about a flaccid renewal of bourgeois narcissism, transforming Deleuze 'into an ideologist of today's "digital capitalism"' (ibid.: xxii). Immanence, then, would simply amount to yet another theoretical path that feigns radicalism, but in fact props up capitalist modes of being.

But what such a reading fundamentally misses – and what has yet to be properly addressed in the related literature – is that the distinction between the virtual and the actual does not amount to an ontological deadlock or dualism, such as the dualism between the One and the Many, or the virtual and the actual, '*but on the contrary, of distinguishing two types of multiplicities*', or rather two types of *production* that form a continuum (Deleuze 1991: 39). The virtual and actual share the same nature, differing only in regime. And the difference in regime *does not exclude the immanence of each to the other*. This conceptual logic, present in Deleuze's early *Difference and Repetition*, forms the conceptual basis for *Anti-Oedipus* and thus the micropolitics of desire. Thus we are given a dynamic relation, upon where microscopic relations of desire can sustain or subvert the power of authority, or macro structures, while these very authorities and structures can exercise their powers in ways that strengthen or undermine the microscopic relations of desire upon which they rely. The one is always in the other, in a dance of immanent causality (where the cause is in the effect); what Foucault (1998: 99) refers to as the principle of 'double-conditioning'. In Deleuze and Guattari's second work, *A Thousand Plateaus*, this entire process is conceptualised and expanded through the concept of the 'assemblage',[13] i.e. a thoroughly heterogeneous ensemble that synthesises and thus consists of divergent multiplicities, be they biological, social, machinic, gnoseological or imaginary, often underpinned and partly shaped by a broader socio-historical substratum, i.e. the axiomatic of capital (capitalism). Each assemblage of 'desire', then, has elements or multiplicities of several kinds, with different elements interpenetrating one another. For this reason, Deleuze and Guattari claim that it is the *assemblage* of both the micro and the macro that is the province of the unconscious, 'the way in which the former condition the latter, and the latter prepare the way for the former or elude them or return to them' (Deleuze and Guattari 2004b: 39). As William Connolly (2002) argues, desire and the micropolitical layer of thinking more generally, can be socially produced in reactive ways, containing sentiments and ways of being that forestall the affirming energies of abundance as genuine love of life-as-difference beyond existential reproach.[14]

This might, in turn, suggest a harmonious circularity between multiplicities, between the conditions of experience and experience itself, between virtual Inside and actual Outside or simply the Other. If that were indeed so, we would still be deprived of the rupture of the Event.[15] But what is significant about a different notion of immanence that I maintain develops from Sartre, Merleau-Ponty and Foucault, and reaches its culmination in Deleuze, is that, despite superficial appearances, it cannot be defined in terms of harmony between the conditions of experience and experience itself. 'Pure' immanence as construed by these four thinkers, entails a notion of a socio-political Outside or Other, and a corresponding excess or disturbance, pluralisation of differences greatly exceeding the representational capacities of language and, as Hardt and Negri (2000) argue, the large-scale contemporary forms of power that produce it, i.e. what they identify as an 'Empire' of global capital.[16] But it is an Other radically reconfigured in terms of a *fold of Being*, as opposed to Hegelian 'holes' of nothingness. The fold is perhaps the central component of the notion of immanence I am advancing via the four thinkers, inasmuch as it denotes a *disjunctive synthesis* that allows one to construct a relational ontology, without for all that evoking negativity and as such a real or formal transcendence.

A disjunctive fold refers to a sort of synthesis that relates divergent series and differences, between and within the Inside/Outside, without subsuming them into a higher dialectical unity, or collapsing them into a total non-relation. It is a synthesis that bypasses the old dichotomy between order and chaos, Apollo and Dionysus. We can, initially at least, understand the fold in a literal manner, as in the folding of a piece of paper. A rather fruitful idea if we are to understand the paper as interchangeable for Being. Two marks on diagonally opposing corners of a piece of A4 paper may be distinguished by their negative difference, in that this primarily demarcates respective locations or identities. Unassuming as the point may seem, it is notable that the opposing marks are still of the same paper, for it is by virtue of this that if I were to fold one side of the paper over to the other, the two opposing marks would still retain their negative difference in one dimension, while gaining a closer connection in another. If this idea of folding is applied to multiple spatial dimensions, as we find in non-Euclidean *n*-dimensional space (and even multiple temporal dimensions), then we can image a highly complex relation of folds as a generative and constitutive process, which is always immanent to itself, and as such beyond any notion of a metaphysical Outside or transcendent Other. We can fold a piece of paper in multiple ways via multiple dimensions so as to generate new divergent relations between and within the marks on it and even the form of the paper itself. Yet the paper shall remain, with no need of extrinsic dimensions. Opposition between two things may still exist, but it is not constitutive or conceptually holistic, inasmuch as it will never delineate the multiple/other meanings or senses that exist between them.[17] An origami.

It is by virtue of this synthetic concept that Deleuze asserts that *Being is difference*. This is a substantial caveat to the notion that being is Univocal or One. As we saw, many have interpreted the One of immanence (or simply 'univocity') in terms of Platonist emanation. Deleuze does indeed claim that all modalities and differences, all individuals and substances, are expressions of a single ontological substance: 'Being is said in a single and same sense, of all its individuating differences or intrinsic modalities' (Deleuze 2004a: 45). That is to say, there is no difference of category, of substance and of form, between the senses of the word 'Being', e.g. for-itself and in-itself, or, ultimately, the *subject* and *object*. But, and this is the crucial point, the single ontological substance relates to itself through a series of disjunctive differentials between and within multiplicities, and it is only by virtue of this differential that it can create differenciated or qualitative distinctions in Being, i.e. beings. The single and same sense is difference in-itself and thus the expression of the multiple, as opposed to the monotony of the One. This point may seem quite distant from the concerns of politics. And yet, it is precisely this univocal, 'pure', disjunctive, immanent take on Being which provides the conceptual basis of a politics without a subject, be it in terms of a positive Body or negative rupture; a politics beyond identity of emancipatory politics, be it essential or differential; and a politics beyond anti-system, oppositional politics. Politically efficacious subjects and the identities by which they are coordinated are constituted in a disjunctive immanent, socio-political relation between the micro–macro continuum of univocity (assemblage). Political resistance is found within this relation. Constituted within, resist within. There is no negative in the first instance.

I believe that this connection between 'pure' immanence and micropolitics so conceived, as far as the concept is concerned, is best understood and appreciated by exploring the genesis or contextual development of the former and *how* and *why* it led to the latter. The point being, of course, that micropolitics is not an arbitrary construction pursued in the interests of propping up bourgeois narcissism, and neither does it arise from arbitrary ontological navel-gazing or an ontological inconsistency. 'Pure' immanence comes as the result of a series of philosophical quagmires, political ambiguities and difficulties that propel new conceptualisations. All this is tantamount to claiming that philosophy, as human ontology, is inseparable from politics – a case I hope will be made more resolute throughout the book.

Thus my post-capitalist emancipatory aspirations are related to the micropolitics of desire, which is hinged on an ontological of immanence. To understand micropolitics, we must understand immanence. And to best understand immanence, we must trace its development. Most philosophical studies that focus on the genealogy of immanence, especially as it is construed by Deleuze, tend to trace its genealogical roots in Kant, Hegel and Spinoza.[18] Though such thinkers are clearly integral to the development of 'pure' immanence, it is my contention, as already suggested, that the transcendental (i.e. the disjunctive Other and its relation to the self) and political aspect of 'pure' immanence (a-subjective and post-identity) truly begins with Sartre, and is carried forth by Merleau-Ponty and Foucault, ultimately leading to Deleuze and his concept of the micropolitics of desire. And although the a-subjective forms of political resistance inherent to micropolitics – as well as its ontological underpinnings – have been articulated before, I believe that by neglecting this genealogy (Sartre and Merleau-Ponty in particular), said studies have yet to articulate these forms of resistance at an adequate level of nuance, failing to draw the crucial connection between existential ethics and micropolitical resistance, and often downplaying the point that we are micropolitical before we are political.[19]

Chapter Outlines

A common thread of immanence unites Sartre, Merleau-Ponty, Foucault and Deleuze; it informs their relations to one another (in terms of what each one picks up and discards from his predecessors), and unifies them in a shared attempt to reconceptualise the terms by which the political is thought. The theme of immanence acts as the primary catalyst or dark precursor to their thought as a whole. Though presented as an evolutionary chronology in the sense that it outlines a series of progressive moves from Sartre to Deleuze, the lineage works by way of a number of productive misreadings each thinker makes of the others. Where a thinker such as Sartre or Merleau-Ponty may have failed to go *far enough* in terms of immanence (either due to restrictions in language or an under-theorisation of force), their successors, such as Foucault, overreach by envisioning the earlier thinkers as *fully trapped* in transcendence. This sort of relation establishes practical foils, in return creating space for new conceptual additions and philosophical advances. In this respect, the lineage accords with Nietzsche's comparison of 'the thinker to an arrow shot by Nature, that another thinker picks up where it has fallen so that he can shoot it somewhere else' (Deleuze 2006b: viii). Each arrow is taken up in part through a misunderstanding, or at least a strained understanding.

Each chapter shall therefore be dedicated to one of these thinkers, with the conclusion identifying the thematic links, so as to present a consistent post-capitalist emancipatory project. With this in mind, the first chapter investigates how Sartre instigates the first few moves of 'pure' immanence. Through following the progression of Sartre's thought, we will come to see a deepening engagement with immanence, which ultimately sets the foundation upon which the later thinkers build. In his early period, Sartre reworks Husserlian intentionality to bring about a repudiation of the transcendental ego. Following on from this, in *Being and Nothingness* and the

Critique, he develops a dialectic in which consciousness, while relating to an 'outside', is construed as also thoroughly embedded in that outside through the subject-body of the flesh and relations of desire. From this comes a conceptualisation of the in-itself and for-itself as simulacra or topological variations of a more primordial intertwining or fabric of univocal Being. In this sense, we are immediately taken away from the subject of social contract theory, insofar as this presumes an asocial self, and the notion of identity as the *sine qua non* of politics, insofar as this presumes the terrain of an inexplicable transcendent Other. This brings with it a new take on politics as an ethical practice – one that will be taken up and extended by the other three thinkers – in which we do not look for a transcendent outside or fracture/break in immanence through which to ground resistance, but rather work *through* and experiment with our situation or condition.

In the second chapter, we turn to Merleau-Ponty to see how, working through a number of issues with Sartre, phenomenology and modern thought more generally, he deepens Sartre's engagement with immanence and the notion of the subject-body and perceptual consciousness as the condition of meaning, negativity and action. Through tracing this development, the chapter elucidates the way in which it sets the basis for Merleau-Ponty's later work. In moving away from the subject-body or an exploration of the phenomenal body to a more direct ontological enquiry into the appearing of the visible-tactile (the actual) field itself, the later works develop an anti-humanist ontology that locates perceiving bodies within a meaning-generating flesh, where the reversibility of Being as 'flesh' establishes a generativity which is always immanent unto itself and as such beyond any notion of a metaphysical transcendent Outside or transcendent Other. It is here that the Outside/Other is first construed as a disjunctive *fold* of immanence itself. Critically, through this Merleau-Ponty provides a conceptual language that avoids the theoretical snares of the traditional dualist language evoked by Sartre, and lays much of the groundwork for the 'pure' immanence of Foucault and Deleuze.

In contrast to Sartre and Merleau-Ponty, Foucault and Deleuze are recognised as avowed thinkers of 'pure' immanence, and because of this they tend to separate themselves from Sartre and Merleau-Ponty by emphasising the latter's continued moments of transcendence, even to the point of caricature. Subsequently, they face the criticisms outlined earlier of being incoherent and of being unable to mount a politics. In Chapters 3 and 4 I argue that the 'pure' immanence of Foucault and Deleuze does not entail apoliticism or self-contradiction. Ironically, their position too is initially developed through a productive misreading of their predecessors, with Foucault presenting a parodied, misleading vision of French phenomenology as meaning-giving (*sens*) and using it as a theoretical springboard for his study of discourse, placing the human subject in immanent relations of production and signification. Such relations entail a Nietzschean conception of force, the development of which in Foucault's thought allows him to account for the conditions under which phenomena are generated, or their ontogenesis. I will argue that this radicalises the decentring of the subject and directly leads to and informs Foucault's later political engagements, wherein the self is placed in relations of transitive, unstable, virtual *forces* constituting actual formations of power, carried out by the formed or stratified relations which make up knowledge (as in formed matters or substances) and relating to extensive processes of organisation and strategy (i.e. bio-power). This, at its most basic, refers to the double-conditioning between the micro and the macro, as described earlier. Contra those who wish to read Foucault within a deeply Althusserian conjecture (i.e. Žižek and Laclau), the nature of this network must be understood according to the immanent logic of dispersion and disjunction underpinning discursive formations in Foucault's earlier work, a logic heavily rooted in Merleau-Ponty's concept of the fold and one that makes strategic possibilities and lines of flight (or lines of escape by which one can exercise a practice of freedom) synonymous with folding, by virtue of being the very excess or discontinuities of the network itself.

In the fourth chapter, I argue that Deleuze combines the essential elements of the three previous thinkers to make an improved politics of immanence, which is to a certain extent more perspicuous, by virtue of being consistent and systematic, specifically with its penetrating account of interiority. Certainly, Deleuze overcomes a number of remaining ambiguities, in particular through addressing an affective and ethical issue evident in Foucault – by turning to schizoanalysis and the incorporation of desire as will to power – pushing the politics of immanence to its ultimate. This argument contends with the misleading but no less prominent view that Deleuzian desire is a pre-symbolic libidinal flux, an asocial essentialist category of idealism and bourgeois ethics. I argue that Deleuzian desire is both instigated by and utilises the ontogenetic conceptual schema of Deleuze's metaphysics (transcendental empiricism) – as derived from an engagement with Sartre, Merleau-Ponty and Foucualt – in which thought and desire are construed as immanent to the real that provokes them, such that they can only have a productive nature.

I argue in the conclusion that taken together the four thinkers of 'pure' immanence offer a new take on ethicality, political analysis and political practice; moving the centre of gravity of analysis and action away from the political triad, towards a subjectivity-without-a-subject, one where we no longer look for a transcendent Outside or rupture in/of immanence to ground resistance in spite of our condition (i.e. dialectical excess), but rather work through our condition and its entangled lines of immanence and 'three' folds of disjuncture, through an affirmative ethics of self-experimentation. When read within a contemporary setting and so within the context of post-industrial capitalism, it offers a unique critique of it, bested in its refreshing radicality only by its accompanying a-systematic (as opposed to anti-system, i.e. dialectical materialism) political praxis. A praxis that, very much in the vein of Gramsci's 'passive revolution', urges us to work *through* capitalism, in order to truly *overcome* its strictures and all that relates to it. What some might view as a self-indulgent Renaissance bourgeois concern of playing with one's sense of self outside of politics is in fact actually the site where the political is most at stake. Politics begins here.

Notes

1. These practices encompass a broad variety of what he called 'Ideology State Apparatuses', i.e. the family, the media, the education system, and so forth; as opposed to the 'Repressive State Apparatus', akin to the 'beastly' half of Gramsci's centaur.
2. Following *material capabilities* and *institutional structuring*, this loosely represents what Steven Lukes (2005) refers to as the 'third' dimension of power.
3. As opposed to *post*-Marxist, which denotes those who, though previously Marxist in some manner, have come to utterly reject it. I am thinking, for instance, of Žižek, Laclau, Mouffe, and to a varying degree Connolly, Hardt and Negri, Patton and Widder.
4. The latter supposedly encapsulates numerous speculations on that which transcends the physical world and in turn grounds it, i.e. foundational and eternal Truths viz. human essence and the highest goods of life. Such speculations were not only considered to present an

outmoded and arcane scholasticism with no basis in verifiable reality, but also precisely that which, by purporting to have reached the absolute truths of human nature and the good life, serves to justify the restriction and contortion of any and all forms of subjectivity and expression inconsistent with said truths. In this sense, the rejection of metaphysical speculation is equated with the establishment of a liberal society, wherein rational subjects of choice are given the right to self-determination.
5. Communitarians such as Charles Taylor and Michal Sandel, for instance, construed the subject as a social and cultural construction, embedded as it were in a rich tapestry of 'constitutive attachments' or shared familial, communal and national histories and understandings. Such attachments are said to constitute a density of character through which the capacity of autonomous subjective choice and personal will is contingently set. Thus the 'anti-metaphysical' minimalist conception of the 'unencumbered self', paradoxically embodies an abstract metaphysical commitment to a subject capable of rational deliberation outside of the very material that makes it possible.
6. See Tønder and Thomassen 2005: 2.
7. As with Kojève's Hegel, Lacan argues that man begins with a primitive, undifferentiated Real, and so a tenuous sense of self in the form of the mirror stage. However, as man's needs are articulated to another (the [m]Other), 'they are subjected to demand', which in turn means, 'they are returned to the him in alienated form' (Lacan 2001: 316). Further, as the demand is universal and requires unconditionality, no *particular* act of love or recognition can satisfy it. As a result, the 'particularity thus abolished should reappear *beyond* demand' (Lacan 2001: 317) in the form of desire. Desire thus becomes a nameless sense of loss or incompleteness that appears even when the subject receives everything it needs and demands from the Other. Desire, in other words, is neither the appetite for satisfaction, nor the demand for love, but the difference that results from the subtraction of the first from the second.
8. In this sense, the subject-centred trichotomy presents not only a three-way classificatory division, but also a triad of elements functionally interrelated in political formations and transformations.
9. However, this immanence retains a negative structure that culminates with a Subject that, on the one hand, transcends what would otherwise be a sterile world of mere Substance, but, on the other hand, is still seen to emerge from immanent conditions of this world. In this way, Hegelian immanence retains a moment of formal transcendence, a moment where, as Hegel says, the divine is realised on Earth. In attempting to conceptualise ideological and hegemonic struggle within a post-Marxist milieu, contemporary thinkers of transcendence/lack

clearly follow this trajectory, while rejecting the idea that the emergence of the Subject from Substance is a completion of immanence, instead seeing it as the moment where immanence is ruptured. As a consequence, they also reject the idea that this completion is a moment of 'positive' Absolute Knowledge, holding instead that it is the recognition of the necessary failure of the Absolute to achieve positive status.

10. The use of the preformative in this context is, strictly speaking, improper and misleading, if by '*pre*condition' we are to understand something that comes before or stands independently and outside of the process, or as that which conditions in advance. The conceptual logic of immanence dictates that there is nothing outside of the process or outside of experience, thus the term 'precondition' cannot be employed without qualification or without the use of parentheses, should there be a syntaxical requirement for its continued usage.

11. According to Badiou (2000: 24), Deleuze's univocity does not signify that Being is numerically one, such that the One is not the one of identity or of number it is nonetheless still a monotonous form of a transcendent One. Each form of Being contains 'individuating differences' that may well be named beings, meaning that beings are merely local degrees of intensity or inflections of power that are in constant movement and entirely singular. The multiple is arranged in the universe by way of a numerical difference that is purely formal as regards the form of being to which it refers, and purely modal as regards its individuation, 'it follows that, ultimately, this multiple can only be of the order of simulacra. And if one classes – as one should – every difference without a real status, every multiplicity whose ontological status is that of the One, as a simulacrum, then the world of beings is the theatre of the simulacra of Being' (Badiou 2000: 26).

12. Quoting Jameson, Žižek (2012a: 63) argues that if 'the mission of the One lies in subordinating illusory pairs, doubles, oppositions of all kind, then it turns out we are still in dualism, for the task is conceived as the working through of opposition – the dualism – between dualism and monism'.

13. Which is equivalent to Foucault's *dispositif*.

14. In a somewhat circular fashion, Connolly maintains that the expansion of deep multidimensional pluralism via the collectivisation and socialisation of the agonistic ethos, into and through a *majority assemblage*, can counter reactive desire, and thus in turn support said pluralism. This displays how, fundamentally, the micropolitical level 'invades and pervades macropolitics' (Connolly 2002: 110).

15. Žižek (1999: 296) makes such a claim with regards to Foucault's 'immanent logic of disciplinary power mechanisms', in which we are faced with a 'vicious cycle of power and resistance' (Žižek 1999: 297).

16. This establishes the basis for the production of a *multitude* as global subject, a cooperative subjectivity that is 'directly opposed to Empire, with no mediation between them' (Hardt and Negri 2000: 393). For thinkers such as William Connolly, abundance suggests an historical contingency and a non-antagonistic differential aspect inherent to identity that, if democratic pluralism is to be effective, requires sensitive fostering and care, empathy and protection, or simply 'agonistic respect'. Agonism moves firmly beyond the liberal virtue of 'tolerance' and the adjacent problematic of antagonistic struggles that, far from being viewed as inevitable at the level of Being, speak to a failure to respect abundant modes of being by forcing them into specific identities of negation, or opposing binary positions. Such antagonistic politics, it is argued, can be spurred on by reactive desire itself.
17. Analogy inspired by Widder (2012: 19).
18. I.e. Beistegui (2010), Kerslake (2009), Lord (2010) and Yovel (1991).
19. Though addressing and expanding on how reactive micro-desire serves antagonistic and exploitative political and social forms, Connolly's work is limited in being chiefly focused on identity and the subject to which it corresponds, as evidenced by the emphasis on agonism and 'critical responsevess' to new identities. Hardt and Negri suffer from a similar limitation, in terms of their emphasis on multitude and Empire, which relies both on identity and opposition.

Chapter 1
Sartre and the Instigation of Immanence

In this chapter, I argue that Sartre's philosophical system instigates the ontology of 'pure' immanence that underpins micropolitics and that is carried forward by Merleau-Ponty, Foucault and Deleuze. But is there indeed such a thing as a Sartrean system, a total *Weltanschauung*?[1] This question touches on one of the foremost debates afflicting Sartre scholarship. A number of interpreters have portrayed Sartre as a sporadic philosopher, void of any underlying and continuous ontology or philosophical and political engagement. His oeuvre, it is said, is punctuated by a series of divergent and conflicting views. In particular, with its emphasis on consciousness, Sartre's early work between *The Transcendence of the Ego* and *Being and Nothingness* is typically taken to represent a deeply subjectivist or even rationalist position, which would later face the axe in Sartre's turn towards a neo-Marxist or even 'postmodernist' dialectic of praxis. Against these interpretations, others have attempted to locate a stable vantage point from which to grasp and fix all of Sartre's thinking under one heading. This is typically identified in the 'dialectic of the self', of which an early formation is evident in *Being and Nothingness*. In this reading, the *Critique* and its 'totalisation-detotalisation' of praxis is said to represent its historico-material fruition. Badiou (2012: 20) goes so far as to claim that Sartre's later encounter with Marxism in the *Critique* was 'unavoidable', precisely due to the presence of the dialectic in *Being and Nothingness*. Thus, as opposed to signifying a radical split, it is supposed that each major work of Sartre's focuses on a particular aspect of the dialectic. Whereas the earlier work can be said to focus more on the nature of existential 'choice', the later work focuses more on its situational or contextual limits.

The true irony here is that despite the divergence of these

interpretations, each unwittingly establishes an overarching image of Sartre as a thinker of formal transcendence. In the first instance, as Deleuze (2004b: 114 n6) puts it, while repudiating transcendence in the version of a field of consciousness immanent *to* a transcendental subject, Sartre retains transcendence's form, insofar as the transcendental field is still determined as a field of consciousness, 'and as such it must be unified by itself through a play of intentionalities or pure intentions'. The transcendental is still individuated at the personal level, as already possessing a subject-predicate structure that goes beyond or sits outside the immanent flux of experience itself. Such a reading is prominent amongst those who privilege Sartre's earlier 'rationalist' works, at the expense of his later 'dialectical' turn.[2] In the second instance, by starting off with this form of the subject, the later Sartre of the dialectic – or rather the 'holistic' Sartre as it is for some – evokes an intentional relation between nomination and the thing, effectively breaking with the univocity of immanence in favour of a metaphysical polarity.[3] In this way, Sartre seemingly pushes forward a formal transcendence of a different sort, in which the Outside/Other replaces the transcendental subject as that to which the field of consciousness is related, entailing a transcendence of the subject and of the object (see Smith 2003: 55). This has led Sartre's interpreters – and at times Sartre himself – unwittingly to endorse a more traditional Marxian politics of transcendence, one that even seems to replicate key aspects of the sovereign-centred juridico-political model of liberalism and social contract theory.[4]

To a certain degree, such a reading can be forgiven, considering that there are numerous occasions on which Sartre, particularly in his early to middle works, explicitly rejects immanence. For instance, in 'Intentionality: A fundamental Concept of Husserl's Phenomenology', Sartre (2013: 4-5) writes:

> Imagine now a linked series of bursts that wrest us from ourselves, that do not even leave an 'ourself' the time to form behind them but rather hurl us out beyond them into the dry dust of the world, onto the rough earth, among things. Imagine we are thrown out in this way, abandoned by our very nature in an indifferent, hostile, resistant world. If you do so, you will have grasped the profound meaning of the discovery Husserl expresses in this famous phrase: 'All consciousness is consciousness *of* something'. This is all it takes to put an end to the cozy philosophy of immanence, in which everything works by compromise, by protoplasmic exchanges, by a tepid cellular chemistry. The philoso-

phy of transcendence throws us out onto the high road, amid threats and under a blinding light.

Against such readings, and indeed Sartre's own statements, I argue that with Sartre there is a total *Weltanschauung*, but it is located in the continuous presence of, and deepening engagement with, immanence. What is important to note vis-à-vis Sartre's express rejection of immanence, is that he is fundamentally referring to phenomenological immanence, as in 'immanent to consciousness'. This is clearly a very different and certainly restricted use of immanence from the one defined at the opening of this work. In fact, despite his rejection of immanence, Sartre moves over time towards a different kind of immanence as fold, or rather he moves away from this rather simplistic understanding of immanence as pure idealist interiority, as 'the pure subjectivity of the instantaneous *cogito*', (Sartre 2008a: 68) to one which is concomitant with, and forms the conceptual basis of, 'pure' immanence.

This 'pure' immanence is ultimately expressed by Sartre through the Heideggerian-inspired notion of 'being-in-the-world'. The basic idea is that though consciousness is empty, for it intends towards its object, it does so through its situation via the body as flesh. This represents the immanent Outside in which it is already embedded, and ultimately this is the meaning of being-in-the-world. There are three critical stages to Sartre's engagement with, and development of, immanence that this chapter will explore and expand upon. Each one corresponds with one of Sartre's published works: (1) *The Transcendence of the Ego* – the displacement of the necessity and centrality of the ego by giving the object itself the role of providing identity for the subject and the flux of consciousness the role of unity through the retention of previous experience. Here we also find a tacit notion of what I identified in the introduction as Deleuze's concept of 'intensive virtuality'; (2) *Being and Nothingness* – the subsequent development of a dialectic premised on a primordial bond of facticity via the flesh and relations of desire, in which consciousness is thoroughly embedded in the Outside/Other to which it relates by virtue of the body as the surface inbetween. Despite being rooted in a problematic dualistic discourse, this greatly anticipates the notion of the fold, again as identified in the introduction, and as first developed by Merleau-Ponty; (3) *Critique of Dialectical Reason* – lastly the materialisation of the dialectic and the flesh within the context of capitalist modes of production (scarcity) and processes of totalisation-detotalisation, which anticipates Deleuze and Guattari's assemblage and their contention that there is a heterogeneous yet immanent relation between micro and macro arrangements or political force relations. It is this aspect of Sartre's thought, in particular, combined with his ethic of authenticity, where we find the instigation of politics of immanence as micropolitics, establishing its philosophical context and paving the way for Merleau-Ponty, Foucault and Deleuze.

The First Stage: Phenomenology and the Transcendental Ego

Deleuze and Guattari (1994: 47) claim that Sartre's presupposition of an impersonal transcendental field 'restores the rights of immanence'. This claim is not followed by any sort of concrete analysis, although it is clear it refers to the way Sartre handles the Kantian legacy of the transcendental field – the 'I think' that accompanies all representations. Specifically, it relates to Sartre's repudiation of Husserl's Kantian categories and the development of an alternative *impersonal* transcendental field as one with the form of neither a synthetic consciousness nor a subjective identity. It is here that our story of immanence begins, for it is here that the legacy of the *I* as indispensable to the coherence of our subjectivity and agency is first displaced. Instead, the ego is envisioned as a simulation, its corresponding agency as a semblance and its central function as a cover.

In striving to take a far more humble and realistic approach to philosophy, Husserl suspends the 'natural attitude' or 'judgement' in favour of the *epoché* ('suspension of judgement'). By following the *epoché*, the philosopher 'brackets out' all the assumptions of the world and the nature of existence and its contents, and instead focuses on experience as an appearance or 'phenomenon'. Through so doing, Husserlian phenomenology attempts to wade through all metaphysical concerns and focus instead on the living human subject, or 'Absolute Being', thereby returning to *concrete* lived human experience. That does not mean to say one makes a judgement towards the 'natural world' by rejecting it, but rather that one is barred from '*using any judgement that concerns spatio-temporal existence (Dasein)*' (Husserl 2012: 59). Even if we bracket the natural world, it 'still remains there like the bracketed in the bracket, like the disconnected outside the connexional system' (ibid.: 57). It is to '*put out of action the general thesis which belongs to the essence of the natural standpoint*' (ibid.: 59). Through this, Husserl (ibid.) establishes a descriptive 'science of consciousness' or a 'new' eidetic science. The central thesis is that through a systematic investigation into 'pure consciousness' we can uncover essential truths about the nature of human experience (ibid.: 62) – thus the clarion cry of phenomenology: 'back to the things themselves', back to the experience of the person, to the 'giveness' (*Gegebenheit*) of experience.

Presupposed in this project is the view that an '*object that has being in itself (an sich seiender) is never such as to be out of relation to consciousness and its Ego*', for the 'thing is the thing of *the world about me*' (ibid.: 91). The hypothetical assumption of a Real Something outside the world of subjective experience is 'indeed a "logically" possible one', but these things have 'purely factual grounds in the factual limits of this experience' (ibid.: 92–3). We cannot grasp the transcendent as it is merely given through certain empirical connections. Thus 'consciousness (inward experience) and real Being are in no sense co-ordinate forms of Being, living as friendly neighbours, and occasionally entering into "relation" or some reciprocal "connexion"' (ibid.: 95). Immanent absolute Being, as with transcendent Being (object), has its objective determining content, but such objective determination bears the same name only when we speak in terms of the empty logical categories – between the 'meanings of consciousness and reality yawns a veritable abyss' (ibid.). As such, consciousness, considered in its purity, must be construed as a self-contained system of Being 'into which nothing can penetrate, and from which nothing can escape; which has no spatio-temporal exterior, and can be inside no spatio-temporal system' (ibid.). The spatio-temporal world, to which man claims to belong as a subordinate singular relation, is in truth intentional Being, and so a Being with a secondary relative sense of being *for* consciousness. Reality so defined has no absolute essence. It has the essentiality of something 'which in principle is *only* known, consciously presented as an appearance' (ibid.: 96). Thus the basic field of phenomenology, when considering consciousness, concerns the bracketing of the nature-constituting consciousness with its transcendent theses.

In bracketing, Husserl effectively sustains a gap between consciousness and reality. Reality is grasped only through consciousness as an aspect of phenomenological experience, or as a phenomenon *for* consciousness, and consciousness as a consciousness *of* reality. That is, the intentional relation is personified by the interplay and separation of the *for* and the *of*, in which case one term of the relation cannot be reduced to the other. Thus we 'fix our eyes steadily upon the sphere of Consciousness and study what it is that we find immanent in it' (ibid.: 62).

In construing consciousness this way, Deleuze (2001: 33 n5) holds, Husserl readily admits that all transcendence is constituted in the *life of consciousness*, as inseparably and intricately linked to that life. However, Deleuze maintains that this plane is immediately related back to a subject, taken as transcendent to the real, in which the empirical is made into nothing more than a double of the transcendental. Thus, in returning to the universal subject to which immanence is attributed, 'the transcendental is entirely denatured, for it then simply redoubles the empirical (as with Kant), and immanence is distorted, for it then finds itself enclosed in the transcendent' (ibid.: 27). Deleuze's view of Husserl is clearly indebted to Sartre's point that with Husserl we find a latent Kantianism, which in turn leads to an unnecessary duplication of the self. At first, Husserl describes a psychical and psycho-physical *me*, but then goes on to add a 'pure' or transcendental Ego (Sartre 2004: 5). In so doing, he creates a point from which various consciousnesses can engage in various acts of apprehension while retaining their coherent unity. Thus we are returned to an internal synthesis, similar to Kant's, in which we must account for consciousness's contact with an object that is transcendent to it, lest we fall into solipsism. Indeed, within the sphere of consciousness, Husserl locates a hyletic structure; structures that effectively mediate the experience of the object, playing 'so great a part in the perceptive intuitions of things' (ibid.: 68).[5]

This subsequently raises the question as to the requirement for the transcendental ego in the first place. As Sartre (ibid.: 6) notes, 'it is usually believed that the existence of a transcendental *I* is justified by the need for consciousness to have unity and individuality'. That is, it is required, first, to overcome confusion between consciousnesses and therefore retain individuality, and, second, to explain how disconnected experiences taking place in a variety of locations and at different times can be attributed to the same individual. Both concern retaining coherent unity, and a subject to which that unity is attributed. The *ego* is introduced in order to retain the unity of self, for the purity of phenomenology risks reducing us to unlocalisable disconnected experiences. In rejecting the transcendental ego, then, Sartre must provide an alternative that can meet these demands.

For Sartre (ibid.), 'phenomenology does not need to resort to this unifying and individualizing *I*', as consciousness is defined by intentionality, and through intentionality consciousness 'transcends itself, it unifies itself by going outside itself'. In this instance, intentionality refers to consciousness as a radical activity that intends towards an object, as opposed to merely synthesising representations, such that consciousness is neither pure subjectivity nor pure objectivity. It is other-orientated, which is to say that all consciousness 'is consciousness *of* something' (ibid.: 10, see also Sartre 2008a: 7). Indeed, 'all that there is of intention in my actual consciousness is directed towards the outside, towards the table' (Sartre 2008a: 76). Insofar as consciousness transcends itself this way, in order to reach an object such as the table and exhausts itself in this same positing, it is non-positional (it is not its own object).

So what of the *I* of consciousness? Sartre (2004: 9) admits 'it is undeniable that the Cogito is personal. In the "I think", there is an *I* which thinks'. If it is asked who has written these very words, I shall be compelled to speak, to identity *myself* as the author of this activity. When confronted with this ego, however, we are not dealing with a pre-existing self; rather, 'we are dealing with a mere appearance' (ibid.: 33) – that is to say, with a semblance that arises when consciousness reflects on itself or on its previous activity (intentionality) during or within the thetic stage.[6] This means that *I* am in fact premised on a 'pre-reflective cogito' or 'pre-reflective being of the *percipiens*' (ibid.: 16), a 'non-thetic' absorption into an activity and awareness of self, which is distinct from the consciousness apprehending the reflection of this activity. The *I* quite simply arises when consciousness reflects on its activity or when it is orientated towards a being (object) which, upon immediate reflection, it discovers *is not* itself. It constitutes itself by a reflective negation of differentiation.

Consciousness, then, is not be a material presence with an Ego or a representational machinary found within. Rather it is something, psycho-physical, found without or out in the world, devoid of content, with nothing lurking behind it. This semblance of an ego is no less functional on that account, offering a sense of agency or a disguise, as if 'consciousness constituted the Ego as a false representation of itself' (ibid.: 48). It is due to the appearance of the ego 'that a distinction can be drawn between the possible and the real, between appearance and being, between what is willed and what is yielded to', through which a grounded self-to-self relation can be sustained (ibid.). Thus, despite its repudiation, there are still experiences in which the ego features.

It is clear that Sartre's concept of intentionality is accorded a radically different meaning to that of Husserl's, for aside from eschewing representational machinery and the transcendental Ego, it results in the principle that the being of knowledge, as in the knowing person insofar as s/he *is* and not insofar as s/he is *known*, cannot be measured by knowledge. The necessary and sufficient condition for a knowing consciousness to be knowledge *of* its object is that it be 'consciousness of itself as being that knowledge', for otherwise it would be consciousness of the thing without consciousness of being so (Sartre 2008a: 8). Pre-thetic or pre-reflective consciousness, in other words, is the basis upon which not only the ego but also *knowledge* can occur. Indeed, the reduction of consciousness to knowledge 'involves our introducing into consciousness the subject-object dualism which is typical of knowledge' (ibid.). But if we accept the law of the knower-known dyad, 'then a third term will be necessary in order for the knower to become known in turn, and we will be faced with this dilemma: either we stop any one term of the series – the known, the knower known, the knower known by the knower, *etc*', wherein 'the totality of the phenomenon would fall into the unknown, in that we would bump up against a non-self-conscious reflection and a final term' or 'we affirm the necessity of an infinite regress (*idea ideae ideae, etc.*)' (ibid.). If an infinite regress is to be avoided, then we must establish an immediate, non-cognitive relation of the self to itself. Thus, Sartre maintains that we must abandon the 'primacy of knowledge if we wish to establish knowledge' (ibid.: 7).

At this stage, we are still left with the question of unity in duration and individuality. As Sartre (2004: 6) notes, it will be objected that 'it is necessary for there to be some principle of unity *in duration* if the continual stream of consciousnesses is able to posit transcendent objects outside itself'. In other words, consciousness must be perpetual syntheses of past consciousnesses with the present consciousness if there is to be a sustained sense of self through time. In recognition of this, Sartre affirms that the flux of consciousness itself participates in this unity by an interplay of 'transversal' intentionalities which are concrete and real retentions of past consciousnesses, and that the reflection through which unity is derived is temporal, and self-referencing: 'consciousness continually refers back to itself' (ibid.: 7). This nature of consciousness retains individuality, for like Spinoza's substance, whose concept does not require the concept of other things from which it must be formed, it cannot be limited except by itself (see ibid.).

This concept of temporality receives its much needed elaboration in *Being and Nothingness*, where it makes up the first of the three ekstases which constitute the for-itself (the second being 'reflection', and the third 'being-for-others'). The main argument is that, in its failed attempt to be totally present to itself in an instant, consciousness nihilates itself from its factitious past, only to flee the present towards a forever unrealisable future. That is, the for-itself arises as diasporic, dispersing itself in the three dimensions of time by virtue of nihilation or the negation of the in-itself. This means that the primary negative structure of the for-itself – its nothingness – is found in temporality. Further, as the subject is temporally spread, it holds it is premised on a fundamental and perpetual fracturing; an ontological becoming that underpins the possibility of transgression, securing the *separation* and conflict of consciousnesses.

Sartre begins his discussion of time by highlighting what he sees as its paradoxical character. Accordingly, temporality cannot primarily be separation, for we have a unity of the *before* and *after*. The problem, however, cannot be referred to a temporal unity as this would risk undermining irreversible succession as the meaning of this unity. But if we are to turn to disintegrating succession as the original character of time, we risk 'no longer being able to understand that there is *one* time' (Sartre 2008a: 159). As a consequence, Sartre asserts that temporality is *not*, and so only a being of a certain ontological structure can be temporal in the unity of its being, as an *internal* relation. 'Temporality is the being of the for-itself insofar as the for-itself has to be its being eksatically' (ibid.). In all its temporal dimensions, the for-itself is always elsewhere, and the separations of the self from the self are the for-itself's temporal ekstasis.

The past, as the first dimension, acts as a kind of facticity, and in this sense a being-in-itself. As with our intentional relation with the table, I am made aware of the past in the form of consciousness (of) not-being, in which case negation is explicit and constitutes the bond of being between the perceived object or past as the for-itself. Thus the past is like the outside, through which my reflective gaze makes a distinction, in the form of the practical *I* that differentiates *myself* from the object or past. However, despite being outside, the connection is not of the exact same type as, say, between a perceived object and consciousness, for a reflecting consciousness recognises that it once was *this* past, as being the past. This is so in two interrelated senses. First, as well as being like the outside, the past is that which reflective consciousness continually uses as its proverbial centre of gravity or point of referral when distinguishing itself from an outside object or subject, so as to gain a sense of unity, i.e. I am not this, I am not that, for this is me, the young man with a certain set of experiences, tastes, preferences and desires. In this case, the past is a thematised one. In the same way, the past also becomes *the object* of a thesis for me, in which case the for-itself affirms itself on the basis of a negation, as in *not being* this Past (any longer) which it posits. As per phenomenological ontology, this refers to a constituent or impure reflection of knowledge on par with a psychic temporality that is premised on the original temporality of which we are the temporalisation (ibid.: 182). Second, the past is 'a thing which one *is* without positing it, as that which haunts without being observed, is behind the for-itself, outside the thematic field which is before the for-itself as that which it illuminates' (ibid.: 163). Much like the tacit awareness of self we have, the past is not just present in the thetic (positional) mode of consciousness, for it also surrounds it, essentially as its virtual double or a kind of latent facticity and in this sense a being-in-itself that is not entirely negated, but which nevertheless situates the for-itself in its flight towards the future, continually and pre-reflectively orientating consciousness's for-itself to the world. It is the 'origin and springboard of all my actions', and my 'contingent and gratuitous bond with the world and with myself inasmuch as I constantly live it as a total abandonment' (ibid.: 164). In the first case, the past is the thing I once was, refer to and continually escape; in the second, it is a background which still exists and insists, but which I continually, though inadvertently, *attempt* to escape by the mere dint of temporalisation.

The second dimension denotes the present, specifically understood as the presence of the for-itself to the world, and as such a presence to being in the form of the being of consciousness, intentionality. It is by this presence that the for-itself effectively attempts to bring totality, and by this attempt brings temporality, into the world. It is the organising centre of the synthetic unity of temporality. Yet, there is a lack of coincidence with self, a nothingness, existing within the present, that equally relates to the lack inherent in the past and future, by virtue of which the totality is simultaneously detotalised, and the duration of temporality guaranteed. To be engaged with drinking a beer, for instance, means, in the present mode, never to have finished drinking, or to have still to be drinking beyond the drinking which I am. I am this drinking, which I have to be, but which I am not, for I am seeking to be the one who has finished drinking. Once I have finished drinking, *I have drunk*, the immediate future of the task, its end, has arrived, and so I am no longer the one drinking the beer; 'the ensemble slips into the past' (ibid.). At the same time, I realise that I was never one who was identified with the drinking, for while drinking I was either the one who has already drunk a certain amount and/or who was seeking to drink more, with the end of having drunk. The activity drives me into the was that I was not, the not-yet and the never-reached. As such 'I' am designated as an unachieved totality, one which cannot be achieved. Thus the presence of the for-itself is always beyond itself, as in the continual flight from identity.

Clearly, the present as presence of lack is already related to the future; it is that being (either immediate or abstract) towards which the present flies, only to discover what it is not-yet-and-never-will-be. That is, the third dimension of the future is the dimension in which the for-itself is present to itself as lacking the self it would be. The future does not cease to be future, for there is always a future in relation to a present or a past, be that immediate or distant. The future, moreover, can never be realised, for by definition it exists only in relation to the present and a future reached is no longer a future but a present. Nihiliation, or active negation, is once more central, in that the for-itself cannot be what the Future promised to be. This creates a split in that the present becomes the former future of the past while denying that it is this future. The unrealised future, the original future, can no longer be the future in relation to the present (which has been surpassed), and so remains the future only to the past, in which case it becomes the 'unrealizable co-present of the Present and preserves a total ideality' (ibid.: 168). In short, the future can only remain a future if the present constitutes itself as the lack of this future, and so one can never really coincide with one's future.

Taken together, the three dimensions of temporality reveal that the for-itself disperses its being in three dimensions of temporality 'due to the fact that it nihilates itself' (ibid.: 165). Or rather, the for-itself is a being of temporal ekstasis, in that it must simultaneously exist in all its temporal dimensions as a distance from the self, as a nothingness which is made-to-be as separation of the self from the self. Each dimension is the for-itself's way of projecting itself 'vainly toward the Self, of being what it is beyond a nothingness' (ibid.: 160). In this sense, the three temporal dimensions are ontologically equal and interdependent; and the subject is fractured, a flight of ecstatic being, spreading itself across the temporal dimensions, and so never one with itself.

What is immediately evident with Sartre's take on time, specifically the view on the non-thetic pre-reflective past, is that it has critical elements that meet the general criteria of a virtual or intensive multiplicity as described by Bergson (2001: 128, 162–4), and as advanced by Deleuze (2006a: 112). It speaks to a mental synthesis in which the three dimensions of time and their corresponding psychic states interpenetrate and melt into one another to establish a forever fluxual synthetic whole (a totalisation), forming an interpenetrating mass as opposed to a discrete series of events spread out in an open field, which is set off from an extensive Outside to which consciousness continually intends in a condemned effort to achieve self-coincidence. That is to say, it is a reality, and a condition of our experience of reality, initially beyond though related to the corresponding symbolic representations of such intensities juxtaposed in an ideal extended space. Thus it is, more specifically, the past that is a virtual realm (in that it is real without being actual), growing without ceasing, and insisting into present such that there is no limit to its preservation. Explicitly employing Bergson's terminology from *Time and Free Will*, this underpins Sartre's (2004: 34) statement, in *The Transcendence of the Ego*, that the ego is an abstract, infinite contraction of the material self, a 'virtual locus of unity' – or, more specifically, it is, in relation to the past as facticity, an 'interpenetrative multiplicity', and in relation to the future, a 'bare potentiality', which is actualised and fixed when it comes into contact with events (ibid.: 38). Here, the ego, 'is apprehended but also *constituted* by reflective knowledge' (Sartre 2004: 34), returning us once more to the practical function of the ego.

Despite this fracturing of time, however, the subject is at the centre of a unifying act, i.e. nihilation; that is, it unifies by individuating. Therefore, it does not so much establish a multiplicity in the strictly Bergsonian sense of unity in memory, as much as establish a quasi-multiplicity, 'a foreshadowing of dissociation in the heart of unity' (Sartre 2008a: 158). Temporality is a 'unity which multiplies *itself*'; that is, temporality can be only a relation of being at the heart of this same being' (ibid.: 159), as in the for-itself insofar as the for-itself has to be its being eksatically, in turn accounting for the irreversible order and unity of time (or the self). Specifically, though holding that the past penetrates the present, which is to 'affirm that duration is a multiplicity of interpenetration and that the past is continually organized with the present', Sartre adds, contra Bergson, that the multiplicity of before and after cannot be accounted for through the unity of memory, for this fails to explain 'how the past can "be reborn" to haunt us, in short to exist *for us*. If it is unconscious, as Bergson claims, and if the unconscious is inactive, how can it weave itself into the woof of our present consciousness? How does it emanate from the past as such?' (ibid.: 132). The multiplicity of before and after, for Sartre, is explained by nihilation or perpetual flight, where, as we saw, the present is the centre of the synthetic unity of the temporal dimensions. It is necessity for being to metamorphosise itself that establishes duration.

Change and becoming, then, is the for-itself, in that the for-itself is spontaneity. Indeed, the 'flight' of the for-itself is the refusal of contingency 'by the very act which constitutes the for-itself as being the foundation of its nothingness', yet it is exactly this contingency that is fled, and it can 'not be annihilated since I *am* it, but neither can it any longer be as the foundation of its own nothingness since it can be this only in flight' (ibid.: 172). The totality of temporalisation is never achieved, such that it is a 'detotalised-totality' (ibid.: 187): it is refused, and flees from itself. Thus, the time of consciousness is human reality which temporalises itself as the totality which is to itself its own incompletion. There is never an instant in and of itself, precisely because the for-itself never *is*. In this way, the for-itself is nothingness, which underpins the possibility of transgression and negates harmonious synthesis.[7] Subsequently, Sartre also meets the first demand that led Husserl to posit the transcendental ego in holding that we are barred from any true interaction: as neither term is of the same order, consciousness is one and shares nothing with other consciousnesses, so interaction of this sort is impossible. There is no real point of encounter, rather a mere crossing.

Given Sartre's deviation from Bergson, it is understandable that there seems to be an ambiguous tension between the notion of the virtual, especially as Deleuze will portray it, and the notion of time as a unifying act by virtue of nihilation as the organisational centre of time. This is undoubtedly true for *The Transcendence of the Ego*. But though consciousness is empty, for it intends towards its object,

Being and Nothingness adds that it does so *through* its situation via the body as flesh, or an Outside in which it is already embedded, in which the subject is not a pre-existing determination that can be found ready-made, but a fluid effect of reflection, in accordance with a dialectical process within an immanent apparatus or order. The 'ego' as a *practical* function is still retained, inasmuch as it assists in conceptualising self-to-self relations (i.e. 'bad faith'), but it has no transcendental significance in and of itself. Alas, it is precisely this retention that Deleuze conflates with a subject-predicate structure, which when read against a fleshless version of Sartre provides an image of formal transcendence.

The Second Stage: the Body and Lived Experience

Before discussing the flesh as an immanent Outside, I wish to address why and how it was developed, so as to foreclose any assumption that this is an arbitrary or inconsistent feature of Sartre's thinking. In terms of the why, it is initially to be found in Sartre's infamous introduction to *Being and Nothingness*. As Sartre therein states, it is precisely the ontological gap or 'veritable abyss' retained by Husserl that he finds problematic and in need of bridging through proper elaboration. Along these lines, Sartre (ibid.: 1) concedes that Husserl made considerable progress 'by reducing the existent to the series of appearances which manifest it', overcoming 'a certain number of dualisms which have embarrassed philosophy', replacing them instead with the 'monism of the phenomenon'. It has allowed philosophy to sidestep Kant by rejecting the dualism of appearance and essence and 'the illusion of worlds-behind-the-scene' (ibid.: 2). With Husserl, the essence of an existent 'is no longer a property sunk in the cavity of this existent; it is the manifest law which presides over the succession of its appearances, it is the principle of the series' (ibid.). Phenomenal being manifests its essence as well as its existence, and so it is nothing but the well-connected series of its manifestations. Yet, by reducing the existent to its manifestations, we overcome one set of dualisms only to establish another: that of the finite and infinite.

Husserl replaces the reality of the thing by the objectivity of the phenomenon and bases this 'on an appeal to infinity' (ibid.: 3). The existent is reduced to a finite series of manifestations. But this is impossible, as each one of them is a 'relation to a subject constantly changing' (ibid.). So, although an object may disclose itself only through a single *Abschattung* (shadow), 'the sole fact of there being a subject implies the possibility of multiplying the points of view on that *Abschattung*', which suffices to 'multiply to infinity the *Abschattung* under consideration' (ibid.). Thus the theory of the phenomenon has replaced the thing's reality with the phenomenon's objectivity, and this has been based on an appeal to infinity. The appearance, which is finite, indicates itself in its finitude, 'but at the same time in order to be grasped as an appearance-of-that-which-appears, it requires that it be surpassed toward infinity' (ibid.). What appears in fact is only an aspect of the object, and the object is altogether in that aspect and altogether outside it. Thus the outside is opposed in a new way to the inside.

Related to this issue is something more fundamental: 'If the essence of the appearance is an "appearing" which is no longer opposed to any being, there arises a legitimate problem concerning *the being of this appearing*' (ibid.: 4). So is the phenomenon of being identical with the being of phenomena? Is 'the being which discloses itself to me, which appears to me, of the same nature as the being of existence of existents which appear to me?' (ibid.). Husserl considers being as an appearance which can be determined in concepts, as opposed to considering being as the condition of revelation. Yet knowledge cannot by itself give an account of being, lest we fall into the infinite regress mentioned above. This relates to the reworking of intentionality away from the question of knowledge. The phenomenon of being, Sartre maintains, requires an appeal to being, to something transphenomenal. Not as something hidden behind phenomena, nor as an appearance as a distinct being. Rather, what is implied is that 'the being of the phenomenon although coextensive with the phenomenon, can not be subject to the phenomenal condition – which is to exist only insofar as it reveals itself – and that consequently it surpasses the knowledge which we have of it and provides the basis for such knowledge' (ibid.: 6).

Although Husserlians may object insofar as the difficulties mentioned pertain to a particular conception of being and that what determines the being of the appearance is the fact that it appears, Sartre (ibid.) feels this is 'simply a way of choosing new words to clothe the old "*esse est percipi*" of Berkley'. Husserl's phenomenological reduction treats the noema as unreal, declaring that its *esse* is *percipi* (or that its existence is perception). Charging Husserl with solipsism, Sartre asserts that though 'every metaphysics in fact presupposes a theory of knowledge, every theory of knowledge in turn presupposes a metaphysics' (ibid.). As such, idealism ought 'first to give some kind of guarantee for the being of knowledge' (ibid.). The being of knowledge simply cannot be measured by knowledge. It is not subject to the percipi. The foundation of being, therefore, must be transphenomenal. Indeed, consciousness 'is the transphenomenal dimension of being in the subject' (ibid.: 7). Thus, rather than dealing with the analysis of a *concept*, Sartre analyses the relation of a being (consciousness or the for-itself) to another being (in-itself), which corresponds to the difference between Husserl's and existentialism's phenomenology. In short, consciousness *cannot be bracketed from reality*, for reality plays a fundamental role in its activity. Subjectivity is consciousness (of) consciousness,[8] and consciousness is the revealed-revelation of existents, whereby existents appear before consciousness on the foundation of their being. Where Kant argues that the transcendental subject is also required to provide a distance between the subject and the world, to keep representations from crowding upon the soul, Sartre argues that this 'crowding' actually personifies our thrownness in or enthrallment with it, requiring us constantly to react. Self-reflection, in this sense, is always secondary, and so the self, though real, is not itself generative. That is, consciousness can 'exist only as *engaged* in this being which surrounds it on all sides and which paralyzes it with its phantom presence' (ibid.: 114).

However, it is on the question of the precise conceptualisation of such enthrallment that a number of interpretative problems and ambiguities arise. The initial stages of the argument in *Being and Nothingness* present such facticity – that is, the necessary connection with the in-itself – through the situation and through our being-for-others (i.e., the look), which themselves are also oppositional relations. At its most basic, this argument holds that elements outside of the self (the situation) structure it, establishing a whole, or what Sartre later calls the 'singular universal', and in some respects, a 'totalisation' (Sartre 1976b: 59–60). However, the self, which is defined by negation, reacts to this situation in continual flux and tension. There is no 'harmonious synthesis" (Sartre 1963a: 338). Therefore, the thesis and the antithesis 'represent the two moments of freedom', which remain 'mutilated and abstract and perpetuate their opposition' (ibid.). As such, existence 'exhausts itself in *maintaining* a conflict without a solution' (ibid.: 273).[9]

This seems to echo the common claim made by contemporary thinkers of transcendence: that there is a rupture between reality and our experience of it, and that it is this rupture that defines and constitutes our subjectivity. Indeed, based on Sartre's section on 'the look', it would seem that he retains a primary metaphysical polarity or rupture of an otherwise insular domain, establishing two different orders of Being through an absolute opposition, wherein I am (the for-itself) absolute negativity and the world is positivity. In reality, this reading fails to appreciate how *Being and Nothingness* strives to move from the abstract to the concrete. As Sartre says, following Laporte, 'an abstraction is made when something not capable of existing in isolation is thought of as in an isolated state', whereas the 'concrete by contrast is a totality which can exist by itself alone' (2008a: 27). Further, from this point of view, 'consciousness is an abstraction since it conceals within itself an ontological course in the region of the in-itself, and conversely the phenomenon is likewise an abstraction since it must "appear" to consciousness' (ibid.). The concrete 'is man within the world in that specific union of man with the world which Heidegger, for example, calls "being-in-the-world"' (ibid.). Being is contrasted with Existence in that it is all-embracing and objective as opposed to individual and subjective. Thus, the first half of *Being and Nothingness* deals with the immediacy of experience, and the second part with the background flesh of that experience, and their mutual imbrication. Now we reach the 'how' of the flesh.

In accordance with the nature of *Being and Nothingness*, this thesis first comes into play halfway through it. Here Sartre (ibid.: 241) begins by conceding that though 'some may be surprised that we have treated the problem of knowledge without raising the question of the body and the senses or even once referring to it', it is 'not my purpose to misunderstand or to ignore the role of the body'. What in fact is important 'above all else, in ontology as elsewhere, is to observe strict order in discussion' (ibid.). Accordingly, the body, 'whatever may be its function, appears [note: not 'exists'] first as the *known*' (ibid.). As such, we cannot 'refer knowledge back to it or discuss it before we have defined knowing, nor can we derive knowing in its fundamental structure from the body in any way or manner whatsoever' (ibid.). The body cannot be *for me* transcendent and known. What I know is the body of another, 'and the essential facts which I *know* concerning my own body come from the way in which others see it' (ibid.). Thus, 'consciousness *exists* its body' (ibid.: 353), for unreflective consciousness is not consciousness *of the* body. The relation between the body-as-point-of-view and things is an *objective* relation, and the relation of consciousness to the body is an *existential* one.

Critically this relation, or passing through, exists on a non-reflective plane, as a fundamental part of the synthetic totality of man's being-in-the-world. It is a non-reflective consciousness, in that quite simply it 'is non-thetically conscious of self' (Sartre 2002: 38). Sartre argues that it is 'a mode of our conscious existence, one of the ways in which consciousness understands ... its Being-in-the-world' (ibid.: 61). This must be the case, for the world is a synthetic totality, and '*man* is a being of the same type as the *world*; it is even possible that, as Heidegger believes, the notions of the world and of "human-reality" (*Dasein*) are inseparable' (ibid.: 5). Within this, it is rightly asserted that there is a 'dual nature of the body, which on the one hand is an object in the world and on the other is immediately *lived* by the consciousness' (ibid.: 50–1). It must *not* be imagined 'that consciousness is spontaneous in the sense that it is always free to deny a thing and to affirm it at one and the same moment ... It *knows* itself only in the world' (ibid.: 52–3).

Here, Sartre starts to develop a theory of the pre-personal unconscious, differing from Freud's, primarily in that it is not closed-off and deterministic but rather ontological.[10] Our state of latency, according to Sartre, is essentially a reflection of our being-in-the-world as a relational state. Indeed, in *Being and Nothingness*, he criticises psychology for viewing desire as something in man by 'virtue of being "contained" by his consciousness', and further for believing that the meaning of a desire is inherent in the desire itself (Sartre 2008a: 578). Through this method, the psychologist makes the abstract prior to the concrete, with the concrete being merely an organisation of abstract qualities. In reference to the case of Flaubert, he states: 'the fact that the "need to feel intensely," a universal pattern, is disguised and channelled into becoming the need to write – this is not the *explanation* of the "calling" of Flaubert; on the contrary, it *is* what must be explained' (ibid.: 579). The psychologist, then, fails to explain why Flaubert turns to writing rather than painting or music. The fact confronted is given as primary and the analysis stops there. The entire complexity of Flaubert's behaviour and actions is reduced to certain properties and an arbitrary referential axis, 'comparable to those of chemical bodies, beyond which it would *be* foolish to attempt to proceed' (ibid.: 581). Love and jealously cannot be reduced 'to the strict desire of possessing a *particular* woman, but that these emotions aim at laying hold of the world in its entirety through the woman' (ibid.: 583). An act reflects my original choice, my project as situated in my context. This choice carries itself through the pre-reflective, so that it can be enacted without reflection or overtly conscious deliberation.

It is for this reason that Sartre develops an *existential* psychoanalysis. The essential task in this instance is 'hermeneutic', that is, 'a deciphering, a determination, and a conceptualization' (ibid.: 590), deciphering the meaning of acts in relation to a synthetic totality. When Sartre says that we must bring our fundamental choice to light, he is paying homage to a method that 'has been furnished for us by the psychoanalysis of Freud and his disciples' (ibid.). Alike with Freud, Sartre's existential psychoanalysis considers all objectively discernible manifestations of 'psychic life' as symbols maintaining symbolic relations to the fundamental, total structures that make up the individual person. There is a need, in this sense, to restore the twofold structure: the event of infancy and the psychic crystallisation around this event. The crystallisation is what takes shape in pre-reflective consciousness, making every act a manifestation of the totality of the existent.

In addition, conscious reflection, or consciousness's non-thetic consciousness of itself, may be able to possess or apprehend all, but this does not necessarily mean that it 'commands the instruments and techniques necessary to isolate the choice symbolized' (ibid.: 591). To be sure, 'if the fundamental project is fully experienced by the subject and hence wholly conscious, that certainly does not mean that it must by the same token be *known* by him' (ibid.). *One has to make a distinction between consciousness and knowledge.* The reflection can only really furnish us with the brute materials 'towards which the psychoanalyst must take an objective attitude' (ibid.: 592). Reflection on its own is only ever quasi-knowing. Subsequently – once more following Freudian analysis – dreams, failures and obsessions are still important to analyse, and still reflect our psychic self. But rather than reflecting the libido, they reflect the totality of the self, the first primary choice, or our total relation to the world and Others.

The concept of *lived experience* (*le vécu*) of Sartre's later period expands on this notion, *explicitly* recognising a 'dialectical process of psychic life' as well as 'processes which are "below" consciousness and which are also rational, but lived as irrational' (Sartre 2008b: 42). In reference to *Saint Genet* and *The Family Idiot*, Sartre states:

> The individual interiorizes his social determinations: he interiorizes the relations of production, the family of his childhood, the historical past, the cotemporary institutions, and he then re-exteriorizes these in acts and options which necessarily refer us back to them. (Ibid.: 35)[11]

Furthermore, such predispositions operate in a *habitual way*, easily recalled into action, *lived* rather than *known*. The 'intellectual's thought must ceaselessly turn back on itself in order to always apprehend itself as a *singular universal*' (ibid.: 249) – a 'thought is secretly singularised by the class prejudices inculcated in him since childhood', (ibid.) and so the 'universality of the idea is limited by the singularity of the fact, a *dated* and *localized* event that *takes place* at a certain point in the history of a nation, and which resumes and totalizes it to the extent that it is a totalized product of it' (ibid.: 251–3). This being the case, it is possible to liquidate forms of bad faith in man, such as 'the traces of racism within him left over by his childhood, by a rigorous investigation of the "incomparable monster" that is his self' (ibid.: 249).

It is only after, or on top of, this initial relation that Sartre construes the transition from the body-*for-me*, to the *body-for-Others*. Then, from the body-for-Others to a third dimension: 'I exist for myself as a body known by the Other' (Sartre 2008a: 375). Overall, the Other's role is bringing our body to reflective consciousness, dragging it out of the non-thetic and transforming it into an object, rather than being the primal form of interaction via alienation. Due to the existence of the Other, my body is 'extended outside in a dimension of flight which escapes me' (ibid.). Through the Other my body is alienated, becoming simply a 'tool-among-tools' or 'a being-a-sense-organ-apprehended-by-sense-organs, and this is accompanied by alienating destruction and a concrete collapse of *my* world which flows toward the Other and which the Other will reapprehend in *his* world' (ibid.: 376). When a person feels embarrassed or feels himself blushing, when he is aware and anxious of a facial scar, acne, bad hair and so forth, he is really 'vividly and constantly conscious of his body not as it is for him but as it is *for the Other*' (ibid.). I cannot be embarrassed by my own body as I exist it, but only as it is for the Other. Thus, when I attempt to hide a scar, acne, or to correct my hair, it is not my body-for-myself which I wish to annihilate, but this inapprehensible dimension of the body-alienated. In this instance, my body becomes another means through which I may be estranged from myself through the Other.

Again in accordance with Sartre's attempt to move from the

abstract to the concrete, his next task, once making us cognisant of *what* the body is, is to uncover our concrete relations with Others. These will 'represent the various attitudes of the for-itself in a world where there are Others' (ibid.: 383). In turning to the attitude of desire, Sartre stumbles upon *where* the body is. The relations uncovered in his analysis of the body, 'presuppose a facticity' (ibid.) – *the flesh*. Here, Sartre envisions consciousness as engulfed in a body, which is engulfed in the world as the surface between the for-itself and in-itself, or the intensive of consciousness and the extensive Outside to which consciousnesses intend. Thus, by flesh, 'we do not mean *a part of* the body such as the dermis, the connective tissues or, specifically, epidermis; neither need we assume that the body will be "at rest" or dozing although often it is thus that its flesh is best revealed' (ibid.: 412). Rather, prefiguring Merleau-Ponty's (1968) use of the concept, the flesh is the fundamental stuff of Being, which the body is in and of.

That is to say, the body is the surface (third term) or interface between, through which the virtual content of the Idea can be actualised in time as extended in space, as its final mechanical movement or contraction. Further, it is by virtue of the body's extensivity and mechanical movement, or rather the way it is *in* and *of* the world's flesh, that we can have an intellectual and intuitive experience of reality as extended, namely in the form of memories as continual recordings of these experiences, and a past as a springboard for my actions and corresponding thoughts and the ability to think reflectively or thetically under the form of extensive homogeneity. Or rather, the body as surface reabsorbs the finished act into the interpenetrative multiplicity (see Sartre 2004: 38), and as such furnishes and informs the direction of consciousness in the form of the pre-reflective past. Life becomes consciousness's immanent Outside, and living thought (as in thetic awareness) becomes an encounter with something substantial, a direct experience of life forces. Indeed, is not the consistent thesis throughout Sartre's work that consciousness, or praxis, exists only as engaged, and it is only in this way that freedom can have any intelligibility? Conscious thetic awareness retroactively creates a fissure (nothingness) between itself and the world. From this comes a conceptualisation of the in-itself and for-itself as simulacra or topological variations of a more primordial intertwining or fabric of univocal Being. It follows that there can be no true self-transparency, or radical choice in its typical sense.

Sartre's main ambition here, however, is to outline how this tactile experience of the fleshly surface comes to my attention as a focus of awareness. For this, he turns to desire, and the act of the caress – touching. As with Sartre's theory of emotions, sexual desire represents a radical modification of the for-itself, wherein the body is no longer grasped as the instrument 'which can not be utilized by any instrument – i.e., as the synthetic organization of my acts in the world' – if it is lived as flesh; so that it is 'as a reference to my flesh that I apprehend the objects in the world' (Sartre 2008a: 414). Thus, in desiring-perception, I discover the fleshy nature of objects, realising my flesh by means of their flesh and so on. And so, here we have the third term, via the flesh, for incarnation is the preliminary condition of the appearance of the Other as flesh to my eyes, which in turn realises my incarnation.

So what are we to make of those moments in *Being and Nothingness* where Sartre depicts the situation as constituted by consciousness, in which case consciousness is made transcendent to its situation (i.e. Sartre's example of Pierre in the café [ibid.: 33–5])? It is notable that such statements and examples are given in the first half of *Being and Nothingness*, in which case we can conclude, in accordance with the comments made earlier regarding analytical priority, that they are designed to depict the phenomenological immediacy of experience as opposed to its ontological housing. That is, such examples reflect the 'strict order of discussion', in which the progression of the text itself reflects the argument it is making, moving from the abstract to the concrete. Though consciousness intends outward to the object, the world of the object already weighs upon it. As said, it is by virtue of the body's extensity and mechanical movement, or rather the way it is *in* and *of* the world's flesh, that we can have an intellectual and intuitive experience of reality as extended, memories as continual recordings of these experiences, the past as a springboard for my actions and corresponding thoughts and the ability to think reflectively or thetically under the form of extensive homogeneity.

So what are we to make of the negative? Though Sartre does indeed argue that for there to be real openness the one who is open to being and who sees must be a partial lacuna in being, wherein the negatite accounts for the way in which the for-itself arises as a knowledge of the in-itself and how this knowledge gives rise to that diversity of things, he goes on to add that negation becomes 'a bond of essential being since at least one of the beings on which it depends is such that it points toward the other, that it carries the other in its heart as an absence' (ibid.: 198). Negation thus depends on something (the flesh of facticity) which exists before the negation and constitutes its matter, in turn making the distinction between the for-itself and the in-itself abstract. For Sartre, the whittling down of the status of nothingness (insofar as it is the abstract moment in the primordial being-in-the-world) does not necessitate the deterioration of the value of negative thinking, in that negativity indeed establishes a this, causing it to exist on the thetic level. But this can only arise on the ground of the presence of all being, understood as flesh. Nothingness can only be human reality apprehending itself as excluded from being and perpetually beyond being, in relationship with that 'nothing', such that nothingness becomes an illusory apprehension of ourselves as transcendent. Through conscious activity it *appears* to us that we are not the world, spatiality, permanence, matter, or, in short, the in-itself in general. Yet the revelation adds nothing to what is reflected, to the in-itself. Rather, it invests it with internal and external negations, in which 'this' and the 'world' arise as distinctions, as things that I am not.

From this, we can also come to understand how the caress is not the realisation of a perfect unity between the in-itself and the for-itself, but rather the realisation and brief capturing of their grounding. Indeed, the impossible unity of the in-itself and the for-itself are two abstracted sides of Being, so to conflate their unity with that of the revelation of univocity of flesh is to neglect the analytical distinction and direction of *Being and Nothingness* altogether. Put differently, the caress is a 'successful' act only insofar as it provides an intuitive moment that serves to deliver us beyond the thetic distinction made in Being, or rather the in-itself/for-itself dualism, wherein our body is actively realised as of the flesh, through which I seek to be with the flesh of the Other. It certainly is not successful in the sense of retroactively unifying the two faces of Being that came out of thetic reflection. In fact, it is the thetic moment of pleasure as nihilation, and so in conjunction with the diasporic nature of temporality, which disrupts the caress and prevents it from enduring through time. Authenticity, after all, is the acceptance that there is no endurance of any essence in Being, or that the essence of Being is its becoming, its constant slide into nothingness via temporality. Bad faith, particularly in the form of the 'impossible' synthesis of the in-itself-for-itself (to become Man-God), then, is precisely the misdirected attempt to realise a static essence, an attempt to realise a concrete Ideal out of a contingent Being, an active denial of what one is, which is what one is not.

The Third Stage: the *Critique* and Sartre's Micropolitics

The key to understanding how Sartre's immanent philosophy of the flesh relates to socio-political matters is to be found in his later works, particularly the *Critique of Dialectical Reason*. This work is marked by the recognition that the formal structure of the situation and facticity, of the flesh, in *Being and Nothingness*, remains somewhat abstract and seemingly apolitical, inasmuch as it is separated from material and social processes. Indeed, most of the reproaches made against Sartre's seminal work following its publication arose more or less from a Marxist understanding of materialism.[12] In his eagerness to retain the singularity of the existential, Sartre sought to defend it on the Marxists' own terms. Two things come as a result of this move. First, is the continuation of his engagement with immanence as depicted in *Being and Nothingness*. In this sense, the *Critique* should be viewed not as a replacement for *Being and Nothingness* as much as a supplement, providing not only a materialisation of situatedness but also a contingent explanation of history and historical struggle. As Sartre makes clear in the second volume of the *Critique*, his position, which opposes Hegelian idealism and external dialecticism, envisions antagonistic reciprocity as a 'bond of immanence between epicenters, since each adversary totalizes and transcends the totalizing action of the other' (Sartre 2006: 5). All determinations are concrete and it is a bond of immanence that unites them. The logic of facticity fleshed out in *Being and Nothingness* is continued, but placed within a particular conceptualisation of history, in this case scarcity (as in the contingent impossibility of satisfying all the needs of an ensemble) (see Sartre 2006: 340). Second, as a result, and though sheathed in dialectical expressions, this serves to anticipate and lay the foundations for Deleuze and Guattari's *assemblage*.

As I said at the start of this book, the political element of 'pure' immanence concerns the material Outside through which the virtual incompossibility of subjectivity is both conditioned and provoked (or 'double-conditioned') into organised actualisation. This is best captured by Deleuze and Guattari's concept of the assemblage. As stated in the introduction, an assemblage is a thoroughly heterogeneous ensemble that synthesises and thus consists of divergent elements, be they biological, social, machinic, gnoseological or imaginary. More specifically, these 'elements' are multiplicities: some are impersonal-intensive/molecular/micro (or, rather, 'virtual'), whereas others are extensive/molar/macro processes of organisation and strategy (or, rather, 'actual'). Immanent in a given assemblage, or rather inhabiting and codifying the mutual imbrication of these two domains like its diagrammatic virtual double, is what Deleuze and Guattari (2004b: 155) refer to as an *abstract machine*, which in *Anti-Oedipus* is construed in terms of the axiomatic of capital, i.e. the ultimate quantitative value that supersedes all other value systems, and redirects subjectivity according to the demands of the market. It is diagrammatic in the sense that it mobilises non-stratified matter and functions, utilising, for instance, various types of discourse and forms of 'scientific' or reified knowledge for a particular purpose, as is the case when the use of police or military force is retrospectively justified according to received notions of civility, justice and authority.

Utilising a formulaic method, this can be related to Sartre's renewed understanding and use of the 'totality', though of course without obscuring any conceptual tensions (i.e. the totality is devoid of the language of 'disjunction' and 'vice-diction' underpinning the assemblage). We can envision the unsurpassable opaqueness of lived experience, including the flesh and totalisations (the latter drawing on and replacing Sartre's previous take on temporality), as making up the 'micro' element; and the totality of the social, and totalisation of the material world as making up the 'macro', with scarcity effectively taking the place of the abstract machine, inasmuch as scarcity acts as a spectre, or a tacit value system, constantly enshrouding the social, operating in the background and thereby influencing (albeit in a mutual reciprocity), orientating, directing and justifying various exercises of force and power.

First, totality. The circularity of the regressive-progressive method underpinning Sartre's approach to totalisation and totality is designed to emphasise that nothing is subordinate to an *a priori*, or that rather the plurality of a multiplicity cannot refer back to a stable unity. Thus totalisation is 'never achieved' and 'the totality exists at best only in the form of a detotalized totality' (Sartre 1963b: 78). Specifically, totalisation is related to totality, as in:

> a being which, while radically distinct from the sum of its parts, is present in its entirety, in one form or another, in each of these parts, and which relates to itself either through its relation to one or more of its parts or through its relation to the relations between all of some of them. (1976b: 45)

In reality this refers to the moment of synthesis, to 'the most rigorous synthesis of the most differentiated multiplicity' (ibid.: 46). In essence, praxis, as in the 'pure spontaneity' of consciousness and the material modification of the world, must be understood as a material totalisation (or synthesis) of its situation, an integration of material multiplicity into a projected totality, or the actualisation of the virtual content of an Idea, immanent to the real Outside that provokes it.

As with the assemblage, this is not to undermine the univocal nature of the elements being brought together. Their disparate nature is only viewed from the vantage point of praxis, or a retroactive identification as a moment of incarnation, wherein a practical reality envelops in its own singularity the ensemble of totalisations in progress – incarnation is totalisation as individuated (Sartre 2006: 28). Furthermore, each struggle is a singularisation of all the circumstances of the social ensemble in movement. By this singularisation, it incarnates the totalisation-of-envelopment constituted by the historical process – 'every totalization is enveloping as a totalization as well as enveloped as a singularity' (ibid.: 49).

Corresponding to the indiscernibility of the assemblage and its corresponding lines of subjectivation (see Deleuze 2007: 345), and in some ways rooted in the conflictual relation in *Being and Nothingness*, this is a never-ending *process*. In this instance, negation exists within the process of totalisation (which is a constant projection into the future) and it is put into opposition with new projects (counter-finalities) that detotalise it. Thus there is a detotalised nature of all totalities and no ultimate teleological movement. In this sense, the totality (a social totality, a political totality, a cultural totality, and so on), as with the assemblage, is relative, a mere 'appearance' of a process that must be upheld for it to appear. Totalisation, then, refers to the process which, through the multiplicities, continues that synthetic labour, 'which makes each part an expression of the whole' (Sartre 1976b: 46). Thus, it is a 'developing totalisation', and the dialectic is a 'totalising activity' (ibid.: 47), in which the 'totality' is a regulative principle. In being an activity related to praxis, it holds that to totalise is to temporalise, which returns us to the immanent movement of consciousness. Or, rather, the human ensemble 'temporalises its (the individual's) totalisation and totalises its temporality' (ibid.: 55).

For this reason, Sartre (ibid.: 113) defines the totality as a 'totalising project'. Furthermore, this totalisation (negation by praxis) exists in a dialectical tension with other totalisations as mediated by the *material world*, and similarly as mediated and conditioned by the totalised and totalising past of the process of human developments: 'I totalise myself on the basis of centuries of history and, in accordance with my culture, I totalise this experience' (Sartre 2004: 54). The individual life becomes 'diluted' in the 'pluridimensional human ensemble', which both temporalises its totalisation and totalises its temporalirity (ibid.: 55). Hence when Sartre speaks of the 'interiorisation of exteriority' and the 'exteriorisation of interiority' (ibid.: 60), he is essentially stating that the wider macro material totality conditions our unique micro totalisation, which in turn conditions the wider macro totality, which in turn conditions us, and so on (what Sartre refers to as 'circularities' and 'feed-back devices' [ibid.: 16]). Such counter-finalities can transform into a practico-inert – a field of activity no longer responsive to the group struggle which founded it (i.e. bureaucracy) – constituting the critical level of 'social Being' (ibid.: 230), in that we all arise in the same field of action or material field of multiplicity. In this way, it is said that beneath the rift of antagonistic dissociation, 'we find not the infinite void but unity again, and human presence. The fissure between the enveloped incarnations allows the plenitude of the unity of immanence to appear as a totalizing and singular incarnation *of all incarnations taken together*' (Sartre 2006: 86). Unity is dissociated within a vaster unity, i.e. that of the totalisation-of-envelopment, which is one of immanence (see ibid.: 85, 448).

Such totalisations do not dissolve the collectives, nor do they unify a multiplicity into a group. Rather, they refer to the way in which every single person defines his or her practical field in a fundamentally univocal relationship, wherein the practical field is engendered by praxis and transformed perpetually by it. Thus, if it 'was right to speak of a transformation of the agents (and of praxis) by the field, this transformation did not break the univocal nature of the fundamental relationship' as a 'synthetic immanence of exteriority' (ibid.: 165). All interior exteriorisations of praxis take place against a 'background of immanence' (ibid.: 231); the agent and the praxis are modified by the practico-inert, 'but in immanence' *inasmuch as they work inside the practical field*. Every person is linked to every person, even if unknown to one another, by an undetermined yet 'reciprocal bond of immanence', constantly ready 'to be actualized', revealing 'the relationship of two persons as having *always* existed' (ibid.: 247, see also Sartre 1976b: 109).

Once more placing the body at the centre of this operation, as the ultimate interface of or surface between interiorisation/exteriorisation, Sartre is led to re-endorse his earlier position on the flesh, but now within the context of a material social reality. The whole event, the process of the social totalisation-of-envelopment, is incarnated, it becomes the body, and will be resuscitated, re-exteriorised, re-produced even, in the form of an enveloped totalisation. Being not inert matter, but rather an affective device, the body will express this immanent bond in its desires. That is, the

> fundamental existence of the sexes as a bond of reciprocity . . . disposes [the individual] in its carnal depth – and within the framework of the historical conjecture – to reactualise, by transcending, the relation of immanence that conditions him in his flesh by means of *that* particular woman: i.e. to realise himself as sexual behaviour at every 'opportunity', in every *encounter*, i.e. (outside of work) in a permanent way. (Sartre 2006: 260)

Thus, once again, the body makes itself flesh, but also the flesh becomes act, 'while retaining the opaque passivity of fleshly thickening to the very point of orientating practically . . . and revealing its own arousal', thus the 'carnal act' (ibid.).

The significance of the assemblage, and more specifically Sartre's prefiguring of it via totalisation, is the way in which its univocal immanence delivers us away from a teleological, segmented and/or subject-based conceptualisation of the social world. The social world is shown to be a fluid process of contingent and heterogeneous connections that permeate various levels of organisation, combining micro and macro elements such that one cannot be truly understood or defined without reference to the other. The subject – though this is already a misleading term – is not an epicentre of social reality, but rather a variant of it, the effect of an immanent generativity. Thus, as opposed to a politics of the subject, this presents us with a micropolitics. That is, instead of focusing on the subject, no matter how contingent or displaced, as the site of primary political transformation and subjectivation, Sartre's totalisation leads us to focus on an immanent or virtual, impersonal and pre-individual life. To put it in more concrete terms, Sartre's totalisation speaks to a micropolitics, as described in the introduction, by:

1. Elucidating an immanent generativity that entirely eschews the subject as a precondition of thought, meaning and action.

Indeed, this in and of itself establishes a direct challenge to social contract theory, and its retention of an asocial 'empirical' subject, or 'chooser of ends'.
2. Connecting this immanent process of subjectivity with a material socio-political reality, such that even one's most intimate and 'private' sense of self can be seen to be politically marked or engaged.

Existential Ethics and Immanent Freedom

A micropolitics of this order, as in one that displaces the centrality to the subject only to expose how even our most intimate and private sense of self is politically configured, raises the question of freedom, or rather resistance. There is clearly no *a priori* transcendental subject of freedom to be had in this philosophy, a basic rational conscious deliberator nor negative rupture in the vein of lack. How does Sartre avoid structural determination and the obliteration of any genuine resistive act of freedom? How do we, in other words, break free of micropolitical subjectification? These are questions that have continued to plague philosophers of immanence and theorists of micropolitics, as we saw in the introduction. But there are answers, the origins of which, once again, we can find in Sartre. Resistance is found in self-experimentation, which is, in effect, an authentic embrace of existential freedom.

In repudiating Husserl's idealism, the early Sartre claims he 'immersed man back in the world', and as such restored to man's 'anguish and his sufferings, and to his rebellions too, their full weight' (2004: 51). With this, he declares: 'Nothing further is needed to enable us to establish philosophically an absolute positive ethics and politics' (ibid.: 52). This ethics is one of authenticity, typically construed as accepting the enduring the responsibility of one's 'radical choice'. That is to say, our ontological condition (nihilation) leaves us utterly responsible for choosing the self we become and the evaluations that emanate from that self. Is authenticity, then, the mere acceptance of this responsibility, conjoined to the idea that the unhappy consciousness, being the axiomatic condition of nihilation, is unsurpassable? No. As far as 'freedom' is concerned, Sartre does not look for a break or fracture in immanence or an outside positive supplement. If the forces at work below the simulative level of the self or I are immanent, *then so too is resistance.* Sartre's valuative ideal of authenticity speaks to the way in which we seek such a practice of freedom, in which we attempt to *recognise* and *utilise* the *conditions* and *factitious limits* that have given form to this semblance of the ego, prior to contractual engagements. As said, the appearance of the ego in this case 'is not so much theoretical as practical', providing a point of reference, or a way to sustain various forms of concrete concerted agency, in turn enabling us to conceptualise self-to-self relations and ethical considerations (ibid.: 48).

It is precisely with this immanent relation in mind that Sartre says the self chooses itself in *situation*, that 'the exercise of this freedom may be considered as *authentic* or *inauthentic* according to the choices made in the situation', that authenticity 'consists in having a true and lucid consciousness of the situation, in assuming the responsibilities and risks that it involves in accepting it in pride or humiliation, sometimes in horror and hate' (Sartre 1976a: 9). Hence the central Sartrean claim: 'man can always make something out of what is made of him' (2008b: 35). That is, man is 'totally conditioned by his social existence and yet sufficiently capable of decision to reassume all this conditioning and to become responsible for it' (ibid.: 34). Sartre asserts that this 'is the limit I would today accord to freedom: the small movement which makes of a totally conditioned social being someone who does not render back completely what his conditioning has given him' (ibid.: 35). Subsequently, man 'cannot be distinguished from his situation, for it forms him and decides his possibilities; but, inversely, it is he who gives it meaning by making his choices within it and by it', which is to say that to be in a situation is '*to choose oneself* in a situation' (Sartre 1976a: 60). Strictly in this sense, it is said that to choose is to invent: 'You are free, therefore choose – that is to say, invent' (Sartre 2007: 43). Choice is a moment of creation and invention precisely because existence is prior to essence. In choosing oneself, then, there is no predefined eternal image or identity to which one could refer. Any such image would therefore have to be created anew, but *only* out of the stuff out of which one has been made (hence why 'Jewish authenticity consists in choosing oneself *as Jew* – that is, in realizing one's Jewish condition' [Sartre 1976a: 136]). For that reason, 'of all the actions a man may take in order to create himself as he wills to be, there is not one which is not creative', and we 'will to exist at the same time as we fashion our image' (Sartre 2007: 32). It is in this way that man is put in possession of himself as he is and 'places the entire responsibility for his existence squarely upon his own shoulders' (ibid.: 31).[13]

We can say, then, that authenticity is understood as a creative task. It recognises that no 'rule of general morality can show you what you ought to do: no signs are vouchsafed in this world' (ibid.: 43). Similarly, it strays away from the Platonic model of 'know thyself' in emphasising that men have a 'condition' as opposed to a 'nature' in common (see Sartre 1976a: 60), in emphasising man's nothingness – existence precedes essence. For this reason, Sartre argues that authenticity is not supposed to refer to an actuality, that 'the authenticity of your previous momentum doesn't protect you in any way against falling next instant into the inauthentic'. Authenticity is 'all of a piece' and so 'it isn't enough to have acquired it once, in respect of a particular, concrete circumstance, in order for it to extend itself spontaneously to all the situations in which we are plunged' (Sartre 1984: 220) – it 'is by no means enough to be authentic: it's necessary to adapt one's life to one's authenticity' (ibid.: 221). The moment a person proclaims to be 'authentic', s/he slips back into bad faith, for s/he fails to negate, taking his or her *self* to be (or to possess) an essence of sorts. In this sense, Sartre's philosophy is one of becoming that never reduces itself to a belief in static being. Its negation is tantamount to Zarathustra's 'active destruction' (see Deleuze 2006d: 167).

Thus, authenticity should be viewed as an attitude and practice not only insofar as any static identity would fall back into bad faith, but also insofar as the limit of freedom ensures that we are never quite completely rid of all social conditioning, that we never quite reach a 'pure' existential state. One must always seek to take advantage of the *small movements* – a constant attempt to gain lucid and attentive consciousness of one's situation and take as much responsibility for it as is possible within these parameters – that is, of the limits that define the self. Authenticity does not refer to the radical dissolution of all that makes up the self, a return to some archaic *tabula rasa* wherein one can create something entirely new and distinct from its past. Authenticity is the moment of creative affirmation, but within the confines of a context.[14]

What the *Critique* adds to authenticity is a material situation in which freedom arises and through which freedom navigates. Thus the self-experimental model of authenticity is clearly not merely ethical, but politico-ethical, seeking to subvert and play with a sense of self constituted through immanent processes of totalisation-detotalisation of praxis. Congruent with Sartre's idea of 'feedback mechanisms' in processes of totalisation, such practices of authenticity alter the feedback or change the resonance of a totality, of an assemblage. Thus authenticity is both a process and a micropolitical ethic that can serve to subvert, undermine and radically alter macropolitical forms. This is perhaps the most important political aspect of immanence. Real change, real resistance, starts at the microscopic level. We must change ourselves, before we can hope to change our politics.

Conceptual Limits

So why not stop with Sartre? Why must we go onto to consider three more thinkers? Out of conceptual necessity. For Sartre fails to complete immanence in any absolute sense. The retention of some form of ontological polarity – at least insofar as the language itself is retained – evokes an image of transcendence. In anticipation of our discussion in the next chapter, we would do well to note Merleau-Ponty's statement that language, much like music, 'can sustain a sense by virtue of its own arrangement, catch a meaning in its own mesh, that it does so without exception each time it is conquering, active, creative language, each time something is, in the strong sense, said' (Merleau-Ponty 1968: 153). That is to say, language signifies existentially according to its expressive styles, conveying a latent existential sensitivity. With specific regard for Sartre, although immanence underpins his ontology he did not escape dualist ways of expressing negativity, perhaps underestimating the difficulty of conveying the chiasmic interworld to which he was reaching. Invariably, this led to an image of subjectivity in which existential processes seem attributed to a subject and in which the philosophical emphasis still *seems* to be on a knowing, meaning-giving (*sens*) consciousness, even though it is precognitive. As mentioned earlier, Sartre's early and middle works are littered with explicit rejections of immanence on the basis that it denies the Outside to which consciousness intends, and which already weighs upon us. It is only in the *Critique*, as evidenced above, that we finally see Sartre move away from this rather simplistic understanding of immanence as pure idealist interiority, as 'the pure subjectivity of the instantaneous *cogito*' (Sartre 2008a: 68), or as some pure internal conditioning that denies any ontological footing for the Other and Outside. Immanence, as expressed and employed in the

Critique, clearly has its own Outside. Even so, the conceptualisation is limited by its dualistic and dialectical expression, in which case some form of the negative (and so a formal transcendence) persists as seemingly integral to the process of subjectivity. As I have argued earlier in the chapter, this has led Sartre's interpreters – and at times Sartre himself – unwittingly to endorse a politics of transcendence.

In addition to this ambiguity of language, Sartre's use of the flesh and the body, without its support or reference to Merleau-Ponty, contains Kantian ambiguities insofar as it retains traces of the very representationalism he sought to overcome, primarily in that the body is given the role of mediation. Given Sartre's commitment to realism, this is not the intention, and though the body appears to mediate, it is envisioned as doing so without, or rather beyond, representation.[15] However, it will take Merleau-Ponty to elucidate this point, and from it to develop a notion of generative flesh/body that moves us as close as possible to immanence within the scope of phenomenology (limited only in straddling too closely to the phenomenon as opposed to its violent genesis or force).

In this respect, Sartre cannot be said to provide a complete or consistent picture of immanence, but certainly he instigates a project of it in both ontological and political terms, already putting into doubt the central premise underpinning liberal politics and transcendence: that of the centred self, and that of the subject-object split or second-order Otherness and the subject of negativity. As I will argue in the next chapter, Merleau-Ponty not only 'fleshes out' the flesh, so to speak, but also develops a language, specifically in terms of the fold, beyond Sartre's dualistic tendencies, one that is capable of conveying immanence. This, if anything, is Merleau-Ponty's advantage over Sartre. To my mind, this is precisely why Sartre, in a number of his later essays, very subtly clarifies his position with reference to Merleau-Ponty.[16] But it is Sartre who instigates this project and sets its philosophical context.

Notes

1. See Hazel E. Barnes (1974: 13).
2. See for instance, Barrett (1990: 245), Craib (1976: 93), Fox (2003: 149) and Warnock (1970: 128).
3. See for instance, Baugh (2003: 101), Catalano (1996: 65, 2005: 28) and Cumming (1979: 181).
4. See for instance, Aronson (1978: 226), Cumming (1979: 193), Flynn

(1997: 50), Gillan (1997: 193) and Martinot (1993: 45). With regards to Sartre, this is most clearly evident in his *Notebooks for an Ethics*, when he speaks of 'converting' the conflictual 'hell' of human passions into a mutually supportive intersubjective city of ends. Sartre thematically links this with socialism, insofar as capitalism is seen to perpetuate oppressive structures and conflictual alienation between the self and the Other (Sartre 1992: 20, 500); and in *A Plea for Intellectuals*, where Sartre speaks of bourgeois humanism as an 'ideology complex' that is formed through superstructures at the hands of the 'ruling class' (Sartre 2008b: 237–8).

5. A '*hyletic* or *material data*' (Husserl 2012: 176) accounts for the way in which sensory data 'offer themselves as material for intentional informing or bestowals of meaning at differential levels' (ibid.: 175), or how 'objective unities of every region and category "are consciously constituted"' (ibid.: 179–80).
6. Forrest Williams and Robert Kirkpatrick's earlier translation of the text indeed renders the French 'apperance' as 'semblance', which seems more appropriate given its use in the context of Sartre discussing the ego's 'pseudo-spontaneity'. See Sartre (1957: 79).
7. It is specifically in this sense that Sartre's take on time is intricately woven into his theory of nothingness, a point seemingly missed by a number of interpreters, i.e. Anderson (1993: 11–14), Catalano (2005), Detmer (2005: 81), Danto (1975: 35–70), Hatzimoysis (2011: 31) and Warnock (1970: 87). In addition to this take on temporality, and contra Hegel's presupposition that Being and nothingness are empty abstractions, it is not the case that Being *is* and that nothingness *is not* (see Sartre 2008a: 39). Nothingness is not an original abyss from which Being arose, but rather is an abyss created by Being; it 'lies coiled in the heart of being – like a worm' (ibid.: 45). The origin of nothingness would then be in the being of Being, in Man as a being-in-the-world.
8. Though the 'necessity of syntax has compelled us hitherto to speak of the "non-positional consciousness of self"', we can 'no longer use this expression in which the "of self" still evokes the idea of knowledge', hence the use of parentheses to show that it merely satisfies grammatical requirement (Sartre 2008a: 10).
9. Sartre as the avowed champion of the unhappy conscious.
10. Sartre (2008b: 199) himself states that he is not 'a "false friend" of psychoanalysis, but a critical fellow-traveler, and I have neither desire, nor the wherewithal, to ridicule it'. Certainly it is not the unconscious per se that he rejects, but rather the 'unconscious in the form in which psychoanalysis presents it to us' (ibid.: 39).
11. Sartre (2008b: 283) goes on to associate interiorisation and lived experience with ideology (in the Gramscian sense), denoting the way

in which 'social past and the historical conjuncture' are '*lived* without being *known*'.
12. That is, Adorno (1973: 50), Lukács (1973) and Marcuse (1948: 311).
13. Subsequently, Taylor's (1976: 293) claims that Sartre's radical choice as regards the option to create oneself anew in a vacuum – that it lacks attention to the background and to pre-established choices, and that it overlooks 'radical questioning' – is evidently misguided.
14. This emphasis on affirmation is important, for it rails again other readings of authenticity as the acceptance of life in a nihilistic conjecture, i.e. Baugh (2003: 117) and Deleuze (2006d: 171). It has been forgotten that Sartre (2013: 89) makes a sharp distinction between anguish and 'neurasthenia', wherein the latter makes 'pathological terror out of this virile uneasiness existentialism speaks of'. Thus authenticity is not only an attitude that embraces this responsibility – seeking constantly to question every motive and every excuse, every attempt to make myself an in-itself, in order to repudiate self-deception and promote creation – but also one that celebrates and revels in this enduring sense of responsibility, where 'true optimism begins: the optimism of the man who expects nothing, who knows he has no rights and nothing coming to him, who rejoices in counting on himself alone and in acting alone for the good of all' (ibid.: 90). It may be observed that there is an apparent paradox underpinning this claim, in that Sartre presents affirmation as inseparable from a preliminary negative condition, that the affirmation of authenticity is in fact premised on another kind of negation: the negatite. We must recognise that there are evidently two senses of negation that must be separated from each other. One, understood as the negatite, is the human activity or act of the for-itself, which does not denote a negative judgement; and the other is an attitude or judgement on existence, which in turn structures our attitude to the original negatite.
15. As Sartre (1969: 46) says himself, all of his work has been underpinned by an attempt 'to provide a philosophical foundation to realism'.
16. See Sartre (2008b: 154, 2013: 316).

Chapter 2
Merleau-Ponty and the Fold of the Flesh

Unlike Sartre, Merleau-Ponty moves towards a more direct ontological enquiry into the appearing of the visible-tactile field – the actual – itself, which results in an anti-humanist ontology (or *real humanism* as he calls it) that locates perceiving bodies within a meaning-generating *folded flesh*; a folded fabric of univocal Being that is beyond any notion of a metaphysical outside or internal transcendent Other. Merleau-Ponty's 'fold' signifies a necessary renewal of philosophical language that entirely bypasses dualism in vernacular form, and subsequently any evocation of transcendence – a limitation that plagues Sartre. This serves to both radicalise Sartre's socio-political ethic of authenticity as an a-subjective form of resistance and set the premise for the development of Foucault's relational understanding of immanent power, and Deleuze's subsequent addition of desire as the *folded* inside of that power. This makes Merleau-Ponty pivotal to the present lineage, where he acts as a proverbial halfway house between Sartre's instigation of immanence through existential phenomenology and its more overt, systemised and politicised form in Foucault and Deleuze.[1] Ultimately, it is through exploring Merleau-Ponty that we may come to understand the necessity and thus importance of the fold in the development of 'pure' immanence and micropolitics.

I begin the chapter by arguing that Merleau-Ponty's early works, particularly *Phenomenology of Perception*, opens the way for the development of the fold, in particular through its anti-Cartesian focus on the subject-body and the related attempt to overcome extreme subjectivism and extreme objectivism via focusing on the non-dualist lifeworld to which the subject-body belongs. This comes out of a direct engagement with Sartre's phenomenological ontology, albeit one partly based upon a 'creative misreading' of it, with its alleged rationalist self-transparency used as a methodological foil. I move on to consider Merleau-Ponty's all-important 'self-criticism', i.e. the realisation that this anti-Cartesian bid for the non-dualist lifeworld, cannot be fully realised without investigating, and correcting, its own presupposition or prejudicative *Logos* to which its expressive style and conceptual apparatus is beholden. The presupposition, in this instance, is that of a dualistic subject-object epistemological starting point that in a circular fashion unwittingly corresponds with and props up a dualistic ontology. Thus to attend to the presuppositions inherent in conceptual language is at the same time to attend to the 'being' that envelops, forgets and obscures it. This opens up Merleau-Ponty to a direct ontological enquiry that though heavily drawing on and therefore intelligible only through understanding Riemman's non-Euclidean geometry, as I argue, is conducted in the field of aesthetics. Through this enquiry, Merleau-Ponty expands Sartre's concept of the 'flesh', and adds to it the concept of the 'fold'. Aside from providing a new philosophical vernacular, or rather because of it, Merleau-Ponty's 'folded flesh' results in a politico-ethics of ambiguity as a radicalised extension of Sartrean authenticity and thus micropolitics. I conclude the chapter by arguing that, though laying the conceptual groundwork for Foucault and Deleuze, Merleau-Ponty's fold is limited in its political vagueness, i.e. that it does not develop a clear and concrete theory of folded force as a political relation. Thus though contributing to the advancement of immanence as both a consistent ontology and as the conceptual basis for micropolitics, there is a tangible need to look beyond Merleau-Ponty, albeit *through* Merleau-Ponty.

The Crisis of Modern Thought

If the tradition of transcendence as a conceptual architecture accompanying subjectivity is traceable and partly exemplified in Descartes, then it is notable that Merleau-Ponty's foray into philosophy is self-identified as wholly anti-Cartesian in its aspirations; a point often missed by those who insist that Merleau-Ponty is a thinker of transcendence.[2] In no way arbitrary or frivolous, the aspiration emanates from what Merleau-Ponty sees as a distinctly Cartesian or dualistic crisis afflicting modern thought. Between the extreme objectivism of empiricism and the extreme subjectivism of rationalism exists a mutual neglect of any kind of interworld or reconciliatory account of an 'in-between' of interiority and exteriority. The result in both cases is an irreconcilable dualism that is incapable of accounting for co-existence or intersubjectivity in any coherent or substantial way.

Empiricism can be defined by the 'constancy hypothesis', which holds that there exists a direct correspondence and constant connection between stimulus and elementary perception. We directly perceive and know objects without representational mediation of an *a priori* synthetic structure. That being the case, there is no concept of consciousness, subjectivity or interiority to speak of, at least not on the terms familiar to rationalist epistemologies. The hypothesis, however, conflicts with the most elementary data of consciousness. If perception of the object is not mediated then it follows that any sense-datum of it is received in atomistic and disorganised form; that is, as a brute perceptual given of the object. Yet it is apparent that, the 'central combination of stimuli can immediately give rise to a different sensation from what the objective stimuli would lead us to expect' (Merleau-Ponty 2002: 9). That is to say, perceptual atomism simply cannot account for the evidence of a perceptual context or background, against which sense impressions are organised into meaningful, cogent spatio-temporal wholes. Such is the case, albeit a simple one, with Müller-Lyer's optical illusion (Figure 2.1), wherein the addition of auxiliary lines makes two figures appear unequal in length even though they are objectively equal.

The question then arises as to how to put, or rather what puts, atomistic sense impressions back together to form a contextual whole. In attempting to salvage its primary theoretical position in the face of this problem, empiricism turns to 'associationism'. At its most basic, associationism holds that atomistic sense impressions

Figure 2.1 The Müller-Lyer illusion

are organised through processes of resemblance. Previous experiences, in the form of memories, project and fill out sense-data and in return bring about a grouping together of a whole whose consistency is relative to the memory it is associated to. Thus, to *perceive is to remember*. But this merely displaces the problem, for though memory arises from the self it continues to refer to an exterior process. The parts of the thing recalled must have already been bound together by external associations in order to function as an *effective projection* by which the present grouping can both draw upon and relativise itself to. Thus, and quite paradoxically, the 'appeal to memory presupposes what it is supposed to explain; the patterning of data, the imposition of meaning on a chaos of sense-data' (ibid.: 23). The significance of the percept, far from resulting from an association, is presupposed in all association. And so it remains to be explained how the relationship 'figure' and 'background', 'thing' and 'nothing', and the horizon of the past appear as meaningful. When pressed on this point, empiricists almost always revert back to a tacit form of rationalism, treating the *a priori* of the structures of consciousness as if the product of mental chemistry.

But what is problematic with rationalism? According to Merleau-Ponty (2002: x) rationalism detaches the subject 'by showing that I could not possibly apprehend anything as existing unless I first of all experienced myself as existing in the act of apprehending'. The analytical reflection underpinning rationalism takes our primary experience of the world and traces it back to the subject as a condition of possibility distinct from that experience, 'revealing the all-embracing synthesis as that without which there would be no world' (ibid.). In this instance, consciousness is presented as the condition of there being anything at all, 'the act of relating as the basis of relatedness' (ibid.). It ceases to remain part of our experience, offering – in lieu of an account – a reconstruction. The reflection remains incomplete in that it loses sight of its own beginning, its own genesis, in the intricate relation between the *naturata* and the *naturans*. The relation signifies the way in which the world is there before any possible analysis of mine, such that it would be 'artificial to make it the outcome of a series of syntheses which link, in the first place sensations, then aspects of the object corresponding to different perspectives, when both are nothing but products of analysis, with no sort of prior reality' (ibid.: xi). Simply put, when I reflect, my reflection bears upon an unreflective experience. What is more, my reflection cannot be unaware of itself as an event, and so 'it appears to itself in the light of a truly creative act, of a changed structure of consciousness' (ibid.).

Aside from neglecting what can be described as the ontological or concrete grounding of epistemic experience, there is also a problem regarding the epistemological aspect of the rationalist conceptualisation itself. If such an activity is posited as taking place in the mind, there is no concrete or viable way of actually knowing whether or not what we perceive is the same as the brute existent actually there, and so we run into solipsistic and epistemological problems associated with Cartesian doubt and Meno's paradox respectively, in which case my existence is reduced to a bare awareness of existing: 'I think, therefore I am.'[3] By the same measure, the Other is turned into an empty word. Which is to say that analytical reflection knows 'nothing of the problem of other minds, or of that of the world' (ibid.: xiii). And here we find the true Achilles heel of rationalism: the only way it can overcome this doubt is by presupposing the very naturalist or positivist attitude it is supposed to account for and, ultimately, transcend. In this instance, it turns to empiricism.

In continuing to refer back to each other in the manner of a circular conceptual constitution, the affinity between empiricism and rationalism is 'much less obvious and much more deeply rooted than is commonly thought', arising as it were 'not only from the anthropological definition of sensation used equally by both, but from the fact that both persist in the natural or dogmatic attitude' (ibid.: 45). Indeed, what is truly interesting is their quiet complicity in establishing an anthro-naturalist transcendence. The dualism established is not just that of two extreme positions, but also that of the extremity of thought that arises from the intellectual bondage of the two positions and the pre-philosophical ground subsequently established from the inconsistencies within and between them. This is a pre-philosophical ground where the self is always already split between an 'outer' (in accordance with the world) and an 'inner' (beyond the world) version. From whatever angle one looks at it, transcendence remains as a formal structure, in that a thing (whether the subject or the world) is constituted by something outside of it, sustaining a rupture of what would be an otherwise insular domain of immanence.

Philosophical thought need not operate within this paradigm. What both positions overlook, according to Merleau-Ponty (ibid.: viii), is 'the central theme of phenomenology': the interworld or lifeworld (*Lebenswelt*) – that which exists in between the two extremes. By virtue of it, I am always already *open to* the world, and I am always already in communication with others taken as similar psycho-physical subjects. Truly, the *cogito* must reveal me in a situation, for it is 'on this condition alone that transcendental subjectivity can ... *be* an intersubjectivity', wherein the world is something I discover in me as the permanent horizon of all my *cogitationes* (ibid.: xiv). Communication – between selves and between 'subjects' and 'objects' – does not happen either just 'out there' or 'in here', but rather 'in-between' the two, such that it problematises the dualism itself. Within this perspective all negation or epistemic doubt, as that which underpins dualistic thought, takes place 'in a field open in advance, and testifies to a self contiguous with itself before those particular acts in which it loses contact with itself' (ibid.: 417). By extension, the socio-political world is, in a vein not dissimilar to Sartre's notion of totalisation, turned into a *permanent* field of existence. I am always situated relative to it. For the alien life, the living being, is an open life.

From this perspective, the principal gain of phenomenology is to have amalgamated extreme subjectivism and extreme objectivism, thereby overcoming dualism. Though Merleau-Ponty consistently credits Husserl with initiating this move, his own phenomenology concretises it by following in Sartre's *existentialist* footsteps, continuing to repudiate representational machinery or *hyletic* structures, positing that the 'external' world is tantamount with the constitution of the self.[4] That is, Merleau-Ponty agrees with Sartre that the real has to be concretely described as opposed to constructed or formed, which means that one cannot put perception into the same category as the syntheses represented by judgements, act or predications, or that one cannot refer to a synthetic ego as that which gives the self subjective unity and individuality. The Sartrean form of intentionality is reintroduced as is the Heideggerian inspired 'being-in-the-world' as the form of the in-between or *Lebenswelt*. We intend outward, towards and sustain the very world or object which in turn weighs upon us and structures the background of these intentional threads. Thus the structure of the *sens* of the object in the world to which we intend is already in consciousness.

For this reason, Merleau-Ponty (ibid.: 413) speaks of an interweaving between the inside and outside, suggestive of a fabric of Being which makes *folding* possible. We 'are inter-woven into a single fabric', such that the world is 'wholly inside and I am wholly outside myself' (ibid.: 474). It is precisely this single fabric that gestures towards immanence, which is our being-in-the-world that makes up the *insular domain*, and, as such, sutures any rupture in/of it. So, though somewhat present in Husserl's own concept of *Lebenswelt*, there is once more a suturing of the 'veritable abyss' of the 'Kantian texts of Husserl', i.e. *Ideas* (ibid.: 321–2 n47). Reality cannot be bracketed; that is the meaning of existential phenomenology, in which primary consciousness is not a transcendental Ego freely positing before itself a multiplicity in itself. The *I* is relative and pre-personal, and it 'dominates diversity only *with the help* of time' (ibid.). That means that to return to the things themselves, as is the clarion cry of phenomenology, 'is to return to that world which precedes knowledge, of which knowledge always *speaks*, and in relation to which every scientific schematization is an abstract and derivative sign-language' (ibid.: x), which is to start with what is concretely primary: the fabric of Being.

Yet it is precisely on this question of primacy, or rather the nature of this fabric, our being-in-the-world and its conceptualisation, that Merleau-Ponty's deviation from and criticisms of Sartre arise. Though the specifics of the criticism vary in accordance with the variation and advances of their respective thinking, the general complaint remains the same: Sartre reinstates the form of transcendence within immanence through a rupture or gap, laying the blame with consciousness as that which generates a split by relating the pre-philosophical ground or plane back to a subject of consciousness. Though overstated, this is certainly true with respect to the dualistic vernacular Sartre utilises. For Merleau-Ponty, two things result from this: first, it is evident that we cannot rely on Sartre to overcome the crisis of modern thought; and, second, to overcome it we would have to start where Sartre ends, and so conceive of an *a priori* Other/Outside (or a 'primordial *We*' [Merleau-Ponty 1964b: 175]) as a fundamental structure of all relations (see Merleau-Ponty 1968: 237). Merleau-Ponty's *Phenomenology of Perception*, wherein primacy and thus the *Lebenswelt*, our being-in-the-world, is given to embodied perception itself, is usually credited with initiating this reversal.[5] It is to this primordial Other/Outside, as the premise for Merleau-Ponty's advancement of immanence, that I now turn.

Phenomenology Reconsidered via the Body

Despite some oversimplifications of Sartre's argument, and the fact that Merleau-Ponty's position is built on top of Sartre's ontology,

Merleau-Ponty creates an unarguably unique image of phenomenology, with a depth of the analysis of embodied perception unparalleled by anything written by Sartre; an analysis critical in the formation of Merleau-Ponty's ontological turn. A turn that provides a new conceptual system or philosophical language no longer caught up in the Cartesian hangover as Sartre's was. What is particularly important in this respect, and certainly it more than makes up the main argument in *Phenomenology of Perception*, is that we always experience things and act within a context, a background, a 'world horizon' of the lifeworld.[6] It is precisely this background, as we will see, that accounts for the primordial, immanent Other/ Outside. As the loci of perception, the body is central in creating a practical field and perceptual context through which we can operate. It is primarily in this sense that our own body is to account for our being-in-the-world: 'in the world as the heart is in the organism: it keeps the visible spectacle constantly alive, it breathes life into it and sustains it inwardly, and with it forms a system' (Merleau-Ponty 2002: 235). It remains that I cannot grasp the unity of an object, the utility of an instrument, the space in which object and instrument are contained and the distance they have from me – or, rather, I simply cannot take action in the world – without the mediation of bodily experience. And the body is only capable of mediating in such a manner, by being geared towards the world, or rather by being in and of the world.

Here, the body is given as both a brute physicality (an in-itself) *and* a psychic determinant (a for-itself), together forming an indistinguishable synergy and thus a site of synthesis, though without recourse to mind or brain representations. With recourse, however, to our being-in-the-world. The ambiguity of being-in-the-world is translated by that of the body. And this, moreover, is understood through, is founded on and cast against the world-horizon, a background structure of the world as related, initially, to the unfolding of time: the body unites present, past and future, secreting time – taken in the Sartrean sense – becoming the location in nature where 'events, instead of pushing each other into the realm of being, project round the present a double horizon of past and future and acquire a historical orientation' (ibid.: 278–9). We can initially understand this role of the body in three interrelated ways.

First, in the sense that the object itself is given to me along with the parts of my body, in a 'living connection comparable, or rather identical, with that existing between my body itself' (ibid.: 237). When I grasp the pen while writing, I am not thetically engaged with it, and so my habitual use of it does not consist in interpreting the pressure it presents on the hand as an indication of the particular positions it takes and as a sign of an external object. Rather, it becomes an extension of the bodily synthesis, an instrument with which one perceives or an auxiliary. I have a certain 'feel' for the pen and its contact with the paper through which my body, in the form of both a perceptual- and motor-intentional habit, reacts to and engages with the world. If the ink is running low, my hand, without positional thought, will press the pen against the paper with greater force, or shake the pen from side to side. If the pen starts to slip, ever so gently, the fingers, again without further positional thought, will adjust accordingly. I may even have a favourite pen, simply by virtue of the frequency of its use: my hand adjusts its writing movements relative to it, reinforcing the desire for its subsequent use. In this case, the pen and so the body as that which the pen is an extension of, gets from things according to the way in which it questions them. And so, to learn to write is to acquire a certain style of writing through the experience of writing itself. The same is true of sight. The gaze is a natural instrument analogous to the pen, where to learn how to see colours, for instance, is to acquire a certain style of seeing, enriching and recasting the body schema.

In any case, I have no need of a clear and articulate perception or abstract thought of my body and the object in order to act in the world. It is enough for me to have the body at my disposal as an undivided power in time. Sensation, then, is also the constitution of habit and lived-through virtual memory (as opposed to intellectual memory), since 'it pre-supposes in me sediments left behind by some previous constitution, so that I am, as a sentient subject, a repository stocked with natural powers at which I am the first to be filled with wonder' (ibid.: 249). Such is the case when I finally learn to drive a car without 'thinking' about the movement of my body in relation to gear changes or the use of the clutch, or the degree by which I should turn the wheel when turning a corner.

Second, in the sense of the extended space in which such operations occurs. As opposed to being derived through a synthesis of the intermittent psychological image or the apparent size of objects and the physical data as it converges on the senses – which either suggests a primary constituting act or that to experience a structure is to receive it into oneself passively – the image and the data are already presupposed in the pre-thetic depth of the embodied and unconscious self, as informed, called forth and motivated by the objects (the 'feel' of the pen and its contact with the paper or the 'feel' of the wheel and its contact with the road) and events I come into contact with (the need to write or the need to avoid a squirrel on the road). Thus even the focus as a focus on something which presents itself to be focused upon is a non-intellectual gaze; it is that 'perceptual genius underlying the thinking subject which can give to things the precise reply that they are awaiting in order to exist before us' (ibid.: 307). Whatever its genetic provocation, this primordial dimension allows the others (height, width, linear time) to come into thetic and intellectual awareness, out of which I can build an image of the world around me. I shall return to this point later, as it concerns the very 'primordial depth', or flesh, underpinning Merleau-Ponty's ontological turn.

Third, time as virtual past via the body. Sedimentation and the habitual lived-through meanings of style of Being do not just concern the immediate practical tasks of the organism and its predisposed movements and gestures:

> All consciousness is, in some measure, perceptual consciousness. If it were possible to lay bare and unfold all the presuppositions in what I call my reason or my ideas at each moment, we should always find experiences which have not been made explicit, large-scale contributions from past and present, a whole 'sedimentary history' which is not only relevant to the *genesis* of my thought, but which determines its *significance* ... whatever I think or decide, it is always against the background of what I have previously believed or done. (Ibid.: 459–60)

And so the 'subject of sensation ... need not be a pure nothingness with no terrestrial weight' (ibid.). A red pen may solicit my gaze according to the practical requirement to write, and my body will know how to write by virtue of past experience, but the way I see and feel its particular shade of red will be determined by my pre-thetic or virtual memory of the shade and by and in accordance with the present context, i.e. time of day, the smell in the room, the particular situation and the recent events preceding it, the people I am with, the objects and colours surrounding it, and so forth. In fact, my gaze may have been solicited by that particular shade, by dint of my preference for it. The body, then, is not just essential in immediate practical matters but also in the constitution of subjectivity, the situation and facticity. I am not '"a hole in being", but a hollow, a perceptual fold, which has been made and which can be unmade' (ibid.: 249–50). Perception, even when seen from the inside, 'expresses a given situation' (ibid.). Between my sensation and myself there stands the thickness of 'some *primal acquisition* which prevents my experience from being clear of itself' (ibid.: 251).

In all three cases, my body establishes a practical field of perception, relative to the world-horizon and the tasks it calls forth and relative to the habitual sediments the world-horizon and my experience of it disposes within my virtual or durational self. It is a constitutive act of synthesis, contextualising the atomistic via the phenomenology of the body and the nexus of living meanings it engages with. This serves to recast intentionality in terms of an arch, as in the pre-thetic connection with the world in which skills and movements are stored not as representations but as dispositions by and through which I intend towards the object; and as related to a phenomenal 'place', our particular and present being-in-the-world (the body's task and situation) which provides a certain 'scope' for our gestures, and a means by which the world is drawn into the 'hold' the phenomenal body takes on its surroundings. The body gears itself into the world, drawing it in and composing it into a context to be explicated, thus providing an intuitive sense of things and a further ability to gear itself into the world, out of which actions arise and upon which reflective thought or the categorial mode of intentionality – where one steps back from actual situations so as to consider other possibilities – is reliant and co-existent.

It follows that a fully constituted subject is one that exists in a world that is simultaneously structured in terms of practical actualities/concrete movements of an habitual sedimented life and abstract possibilities/acts of intellectual grasping. Hence the case of Goldstein's brain damaged patient Schneider, whose inability to integrate abstract possibilities into the space of his practical engagements with the world resulted in a number of odd behaviours, i.e. an inability to point to a part of his body as requested, though with an ability to instantly swat a biting mosquito on his body, with his hand (see ibid.: 118–21). Similarly, in the case of the phantom limb, it is able to exist, primarily because the consciousness of a limb is immediately unclear and nascent. One does not need a clear and articulate perception of his body in order to set off walking. It is enough to have the body at ones disposal, as an undivided power. The phantom limb is not a deliberate decision, it does not take place at the level of positing consciousness, and so it is neither the actual presence of a representation nor a representation of an actual presence. The denial of mutilation speaks to our being-in-the-world, the Sartrean original choice, a habitual and meaningful commitment to a certain physical and inter-human world, with its own tasks, cares, situations and familiar horizons. Simply, to 'have a phantom arm is to remain open to all the actions of which the arm alone is capable; it is to retain the practical field which one enjoyed before mutilation' (ibid.: 94). The fact that severing afferent nerves can 'kill off' the phantom limb implies that the impulses arriving from the stump aids in the preservation of the virtual side of the amputated limb in the circuit of the bodies existence, keeping empty an area that the subjects' history fills, allowing for existential constructions.

We can see that the body, as with Sartre's fleshism, is *in* and *of* the world, such that external perception and the perception of one's own body vary together because 'they are the two facets of one and the same act' (ibid.: 237), such that every 'external perception is immediately synonymous with a certain perception of my body, just as every perception of my body is made explicit in the language of the external perception' (ibid.: 239). Indeed, this is what is meant by Merleau-Ponty (ibid.: 115) when he refers to the body as the 'third term', 'always tacitly understood, in the figure-background structure, and every figure stands out against the double horizon of external and bodily space'. A thing exists in-itself because it resists my knowing it with total certainty, and yet the thing exists for me because I can always experience it through my own body. It is the common middle term where the psychic determining factors and the physiological conditions of an experience gear into each other. We arrive, then, at the 'in-itself-for-me': the re-examination of the dilemma of *for-itself* and *in-itself*.

The conceptual argument has an intriguing effect on our understanding of social subjectivity. Inasmuch as the ego and the alter ego or Other have parallel destinies, it holds that perceptual being-in-the-world additionally necessitates a renewed approach to the problem of the Other and intersubjectivity. Merleau-Ponty (ibid.: 251) claims that the Other is known to me precisely because I am not transparent to myself, and in addition because my subjectivity 'draws its body in its wake'. To the extent that around the perceived body 'a vortex forms, towards which my world is drawn and, so to speak, sucked in', it is no longer just mine, and merely present; rather, it 'is present to x, to that other manifestation of behaviour which begins to take shape in it' (ibid.: 412). The other body, then, is no mere fragment of the world, but 'the theatre of a certain process of elaboration' (ibid.). It is my body which perceives the body of another and 'discovers in that body a miraculous prolongation of my own intentions, a familiar way of dealing with the world' (ibid.). Again, the caress!

Merleau-Ponty (ibid.: 411) believes this once again places him up against Sartre, who apparently tries to overcome solipsism via the dialectic of the look, turning subjective experience into a purely private spectacle, 'since it would no longer be co-extensive with being'. Yet for that Hegelian-type struggle of the look to ever to be possible, 'all must necessarily have some common ground and be mindful of their peaceful co-existence in the world of childhood' (ibid.: 414). The unbearable gaze of the Other is possible only because 'it takes the place of possible communication' (ibid.: 420). Because of my body, my sensory functions, the visual, auditory and tactile field, I am open to the world, already in communication with others taken as similar psycho-physical subjects. Thus we not only weave into the world, but also into each other: 'the experience of dialogue there is constituted between the other person and myself a common ground; my thought and his are inter-woven into a single fabric' (ibid.: 413). The other is no longer a mere bit of behaviour in my transcendental field, nor I in his; 'we are collaborators for each other in consummate reciprocity', our 'perspectives merge into each other, and we co-exist through a common world' (ibid.). The Other, as with the Outside, is primordial.

In truth, Merleau-Ponty (ibid.: 417) is once again not far off from Sartre in concluding from this that all negation and doubt takes place in a field open in advance, and testifies to a self contiguous with itself 'before those particular acts in which it loses contact with itself'. Indeed, for Sartre, as we saw, the look does not constitute an intersubjectivity, it is merely one of its after-affects, or a concrete realisation of it. Further, Merleau-Ponty also follows Sartre in seeing the ego and the alter ego as semblances or as 'merely a little shadow which owes its very existence to the light', which means to say 'they have validity rather than existence' (ibid.: xv). As Merleau-Ponty (1964b: 175) puts it in *Signs*, the 'reduction to "egology" or the "sphere of belonging" is, like all reduction, only a test of primordial bonds, a way of following them into their final prolongations'. As was the case with Sartre, when applied within a socio-political context, specifically the way in which social forces act upon the body, we can begin to contemplate the way our (inter)subjectivity is always already socially and normatively mediated, raising numerous questions – questions I raised at the end of the last chapter – about our subjective sense of freedom.

Existential Ethics and Authenticity Revisited

How does one gain freedom in this situation? Is Merleau-Ponty's position identical to Sartre's? In the broad sense, yes. The principle is the same. Changes to self, at the most microscopic level, on and through the body as the pivot or hinge between inside and outside, have profound consequences beyond the self. They can alter the resonance, so to speak, within an assemblage. The *sens* of the self can feed back into the very social that acts on it. If the body is the supreme site of immanent forces, transformations and constitution, it is also the site of resistance. Transformation is not unidirectional, after all. It is fluid. But though both Sartre and Merleau-Ponty are concerned with the body, its position in phenomenological analysis is clearly different in each case, subsequently affecting the nuances of existential freedom. For Sartre, as we saw, the body is that which is lived or passed through when engaged in activities. As we are not explicitly aware of our perception as coming from a perspective, it follows that 'pure reflection' would initially have to suspend the body. Thus we cannot phenomenologically start with sensation. In this way, Sartre is able to sustain the negative in the form of the negatite, while denying that it is generative of being. This is to come back to a point made in the previous chapter: negation is secondary, depending on something (the flesh of facticity) which exists before the negation and constitutes its matter, in turn making the distinction between the for-itself and in-itself abstract.

The idea is not to eliminate nothingness but rather to incorporate it into the idea of being, insofar as all thought of the void is the thought of a certain plenitude. Thus, for Sartre, the whittling down of the status of nothingness (insofar as it is the abstract moment in the primordial being-in-the-world) does not necessitate the deterioration of the value of negative thinking. Specifically, the negatite as that which comes with thetic or reflective thought, accounts for the way in which the for-itself arises as a knowledge of the in-itself and how this knowledge gives rise to that diversity of things, the world. To know things (thises) as distinct is the pure revelation of the in-itself by the for-itself. It is in this way that the for-itself is understood as a being such that in its being its being is in question insofar as this being is essentially a certain way of *not being* a being, which it posits simultaneously as other than itself. So Sartre (2008a: 197) puts it, 'the for-itself can be only in the mode of a reflection (reflect) causing itself to be reflected as not being a certain being', that is, the 'reflected causes itself to be qualified *outside* next to a certain being as *not being* that being; hence what we mean by "to be consciousness *of* something"'. This refers to an internal negation, as a relation between two beings: the one which is denied to the other qualifies the other at the heart of its essence by absence. Sartre resists thetic or intellectualised fusion of the two abstracts, as it 'would signify the solidification of the for-itself in the in-itself, and at the same stroke, the disappearance of the world and of the in-itself as presence' (ibid.: 201); but this is not to deny ontological univocity, only epistemological sameness.

It seems clear to me that Merleau-Ponty is not completely correct to identify Sartre's mistake as making this bond the primary opening of being towards the world, such that the being that I am not is in actuality *not* me in any way, with any relation thus establishing an ontological gap or hole. For Sartre, negativity indeed establishes a 'this', causing it to exist on the thetic level. But this can only arise on the ground of the presence of all Being, understood as flesh. The real difference between Sartre and Merleau-Ponty lies in Merleau-Ponty starting with a Gestalten-inspired take on perception as analytically primary, leading him to a notion of life understood as pure ambiguity and contingency – as the ambiguous reciprocity between the world and the body and the contingent nature of our freedom – that is not different to Sartre's, but perhaps more radical in leaving 'pure' consciousness behind. It has a different emphasis. With such a view, Merleau-Ponty asserts that it is improper to privilege consciousness over the body and perception in phenomenological reduction. Contra Sartre, the body is not passed through and then found in the world; it is quite simply the world as is. Just as consciousness cannot be bracketed from reality, it cannot be bracketed from the body as part of that reality. With this in mind, it comes as no surprise that Merleau-Ponty places far greater emphasis on the way in which our body and our habits nondeterministically shape our lives below the level of thetic awareness, and that he is looked to concerning questions of immanence within phenomenology.[7]

Initially, however, Merleau-Ponty follows Sartre on the very simple point that what we call obstacles to freedom are in reality deployed by it. There is, then, 'nothing that can set limits to freedom, except those limits that freedom itself has set in the form of its various initiatives, so that the subject has simply the external world that he gives himself' (Merleau-Ponty 2002: 507). This may risk making the concept of freedom redundant, for if it is everywhere and therefore not something to be measured in terms of our conduct, it is anterior to all actions. The point, however, is that freedom finds its fulcrum in our general commitment to the world, making for a concrete subject (another way of saying the 'subject' emerges after the primordial experience of being-in-the-world). Our freedom does not destroy our situation but gears itself to it.

This supposedly is not a return to Kantian idealism, where consciousness finds in things only what it has put into them. Merleau-Ponty's entire point is to seek the conditions of possibility while concerning ourselves with the conditions of reality, thereby resuming the analysis of *Sinngebung*. It is freedom which brings into being the obstacles to freedom – as it is reflex that returns to and signifies the objective stimulus – so that the latter can be set over and against it as its bounds. Merleau-Ponty thus comes to also endorse Sartre's notion of facticity, with specific reference to the crag on a mountain. As Sartre (2008a: 510) argues, to the climber who wishes to climb the crag, or stand on top of it, or who perhaps has to cross over it to get further up a mountain, it presents itself as an obstacle. But it is an obstacle only in relation to this end. To another, the crag is nothing. A passer-by may be in the area, with the aim of sightseeing, meaning that the existence of the crag poses no obstacle to him. The crag may be easier to climb for some than others, representing a 'residue' limitation, as opposed to an obstacle in-itself.

Yet, Merleau-Ponty (2002: 511) goes on to add that we must 'distinguish between my express intentions, for example the plan I now make to climb those mountains, and general intentions which evaluate the potentialities of my environment'. Whatever decision I made with respect to the mountain, it is clear that it will appear high to me insofar as it literally exceeds my body's power to take it in its stride. I am still destined to see things from the point of view of my terrestrial experience. The broader significance is that, though perceptual structures do not always force themselves upon the observer, there are some which are *ambiguous*, which reveal even more effectively 'the presence within us of spontaneous evaluation: for they are elusive shapes which suggest constantly changing meaning to us' (ibid.: 512). We see the same thing with respect to Gestalt psychology. The grouping of dots

.. ..

is always perceived as six pairs of dots. It is as if, 'on the hither side of our judgement and our freedom, someone were assigning such and such a significance to such and such a given grouping' (ibid.: 511–12). There are no obstacles in themselves, but the self who qualifies them as such is not some a-cosmic subject. It 'runs ahead of itself in relation to things in order to confer upon them the form of things' (ibid.: 512). There is an autochthonous significance of the world, which is constituted in the dealings which our incarnate existence has with it, and which provides the ground for every deliberate *Sinngebung*.

This is true of an impersonal and abstract function such as 'external perception'. If I give in to my fatigue during a walk, that is because I dislike the feel of it, and so have chosen differently to someone who likes the clamminess of his body and feels himself in the midst of things when fatigued. My own fatigue brings me to a halt in that I have chosen differently my manner of being-in-the-world. Nevertheless, we must recognise, says Merleau-Ponty, 'a sort of sedimentation of our life: an attitude towards the world, when it has received frequent confirmation, acquires a favoured status for us' (ibid.: 513). Our habitual and sedimented being means that, even with an inferiority complex or other sort of psychological hang-up that a free act can in theory 'blow sky high', it is improbable that we should change and problematic to presuppose we can measure the act in terms of linear cause and effect. Following Bergson's intensive and durational concept of free will, the 'probability' of rationalism becomes redundant, for it is a notion of statistical or extensive thought which is 'not thought at all, since it does not concern any particular thing actually existing, any movement of time, any concrete event' (ibid.). Indeed, there is a phenomenological basis for statistical thought, in that it belongs to a being, which is fixed, situated and surrounded by things in the world. Number is abstract.

The same is true with respect to our relation to history. I am represented to myself in concrete reflection, and so I find that I am an anonymous and pre-human flux, as yet unqualified as a 'working man' or 'middle class'. I am never truly one of these identities, but nevertheless I freely evaluate myself as one of them. Yet again, that does not slip us back into a dichotomous logic from which we would conclude that history by itself has no significance except for that conferred upon it by our will. Objective thought derives class consciousness from the objective condition of the proletariat, whereas idealist reflection reduces the proletariat condition to the self-awareness arrived at by the proletarian. That is, the former traces such consciousness to the class defined in terms of objective characteristics, whereas the latter reduces being a working man to the commonness of being one. In each case we are in the realm of abstraction, torn between the in-itself and for-itself.

In response to objective thought, then, Merleau-Ponty offers an existential method – existential in the sense that existence, including our enthrallment via bodily perception, cannot be bracketed. I am not conscious of being working class or middle class by virtue of fact (I sell my labour, I buy labour, etc.), nor do I become one or the other on the day on which I elect to view history in the light of class struggle and so on. What makes me belong to a certain class

> is not the economic system or society considered as system of impersonal forces, but these institutions as I carry them within me and experience them; nor is it an intellectual operation devoid of motive, but my way of being in the world within this institutional framework. (Ibid.: 515)

In order for there to be a revolution, the social space must acquire a magnetic field, wherein a region of the exploited is seen to appear. Thus, the process of regrouping is discernible beyond ideologies and various occupations. Class comes into being and a situation is revolutionary when the connection objectively existing between the sections of the proletariat is finally experienced in perception as a common obstacle to the existence of each and every one. We cannot rely on the *representation* of revolution, nor is revolution the result of a deliberate judgement or the explicit positing of an end. The worker does not make himself into a revolutionary *ex nihilo* but on the contrary on a certain basis of co-existence. This returns us back to the difference, as discussed in the introduction of this work, between pre-conscious interests of ideology and the unconscious or pre-reflective grounding of it. Though we have yet to touch on desire itself, we are here in touch with its conceptual base. Devoid of affectivity, this is still a micropolitics inasmuch as it speaks to an unconscious layer of political and social thought, meaning and action.

In anticipation of idealist objections – that I am not a particular project but rather a pure consciousness, and that the attributes of class belong to me only to the extent that I place myself among others and see myself through their eyes – Merleau-Ponty (ibid.: 521) maintains that the other-as-object is nothing but an 'insincere modality of others, just as absolute subjectivity is nothing but an abstract notion of myself'. I must, in my most radical reflection, apprehend around my absolute individuality a 'halo of generality or a kind of atmosphere of "sociality". This is necessary if subsequently the words "a bourgeois" and "a man" are to be able to assume meaning for me' (ibid.). In other words, the For-Themselves – me for myself and the other for himself – must stand out against a background of For-Others. My life, in this sense, has a significance which I do not constitute, entailing an intersubjectivity wherein each one of us must be anonymous both in the sense of being absolutely individual and in the sense of being absolutely general. Our being-in-the-world is the concrete bearer of this double anonymity. I am all that I am and see, an intersubjective field, not despite my body and historical situation, but because of them.

This theme of ambiguity and contingency is constantly played out through Merleau-Ponty's more directly political writings between his early and middle period. Indeed, we see Merleau-Ponty constantly trying to find a political figure to which he could attribute this take on subjectivity. Initially, as with Sartre and in accordance with the post-Marxist theme of the present study, this figure is Marx – a Marx who, as he makes clear in *Sense and Non-Sense*, rails against typical Marxist readings we find in the likes of Garaudy, with Merleau-Ponty (1964b: 127) denouncing it as a '"fleshless Marxism" which reduces history to its economic skeleton'; a 'pseudo-Marxism according to which everything is false by the final phase of history and which corresponds, on the level of ideas, to that rudimentary communism – the "envy and desire for levelling" – for which Marx had no kind words' (ibid.: 128). Instead, Merleau-Ponty understands Marx as presenting the individual as a social being, in that he is 'not in society as an object is in a box; rather, he assumes it by what is innermost in him' (ibid.: 129). *Innermost in him.* He assumes it in his being. There is, then, neither a social nature given outside ourselves, nor a World Spirit, nor a movement appropriate to ideas, nor collective consciousness. Rather, the vehicle of history and the motivating force of the dialectic is

> man involved in a certain way of appropriating nature in which the mode of his relationship with others takes shape; it is concrete intersubjectivity, the successive and simultaneous community of existences in the process of self-realisation in a type of ownership which they both submit to and transform, each created by and creating the Other. (Ibid.)

The Marx of Merleau-Ponty's (ibid.: 130) existentialism understands that the bond which attaches man to the world is at the same time his way to freedom,

> of seeing how man, in contact with nature, projects the instruments of his liberation around himself not by destroying necessity but, on the contrary, by utilizing it; of comprehending how he constitutes a cultural world in which man's *'human nature* has become his nature'.

To resist, is to *resist through* the environmental powers that be. This environment is history, and so, for Merleau-Ponty, Marxism must be understood not as a philosophy of the subject, nor of the object, but rather as a philosophy of history, which consists of binding the two together. This represents a 'concrete thinking' of praxis, away from idealism and metaphysical materialism, towards a form of 'critique' which shares strong affinities with 'existential philosophy' (ibid.: 133). Merleau-Ponty's recourse to Marx clearly anticipates (and, as we know, influences) Sartre's later turn to him and confirms, as said, the tacit relation between ontologies of immanence and Marxist political theory posited at the start of this work.

However, though gaining ground via Marx, we find Merleau-Ponty, in his later *Adventures of the Dialectic*, shift towards a Weberian-inspired liberalism; from a concentration on Marxism towards a more reflective view of history. The themes of ambiguity, contingency and local particularities are all carried forth, but now dressed in new conceptual clothing. As with Marx's general idea, the central ethic Merleau-Ponty derives from Weber's approach is that 'it is not superficial to base a politics on the analysis of the political animal' (Merleau-Ponty 2004b: 344). However, with his analysis of capitalism and its religious (Calvinist) origins, Weber does not simply integrate spiritual motives and material causes. He renews the concept of historical matter itself by posing the economic system as a 'human choice become a situation; and that is what allows it to rise from worldly asceticism to religious motives, as well as to descend toward its capitalistic decay: everything is woven into the same fabric' (ibid.: 333). Thus contra what Merleau-Ponty finds in Marxism, Weber teaches us that history does not work according to a model, but rather is the advent of meaning. To say 'the elements of rationality were related to one another before crystallizing into a system is only a manner of saying that, taken up and developed by human intentions, they ought to confirm one another and form a whole' (ibid.: 344). There is, then, an 'elective affinity' between the elements of a historical totality, which in turn confirms the ambiguity of historical fact and the plurality of their aspects. Far from condemning historical knowledge to the realm of the provisional, it is 'the very thing that agglomerates the dust of facts, which allows us to read in a religious fact the first draft of an economic system or read, in an economic system, positions taken with regard to the absolute' (ibid.: 335).

Ultimately, Weber's liberalism is favoured over Marxism because his 'phenomenology is not systematic ... It does not lead to an absolute knowledge' (Merleau-Ponty 2004a: 341). Man's freedom and contingency exclude the idea that the goal of cultural sciences is to construct a closed system of concepts that confines reality according to a definitive order. The intelligible wholes of history can never be thought of outside of their contingency and the movement by which history turns back on itself in an attempt to grasp itself. For such reasons, 'Weber is not a revolutionary' (ibid.) as much as he is a liberal who does not aspire to and demand a political utopia, falling fowl of an historical or teleological naiveté that considers the formal universe of democracy to be an absolute. His is a liberalism that admits, rather pessimistically, that all politics is violence — violence of the flesh, be it physical or metaphysical. His liberalism 'is militant, even suffering, heroic' (ibid.: 342). It is a liberalism of a micropolitical kind; of colliding and conflicting haphazard micro-macro forces.

Merleau-Ponty's Self-Criticism and Immanent Critique

In reaching for the lifeworld through the priority of perception and a subsequent investigation of the pre-personal embodied consciousness, or the tacit body-cogito as the third term lying in between the subject and object, Merleau-Ponty went considerably far in suturing the gap or rupture in/of the immanence that Sartre himself tried to overcome. They both follow extremely similar paths in this respect. Whereas for Sartre it was critical in ironing out inconsistencies in Husserlian phenomenology, for Merleau-Ponty it was similarly considered necessary for overcoming what he saw as the crisis of modern philosophy and its troubling Cartesian heritage. Though instigating this move through a mutual interlocutor (Husserl), Sartre is envisioned by Merleau-Ponty as the last, though unintentional, bastion of rational Cartesianism. A somewhat overtly simplified criticism of Sartre, it nonetheless provides the contextual foil required for a project that ironically furthers Sartre's own project, specifically through concretising themes of embodiment, ambiguity, contingency and an anti-juridical ethico-politics, i.e. micro 'practices of life' (Merleau-Ponty 1964b: 5), and by introducing the 'fold' of subjectivity – all central themes in micropolitics.

The crux of this anti-Cartesian project is carried forward in all of Merleau-Ponty's subsequent works, to such a degree that we can venture so far as to say that the body (as that which is supposed to realise it and suture, as it were, the 'dualistic rupture') is the linchpin of Merleau-Ponty's oeuvre. Nevertheless, the body and its corresponding concepts receive a fundamental reworking in 'Eye and Mind' and his unfinished posthumously published *The Visible and the Invisible*, pushing thought even closer to a position of 'pure' immanence, and even to a fully-fledged micropolitics. At its simplest, through embarking on a direct ontological enquiry, ambiguity is no longer understood as that which exists between the world and the body. Rather ambiguity is understood in terms of the relation between the visible and the invisible of the flesh, in which case the 'body belongs to the order of the things as the world is universal flesh' (ibid.: 137).

Though it may be tempting see the ontological turn as personifying a radical deviation from Merleau-Ponty's previous phenomenological project, it in fact arises from an *immanent critique* of it, which also explains how the body continues to serve as the loci of investigation. The crux of the critique regards the realisation that the anti-Cartesian project, and the subsequent bid for the non-dualist lifeworld, cannot be fully realised without investigating, and correcting, its own presupposition or prejudicative *Logos* to which its expressive style and conceptual apparatus is beholden (see Merleau-Ponty 1968: 200). The presupposition, in this instance, is that of a dualistic subject-object epistemological starting point that in a circular fashion unwittingly corresponds with and props up a dualistic ontology. Together, this serves to resurrect a subverted Cartesianism and subject of form, inconsistent with the principle of the lifeworld.

In the first instance, this concerns the issue of comprehension and the latent disjunction between intellectual consciousness and perceptual consciousness present in *Phenomenology of Perception*: 'To comprehend is not to constitute in intellectual immanence ... to comprehend is to apprehend by coexistence, laterally, by the style, and thereby to attain at once the far-off reaches of this style' (ibid.:

107). The 'style' and its 'far-off reaches' both refer to conceptual language as the prime medium of comprehension and expression, and the underlying ontological condition that simultaneously envelops and is obscured by it. As we noted in the previous chapter, philosophical language, like all praxis, 'supposes a **selbstverständlich** [self-evident], an instituted, which is *Stiftung* [foundation] preparing an *Endstiftung* [final foundation]' (ibid.: 176). All language, in fact, signifies existentially according to its expressive style. Such are the 'sedimented significations' underpinning language, that it can prevent it from later achieving a 'positive signification' (ibid.). The problem for Merleau-Ponty in this respect is that his anti-Cartesian project still defined itself 'in terms of reasons which owe a lot to Descartes' (Merleau-Ponty 1964b: 11).

Specifically, though Merleau-Ponty (1968: 179) did much to convince us of the naiveté of Descartes, 'who does not see a tacit cogito under the cogito of *Wesen*, significations', he now speaks of the naiveté of his own silent cogito 'that would deem itself to be an adequation with the silent consciousness, whereas its very description of silence rests entirely on the virtue of language'. Although *Phenomenology of Perception* establishes a notion of structure or *Gestalt* as a third notion between facticity and ideality, it fails truly and positively to define *Gestalt* beyond being a spatio-temporal juxtaposition of parts, an exterior designation, and further fails to understand what makes the *Gestalt* a sensible thing (see ibid.: 204). In remaining within the exterior designation, the sensible thing is made transcendent and thus exterior, in terms of the position of its being, assimilating the sensible to the objective. The result was the placing of the '*Gestalt back into the framework of "cognition" or "consciousness"*' (ibid.: 206) (in the form of a tacit cogito), presupposing a pre-reflective contact of self with self, in which processes are still attributable to a subject. Thus, though striving to describe an interworld, or a chiasm between mind and matter, the project did not practice or exemplify the lifeworld in the appropriate philosophical lexicon. It even propped up a form of rationalism in its analysis by striving to provide a 'top-heavy' account about, as opposed to an (appropriate) expression of, Being (ibid.: 178). In either case, this is a failure to attune to the problem of the passage from the perceptual meaning to the language meaning, from behaviour to thematisation, which is also a failure to attend to the projects own conditions of possibility, its own 'non-explicated horizon' (ibid.). Starting with bodily perception and embodied consciousness, as opposed to the world of silence, and developing a language reflective and supportive of that fact, *Phenomenology of Perception* does not fully open us up to a plane of immanence, and in fact ultimately reinstates a form of transcendence within immanence, resulting in the re-emergence of a Cartesian rupture or dualism.[8]

Merleau-Ponty's self-criticism follows a deliberately circular logic. To attend to the presuppositions inherent in his language is at the same time to attend to the 'wild being' that envelops it, and that, more importantly, it forgets and obscures. Only a direct ontological enquiry will complete the anti-Cartesian project by elaborating 'the notions that have to replace that of transcendental subjectivity, those of subject, object meaning' (ibid.: 167): thus the necessity to return to it (ibid.: 165). In other words, the question of language and the question of Being that lies behind it are mutually inclusive, for it is only through addressing both simultaneously that we ultimately reach the lifeworld that previously eluded Merleau-Ponty. It is the investigation of language, then, that ultimately prompts Merleau-Ponty to conduct a direct ontology enquiry.

The wild being to which Merleau-Ponty refers is that of the flesh: language is of the flesh (see ibid.: 205)! With echoes of Sartre's thesis, Merleau-Ponty (ibid.: 136) defines the flesh as a 'carnal being, as a *being of depths*, of several leaves or several faces, a being in latency, and a presentation of a certain absence', which 'is a prototype of Being, of which our body, the sensible sentient, is a very remarkable variant, but whose constitutive paradox already lies in every visible'.[9] Obscure though this definition of the flesh may seem, Merleau-Ponty gives the concept a more thoroughgoing treatment than it receives in Sartre. Presumably for this reason, Sartre had to clarify his position through reference to it, readily linking his notion of the situation of lived experience to Merleau-Ponty's understanding of the flesh and envelopment.[10] It is through the concept of the flesh as one of depth, moreover, that Merleau-Ponty develops the concept of the fold. The flesh is a folded flesh.

Folded Flesh as n-dimensional Depth

To truly grasp the flesh as folded depth, we must turn to the non-Euclidean geometry of Bernhard Riemann; specifically, his concept of a multiply extended manifold and its reworking into metaphysics by Bergson. For though not that which instigates or provokes the development of the flesh – which arises from a very particular anti-Cartesian self-criticism – the manifold is nevertheless its conceptual source. According to Riemann, a multiply or n-fold extended manifold is defined by the fact that position fixing in the manifold can be reduced to n numerical determinations. A manifold, for Riemann, is the area over which varies an extended magnitude or quantity. A magnitude or quantity is 'n-fold extended' when it can be extended in n-ways, and the manifold to which it corresponds is 'n-dimensional' when it contains n-number of dimensions. In the case of pure musical tones, for instance, they are determined or individuated by intensity of sound and tonal pitch, both of which contain a one-dimensional movement, i.e. increase/decrease in intensity and pitch. Together this constitutes two-fold extended magnitudes composing a doubly-extended manifold. In a similar way, 'one obtains a triply extended manifold when one imagines that a doubly extended one passes in a well-determined way to a completely different one' (Riemann 2007: 25). The construction can be continued to reach an n-fold extended manifold.

What is important to consider here, according to Riemann, is the type of magnitude or quantity, or the particular instances of the general concept, in question. To return to pure tonal music as a manifold, inasmuch as its magnitudes are capable of varying without sudden jumps the manifold is continuous. Continuous, that is, for there are no perceivable gaps in dimensional movement or change. Think of the way a musician may shift his or her fingers from the top of a fretless stringed instrument, such as a violin, to the bottom, accompanied by a steady stroke of the bow, so as to effectuate a continuous shift in pitch. This stands in contrast to what Riemann deems a discrete manifold, i.e. those that are associated with magnitudes that jump discontinuously, such as the number of petals on a flower. For Riemann, this presents an issue of metric and measurement. The n-fold quantities need to be specified so as to fix a value onto the magnitude. The size of the parts of discrete manifolds can be compared to each other by straightforward counting as value, i.e. 'this flower has five petals'. The magnitudes of continuous manifolds, however, can only be compared by measurement. As measurement requires 'the superposition of the quantities to be compared', or the positing of some magnitude independent to its place in the manifold, there is required a 'means of transposing one quantity to be used as a standard for the others' (ibid.: 24). Without this transposition, one can only compare continuous quantities in terms of 'more' or 'less', as opposed to 'how much' or 'how many'.

Thus, when considered in terms (particularly the infinitesimal), quantities are regarded as existing relative to position, as opposed to independent of position; expressible in terms of regions, as opposed to unit (such as a musical scale).

The problem here is one of fixing position for the sake of measurement onto a continuous manifold. When the continuous manifold in question is made up of n-dimensions (thus presenting a multiply extended manifold), it follows that position fixing in the manifold can be reduced to n numerical determinations, or individuations. That is, *there is an endless possible variety of determinations*. Though metric relations of a multiply extended manifold can be investigated 'only in abstract terms and their interdependence exhibited only through formulas', Riemann (ibid.: 8) holds that the results can still be presented in 'geometric garb'. The foundation for this 'garb', Riemann locates in Gauss's differential geometry, which at its most basic is the study of the infinitesimal points within space or, in Gauss's case, infinitesimal points on a two-dimensional curved surface without any reference to a 'global' embedding space or universal container, i.e. a dimension external to the surface, to which measurement of the surface can be made relative, such as found in Cartesian coordinates of analytical geometry. Every infinitesimal point of the manifold has a small neighbourhood, or a subspace, that can be mapped as Euclidean on a local level, i.e. without being universalised to the entire manifold. From this, we are able to describe a complex *local* surface without having to add an extra or transcendent *global* dimension of geometric properties.

Though exploring both the curvature and its rate of change in Gauss's fashion, Riemann (ibid.: 24) departed from an empirical intuition that would have otherwise dictated the study of three-dimensional curved surfaces as the next logical step. As we saw, he moved on to consider n-dimensional spaces (again, n designating any integer and dimensions the coordinates upon which phenomenon, or rather the manifold, depends). This accords with the simple yet breathtakingly original distinction he made between the 'unbounded' and the 'infinite'. A circle, for example, is unbounded for one can traverse it endlessly, but it cannot be said to be infinite in length. Against Euclid's second axiom of infinity, upon which his fifth axiom concerning parallel lines is dependant (the lines must be infinitely straight so as to never cross), Riemann postulates that all straight lines are finite, but unbounded/endless. Looking at Figure 2.2, if we imagine L as a finite, though endless circle, it follows that

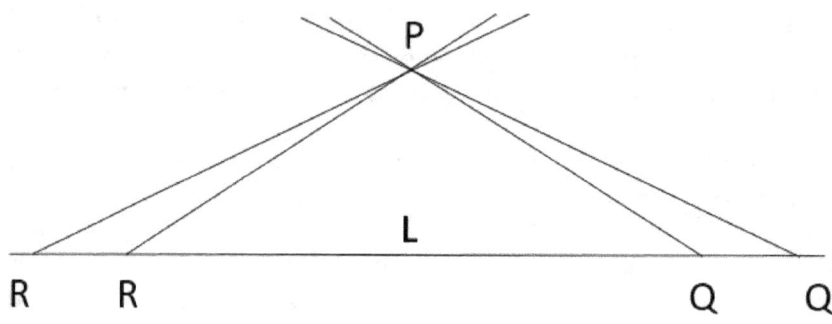

Figure 2.2

we cannot move Q an infinite distance to the right from P along L, without Q, when moved far enough, coinciding with R. There are thus no parallel lines, except, once again, locally. Going further, Riemann allows for the possibility that the points comprising subspaces of a manifold may vary, as the curvature of a surface may vary. If the curvature is not constant but variable, then the shortest distance between two points (the geodesic) will differ between different points in the space.

The crucial point here is that the surface itself becomes space and space becomes abstracted, in that its parts are capable of being linked in an infinite number of ways through non-localisable relations. This presents us with a non-homogenous notion of space, in which it is itself curved, folded in a variety of manners and disconnected from any higher dimension. Thus absolute metrics no longer hold. Developing Riemann's idea by leading it into the topological and, ultimately, the physical, William Kingdon Clifford (as quoted in Kline 1990: 893) compares this idea to hills on a landscape:

> (1) That small portions of space are of a nature analogous to little hills on a surface which is on the average flat.
> (2) That this property of being curved or distorted is continually passed on from one portion of space to another after the manner of a wave.
> (3) That this variation of the curvature of space is really what happens in that phenomenon which we call the motion of matter whether ponderable or ethereal.
> (4) That in this physical world nothing else takes place but this variation, subject, possibly, to the law of continuity.

Any shape (a triangle, a square) is subject to change and distortion when moved across such a space. Such movement constitutes a motion of matter or a movement of time through space – hence

Einstein's notion of a curved space-time continuum and relativity. Indeed, quite prophetically, Riemann (2007: 33) ends his discussion on manifolds by stating that 'either the reality underlying space must form a discrete manifold, or the basis for the metric relations must be sought outside it, in binding forces acting upon it'. That is, the ground of metric relations is to be found in physics.[11]

The immediate effect of Riemann's meditations, generally speaking, is the instigation of the notion that there can be, and that there is, a difference between the mathematical Idea of space (continuous manifold) and actual/metric space (discontinuous manifold). As is known, Bergson translates this into metaphysics, proclaiming that there is a difference (seemingly of kind, but actually of degree) between an intensive/virtual Idea or *multiplicity* and an extensive/actual reality or *multiplicity*, which together define the Absolute as a continuum. Indeed, Bergson goes on to loosely define the intensive or virtual multiplicity in the same terms as the continuous manifold, i.e. it is non-homogeneous and non-metric (which we link with qualitative difference, i.e. *difference in kind*) and intrinsically coordinated, as in without a supplementary higher dimension and definitive cause imposing an extrinsic coordination. And given Bergson is constructing a metaphysics of the subject that can complement science, this is to be understood in terms of the psyche and subjective temporality, rather than space; or rather as a subjective notion of time no longer beholden to that of extensive space. The 'virtual' intensive refers to 'pure' duration as a process by which a series of relations, divergent experiential traces or multiple internal psychic states as recorded and shaped through sensuous experience melt and permeate one another in a process prior to any extension in time as space. The traces are incorporated into one psychic or unconscious whole, forming an interpenetrating mass that ensures the *continuous* progress of the past which 'gnaws into the future and which swells as it advances' (Bergson 1998: 4). It is the past, then, that is a virtual realm (it is real without being actual), growing without ceasing, and insisting into present such that there is no limit to its preservation. The virtual so defined, as we saw, is central to Sartre's notion of time, and pre-reflective consciousness/lived experience.

Though each trace represents a sub-space or dimension within a multiply extended manifold, or virtual multiplicity, Bergson and by extension Sartre end up completely de-spatialisaing the intensive via temporality as pure duration. The virtual unconscious is purely temporal. This move not only proves to be unnecessary – given that non-Euclidean geometry allows for a construal of space beyond that of homogeneity and juxtaposition – but also problematic. Contra Kant, Bergson holds that spatial intuition, and in fact all representational machinery, is established through and by our experience of the extensive and retained to function as representations on the mind via duration (ibid.: 202). This *atmosphere* of spatiality, our intellect and thus our affinity to the Euclidean as the proper idealisation of space, has its own ontogenesis, and so is not derived *a priori*. But in de-spatialising the intensive, Bergson deprives himself of the ability to account for the ontogenesis and differentiation of this atmosphere itself. Either we are left with an undifferentiated and chaotic mess or we come to rely on the very qualities and extensities of space that the virtual is supposed to ground, as a way to conceptualise said ground. Relatedly, this move deprives us of the conceptual tools by which we can think through the process of individuation (the mode of determination), without returning to an ego of endurance as that which provides the practical function of transcendental unity.[12]

As is often recognised, this problematic relates to Merleau-Ponty's claim that there is a certain ambiguity in Bergson's philosophy of the multiplicity regarding precisely how extensive space (breadth, height, depth), time (as durational) and movement (across space in time) co-exist or interact on an intensive level, and relatedly how they are generated or exist so as to act back onto the extensive as the transcendental conditions of possibility for experience or rather to provide a subjective and cogent representation of sensation.[13] The ultimate question, then, is this: how does this familiar setting of extensive space, movement and time (structured spatiality), which Bergson argues is recorded and stored via duration to form a background pre-thetic structure of experience to every act of consciousness, come to be constituted and differentiated (Merleau-Ponty 2002: 321)?[14] Where is the space that makes this space possible?

Merleau-Ponty accounts for this background by re-spatialising the intensive, *virtual* multiplicity, or rather through the introduction of a properly Riemannian notion of space as *depth*. A true depth of self. Depth is no longer tacitly equated with breadth seen from the side, the construction of which would be based upon extensive magnitudes that are visible to us, and which would require the subject to 'abandon his point of view on the world, and think of himself a sort of ubiquity' (ibid.: 309). Depth is an intensive *and* temporal space of interior embodied existence, and thus the experience of the reversibility of dimensions, of a global locality – 'everything in the same place at the same time, a locality from which height, width, and depth are abstracted, of a voluminosity we express in a word when we say that a thing is *there*' (Merleau-Ponty 2004b: 311). It is a truly *n*-extended manifold.

Though latently evident in *Phenomenology of Perception* via embodied consciousness, this notion of depth is first truly realised through an analysis of aesthetics in 'Eye and Mind', and Merleau-Ponty's posthumously published *The Visible and the Invisible*. As said, it is in these works that Merleau-Ponty embarks on a direct ontological enquiry, where ambiguity is no longer understood as that which exists between the world and the body, as was the case in his early *Phenomenology of Perception*, but rather in terms of the relation between the visible (actual) and the invisible (virtual) of the *flesh* or depth of Being. The flesh as depth is for itself the exemplar sensible, an elemental manner of being. It is not matter, mind or substance, but quite simply an element

> in the sense it was used to speak of water, air, earth and fire, that is, in the sense of a general thing midway between the spatio-temporal individual and the idea, a sort of incarnate principle that brings a style of being wherever there is a fragment of being. (Ibid.: 139)[15]

Thus Being is not taken as substance but rather a relationship between the body and the world or between the flesh of the body and the flesh of the visible, 'the coiling over of the visible upon the seeing body, of the tangible upon the touching body, which is attested in particular when the body sees them and touches them' (Merleau-Ponty 1968: 137). The perceived world is, as such, an 'ensemble of my body's routes' or an intertwining of routes and levels with the world, such as space, time, colour and lighting, as lines of force uniting the two fleshes. This means that the body and the world belong to the same flesh, the same Being, such that it can be said the body is *in* and *of* the world. Indeed, the encounters that force *explication* of depth into extensive visible expression, or unfolding and actualisation of virtual depth on the level of consciousness, in turn feed back into depth, implicating or infolding and thus adding an extra element to it and in turn altering the visible. The process continues, such that we are only ever given a constant becoming of *folds*.

Truly, it is only by retuning to space and depth in this vein that Merleau-Ponty can establish a topology of the fold, beyond a

Euclidean and physical understanding – an understanding latently expressed in the English word 'fold' itself – as that which can help us in conceptualising the continuum between multiplicities, or rather the generative and mostly immanent virtual-actual process of flesh.[16] As said in the introduction, the fold here is employed in literal manner, as in the folding of a piece of paper, where the paper as interchangeable for the fabric of Being (flesh). Two marks on diagonally opposing corners of a piece of A4 paper may be distinguished by their negative difference, in that this primarily demarcates respective locations or identities. Unassuming as the point may seem, it is notable that the opposing marks are still of the same paper, for it is by virtue of this that if I were to fold one side of the paper over to the other the two opposing marks would still retain their negative difference in one dimension, while gaining a closer connection in another. If this idea of folding is applied to a non-Euclidean n-dimensional space, or a pluri-dimensional flesh, and if depth is understood to denote an interior created by a process of (in)folding or doubling of the Outside (which is its own surface) then it follows that it is a generative process which is always immanent to itself, and as such beyond any notion of a metaphysical Outside or transcendent Other. We can fold a piece of paper in multiple ways via multiple dimensions so as to generate new divergent relations between and within the marks on it and even the form of the paper itself, yet the paper shall remain, with no need of extrinsic dimensions— if the flesh is Being, then the same remains true of it: an origami of flesh.

To be more precise, an origami of flesh is a pleated n-dimensional unconscious space, in which there is a variety of modalities of folds and seemingly folds of/in folds; much in the same way Riemann (2007: 39 n14) envisions sub-curvatures along all possible orthogonal directions within a continuous manifold, i.e. variable curvature barring stable metrics. Thus the fold not only refers to the Outside extensive world, the sensuous experience of which is folded over to create an Inside subjective world of the virtual self, which is folded back out or into the Outside – the 'big' fold – but also to the multiple and infinitesimal folds of traces and perception that take place within/without this folding, between which is a mutual reliance in the form of double-conditioning (or immanent causality). For instance, the notion of the fold applies to both the dimension of touch and vision, except that here the exploration and the information gathered from the two do not belong 'to the same sense'

(Merleau-Ponty 1968: 133). Even so, the delimitation of the sense is crude, to the point that the intertwining between touch and vision leaves neither of them self-identical: there is a 'double and crossed situation of the visible in the tangible and of the tangible in the visible; the two maps are complete, and yet they do not merge into one' (ibid.: 134). That is to say, they are synthesised or related without for all that being subsumed or collapsed into a higher unity, making a totality that is not superposable. Thus, like a pure manifold, there are *n*-dimensions that present an endless possible variety of determinations or expressions.

Pluri-dimensionality pre-empts Deleuze's notion of 'disjunction', though it receives no further elaboration and so the precise nature of this synthesis remains ambiguous enough to allow some to interpret it as a moment of ideal coincidence.[17] The more general point, however, is still important: the fold. The visible and the tangible intersect and fold into each other, and our experience structures its own metastable potentialities insofar as the intertwining is sensed: 'he who sees cannot possess the visible unless he is possessed by it, unless he is of it' (Merleau-Ponty 1968: 134–5).

Merleau-Ponty explicates this idea through, and thus relates it to, aesthetics by following Riemann's (2007: 24) assertion that a continuous manifold, and thus depth, is only truly captured in colour. Colour is 'the place where our brain and the universe meet', as Merleau-Ponty (2004b: 321) states, quoting Klee. The property of colour does not rely on solid boundaries and so gives rise to an interpenetrative and ambiguous space which draws our attention to primordial depth. Mark Bradford's *Riding the Cut Vein* (Tate Modern, London) provides an excellent example of how colour operates in this fashion. The sheer size of the piece (roughly 3,350 x 6,100 mm) bars the gazing subject from immediately or prethetically gripping it as a working contextual structure (unless of course s/he is viewing a miniaturised reproduction or computerised image of it). As our eyes make the journey across the canvas, the almost indiscernible zones of colour continually provoke a new affective sense, a new dimensional perspective and, eventually, a new representation. These slowly build together to make a total, though still contingent, impression. For me, it is one of the dark and varied forces of the future bearing down on the present, separated only by the river-like horizon in the centre, whose tone is calming and sedate. The point is, however, that another might see something quite different, in that his or her intensive-virtual-depth is composed of different experiences and existential traces, and indeed will be actualised in an entirely different temporal-wave, reacting to and forming the colours in an entirely singular way. As with cloud-spotting, there is no consistent interpretation to be had.

The human visual system picks an interpretation of each part that makes the whole consistent in a manner relative to one's own subjectivity, i.e. their own flesh via the world's flesh. This fact alone demonstrates that our relation with the object and with space is not only non-intellectual (at least initially), but also generative, with colour being the exemplary form of this process. The same is evident in various optical illusions, such as Wittgenstein's rabbit/duck or the Necker cube, where ground and field are confounded, conveying that optionality does not describe space with identical distances and that works of art provoke different perspectives and sensations in different people. Colour even affects extended or 'classical' depth, as is evident in Paul Klee's *Wintry Mask*. The shading itself creates a depth in a two-dimensional painting without perspectival geometries, i.e. the appearance of sunken eye-sockets. Similarly, once one shades a Necker cube in a particular way (see Figure 2.3) it forces it into one visual perspective, determining one face to forever act as its front, in turn negating the cube's previous interchangeability and ambiguity.

In reconnoitring this ambiguity, Merleau-Ponty concludes that we must see space and its content as together. The problem is generalised. Colour is not the dimension of depth. Depth is the 'dimension of colour, that dimension which creates identities, differences, a texture, a materiality, a something – creates them from itself, for

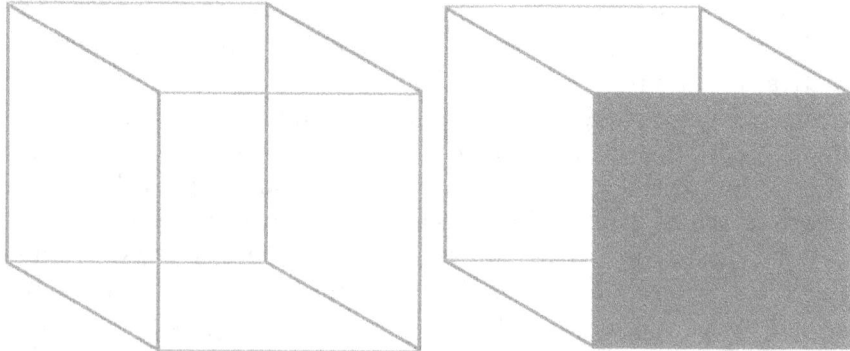

Figure 2.3 An ordinary Necker cube, accompanied by a Necker cube with a coloured front

itself' (ibid.). The painter's vision is not a view upon the outside, or a 'physical-optical' relation with the world. The world 'no longer stands before him through representation' (ibid.). It is the painter to whom the thing of the world gives birth by a sort of concentration, a 'coming-to-itself of the visible' (ibid.). The painting relates to nothing at all among experienced things unless it is 'autofigurative', breaking the 'skin of things' to show how things become things, how the world becomes world (ibid.).

Art, then, cannot be a construction of an artificial relationship to a space and world existing outside; it rather 'awakens powers dormant in ordinary vision, a secret of pre-existence', an Idea or metastable of flesh (ibid.: 313). And where art captures the process of Being and the pre-personal perceptual emergence of everyday objects, the artist him-/herself personifies the hinge or fold between the creator and the created, between the self and world as well as the self and other, between interiority and exteriority – a fold that essentially exceeds these terms, effacing any rigid distinction between the two – out of which art can be and is created. In some sense, then, the artist's body is the proverbial vestibule or interface sitting 'in between' the seeing and the seen, dragging in its wake (and even folding) the visible-invisible, which itself it devised of infinitesimal folds. Art overcomes the existential restrictions of language that tend to conjure up a two-dimensional Euclidean space, to present us with the fold itself. That is, it is through the artist's body – the fact that s/he is *in* and *of* the world as flesh, his or her giving him-/herself up to the nature to which s/he belongs and his or her re-exteriorisation of it, the intertwining between vision and movement experienced by the lived body, this folding of the flesh – that art and even reality as experienced can be created and sustained, and returned back into the process.

Tender is the Flesh

With Merleau-Ponty's analysis of aesthetics and his turn to ontology itself, we are presented with an image of subjectivity not as a hole that punctures or disrupts the fabric of Being but rather as a fold of that very fabric, a topography unfolding by differentiation. Against both positivist and negativist conceptions of being that preconceive being as objectivity posited before a subject around which the visible can spread, we see a world of degrees, distance, depth and difference, an ensemble of my body's routes. Indeed, there are other landscapes besides my own, which means that there are no rigid borders around my expressive body as it takes up its own trajectory; such that the domain of the flesh is unlimited, an 'ultimate notion' (Merleau-Ponty 1968: 140). It remains open to the encroachments of others, expressing an intercorporeality, a primordial We. This in turn overcomes the problem of the *alter ego*, because

> it is not *I* who sees, not *he* who sees, because an anonymous visibility inhabits both of us, a vision in general, in virtue of that primordial property that belongs to the flesh, being here and now, of radiating everywhere and forever, being an individual, of being also a dimension and a universal. (Ibid.: 142)

It also remains open to constant change. For aside from always being affected by the first opening, folding itself is never exact, it never 'coincides', such that an excess is created through which renegotiations of said (inter)subjectivity may occur. Merleau-Ponty relates this anonymous visibility, openness and folded ambiguity of change to a certain concept of life. A life not of the subject with his identity claims and conscious sense of self, but a life of 'an atmosphere' in the 'astronomical sense', enshrouded, as it were, by those mists we call the sensible world or history, enshrouded by the fold of folds, 'the *one*, of the corporeal life and the *one* the human life, the present and the past, as a pell-mell ensemble of bodies and minds' (ibid.: 84). Here, the 'one' refers to the indefinite pronoun *on*, which refers to the anonymous, pre-personal subject. An All-One.

A pre-personal, non-negative anonymous life, a primordial or virtual depth of folded transformation, folded ambiguity and contingency. The relation this idea has to Merleau-Ponty's Marxist and Weberian politics as elucidated earlier is quite self-evident. Merleau-Ponty's last works go further in railing against what he describes as the illusion Valéry depicted in speaking of 'that little man within man whom we always presuppose', instead coming to understand how a body becomes animate and how these blind organs end up bearing a perception. Thus the 'little man within man' is only a phantom. The *real humanism* is an anti-humanism, in the tradition of Machiavelli, insofar as it evokes a philosophy which confronts the relationship of man to man and the constitution of a common situation, a common All-One and a common social, historical and political contingency 'between men as a problem' (Merleau-Ponty

1964b: 223). Such a 'humanism', therefore, no longer loves man in opposition to his body, mind in opposition to its language, values in opposition to facts. Mind and man never simply are. Instead, they are shown in the movement by which the body becomes gesture, language an oeuvre, and co-existence truth. The movement of folds, i.e. contingency as the continued confirmation of an astonishing junction between fact and meaning, 'between my body and my self, my self and others, my thought and my speech, violence and truth' (ibid.: 240–1). In this sense, Merleau-Ponty's fleshism provides a radicalisation of Sartre's ethic of authenticity as the continual process of creating within one's situation, though now within one's folds and through one's folds. The ethic amounts to a more resolute rejection of the very subject upon which social contract theory and especially theories of lack rely (subjects of negativity), that completely eschews, as Merleau-Ponty (ibid.: 235–6) admits, 'juridical politics'.

Although Merleau-Ponty's fold is critical in providing a new language not caught in the trap of Cartesian dualism (thereby radicalising Sartre) and in furthering our understanding of virtual and generative processes in a world of immanence that operate below the epiphenomenal level of the self and Other, he lacks a proper elucidation of politicised intensive forces.[18] It is in this sense that Deleuze and Guattari (1994: 178) argue that the flesh 'is only the thermometer of a becoming. The flesh is too tender.' In developing this point, Deleuze and Guattari make clear reference to Merleau-Ponty's analysis of art via flesh, and subtly compare it to Deleuze's own notion of *meat*, as introduced in his monograph on Francis Bacon. Following Merleau-Ponty in seeing that every theory of art posits a metaphysics, Deleuze (2013: 37) categorises painting as an act that directly attempts 'to realise the presences beneath representation, beyond representation'. However, through an analysis of Bacon, Deleuze moves beyond Merleau-Ponty, depicting painting as presenting something more profound than the invisible that pervades its geometric forms and narratives: the *intensive forces* – the socio-politics – acting upon the body and climbing through its flesh. The bone in the flesh and the violence of sensation. Bacon's contorted figures reveal this vitality, the powerful non-organic life that lies beyond the organism, particularly through the deformations which the body undergoes via animal traits of the head and through 'the techniques of rubbing and brushing that disorganize it and make a head emerge in its place' (Ibid.: 15). This constitutes 'a *zone of indiscernibility or undecidability* between man and animal' (ibid.: 16). This accords with Deleuze's Nietzschean twist of the virtual notion of the transcendental field. Force is the transcendental condition of sensation. Thus, though both Merleau-Ponty and Deleuze characterise being in terms of a genetic potential as a field of pre-quantitative and pre-qualitative processes, Merleau-Ponty appears to side more with the theatre of images, of visibility, with meagre gestures to its political significance, or at least devoid of a systemised relation to, and theory of, the political.

Foucault's work represents an advance in our lineage in just the same way that Merleau-Ponty represents an advance over Sartre. He is the first to add a politicised, *folded* force, and connects this with broader political strategies and historical movements. Indeed, Foucault develops force as an addition to the fold via Nietzsche's will to power, in tandem with Deleuze. Whereas Deleuze develops Nietzschean folded force in terms of the intensive, in terms of interiority, Foucault adopts and connects it with the actual, with exteriority. Deleuze's work with Guattari seeks a coherent unity between both, with desire demarcating the pivot point, the inside crease of the fold. The more general point is that where with both Sartre and Merleau-Ponty we have been dealing with a very conceptual understanding of subjectivity and how it affects politics, with Foucault, and later Deleuze, we come to a more concrete micropolitical theory of immanence or *political* subjectivity that is nevertheless indebted to Sartre and Merleau-Ponty and intelligible only with this context in mind.

Notes

1. This is typically why Merleau-Ponty is looked to concerning questions of immanence within phenomenology, i.e. Deleuze (2004a: 77).
2. The crucial difference with Sartre, on this account, is said to regard the nature of intentionality and consciousness. Sartre, as we know, is said to retain consciousness as a negation and thus the dialectical counterpoise of Being. In this instance, the only true relation with the in-itself is one of constitutive differentiation or opposition. In entrusting the body with the synthesis of the perceived world, not as pure datum but rather as a temporal synthesis and subjectivity, Merleau-Ponty is said merely to invert Sartre's argument. The for-itself is made immanent to a body as mediation of experience, as opposed to the Outside or object, allegedly establishing a dialectic of embodied

existence reminiscent of Sartre's dialectic of the self. See, for instance, Grosz (1999: 149), Kazashi (1999: 113) and Silverman (1993: 272).

And as with Sartre, many commentators have mistaken Merleau-Ponty's simplified understanding of immanence as pure interiority and his subsequent rejection of it as a basis upon which to argue that Merleau-Ponty is incompatible with *any* notion of immanence (i.e. Smith 1999: 35, Weiss 1999: 125).

3. As in the Socratic dialogue by Plato (1980: 80) in which it is observed that one 'cannot search either for what he knows or what he does not know. He cannot search for what he knows – since he knows, there is no need to search – nor for what he does not know, for he does not know what to look for.'
4. As John Stewart (1998: 197) correctly asserts, 'Sartre is Merleau-Ponty's chief interlocutor.' See also Barbaras (2004: xxviii).
5. Alleging that he simply follows Husserl and Sartre, Habermas (1987: 317) criticises Merleau-Ponty for failing to bypass the 'dicthomotizing basic concepts', wherein the quasi-solipsistic subject is central. This misses the entire point of Merleau-Ponty's position, and indeed that of existentialism as a whole, apropos being-in-the-world.
6. Aside from the phenomenological tradition, we can see here the influence on Merleau-Ponty (2002: 9) of Gestalt theory, carried over from his previous *The Structure of Behaviour*, where it is argued that 'a figure on a background is the simplest sense-given available to us', and yet it is also a *contingent* characteristic of factual perception.
7. I.e. Deleuze (2004a: 77). This relates to the view that Sartre lacks the very notion of sedimentation that is central to Merleau-Ponty's concept of freedom (i.e. Compton 1998: 175, Hall 1998: 187, Stewart 1998: 200). Once again, it is evident that such a reading is caught up in an erroneous understanding of Sartre's ontology, and subsequently his take on authenticity, the consequence being that Merleau-Ponty's take on freedom is held to differ not in emphasis and radicality but rather in its conceptual framework. This goes right to the heart of the Beauvoir/Merleau-Ponty debate, in which Beauvoir reproaches Merleau-Ponty for creating a 'pseudo-Sartreanism' insofar as it neglects the 'interworld' in Sartre's own thought (see Catalano 1998, Langer 1998).
8. See Deleuze and Guattari (1994: 46). Barbaras (2004: 16) makes a very similar point, in particular emphasising that the *Phenomenology* fails to establish a positive characterisation of the perceptual field.
9. Emphasis added. Despite the fact that Merleau-Ponty's ontology has influenced feminists such as Butler, Young and Irigaray they have also all been highly critical of it. Following Butler, Young and Irgaray, Grosz (1999: 1555) argues that fleshism represents a latent phallocentrism. See Coole (2007: 212–20) for a detailed discussion of this

debate and a good defence of Merleau-Ponty on the basis that the flesh is a temporal and relational existence, and as such it refers to the intercorporeity and intersubjectivty of an interworld as opposed to the opacity of an intraworld.
10. See Sartre (2008b: 154, 2013: 316).
11. Mass can be considered the binding or individuating force here, inasmuch as, according to the theory of general relativity, it bends spacetime to create the effects of gravity. In Deleuzian metaphysics, as we will come to see, the 'force' of gravity or rather mass is in part analogous to that of the Outside fold as the will to power. As with mass, it arises from the same plane or level of reality that it effectuates – albeit it on the side of the extensive – in the manner of an immanent causality, i.e. cause in effect.
12. Concerning Bergson's ego of endurance, see Widder (2012: 138).
13. For more on the phenomenological critique of Bergson, and the relation between Bergson and Merleau-Ponty, see Ansell-Pearson (1999: 23, 50–9, 71–9); Barbaras (2004: 99, 225); Landes (2013: 171); Somers-Hall (2006: 215–18) and Wambacq (2011: 237–46).
14. Deleuze (2004a: 111) advances a strikingly similar reproach against Bergson.
15. For more on the flesh, see Barbaras (2004: 153–229); Coole (2007: 233–41); Landes (2013: 151–81).
16. As Deleuze (2004a: 77) rightly points out, Merleau-Ponty's use of the fold has a clear affinity with Heidegger's notion of dwelling, unfolding and the four-fold, as developed in *Contributions to Philosophy* (Heidegger 2012: 174) and 'Building, Dwelling, Thinking' (Heidegger 1971). That said, it is clear that Merleau-Ponty develops the fold within the context of Riemannian geometry as conceived by Bergson.
17. I.e. Deleuze and Guattari (1994: 178).
18. Although Coole (2007: 232) is right to assert that a notion of force is evident in Merleau-Ponty's thinking (indeed, it features in his adoption of the Gestaltent field), it is not clear how, or indeed where, Merleau-Ponty actually proposes this as an alternative. Neither does it receive the same elaboration as flesh, with only a few passing references to force made in *The Visible and the Invisible*.

Chapter 3
Foucault and the Force of Power-Knowledge

Sartre radically displaces the centred self and begins to reconfigure the Outside/Other through his fleshism. This is advanced by Merleau-Ponty, who in reaching for the *Lebenswelt* as a means to bypass the crisis of modern thought, ultimately provides the conceptual notion of the fold. The fold, in turn, allows us to overcome some of the more ambiguous elements in Sartre's thought, particularly insofar as his retention of a dualistic vernacular evokes a problematic image of transcendence and therefore remains trapped in this crisis. The remaining issue with Merleau-Ponty concerns his lack of a worked-out conception of force, particularly within a political context. Though he made steps towards an account of the politico-genetic underpinning of phenomena, he failed to go far enough. In some respects, this is due to the fact that, despite developing a new conceptual language, Merleau-Ponty remained in a phenomenological frame of reference, emphasising more the conditions of possibility of knowledge and experience, as opposed to the conditions (particularly the political conditions) under which they are generated. By incorporating and profoundly politicising Merleau-Ponty's concept of force as a disjunctive fold of the Outside, Foucault elaborates a truly immanent concept of political power and resistance and connects this to broader capitalist sociopolitical processes and strategies.

There are several stages to this argument that this chapter will follow. First, despite distancing himself from the phenomenology of Sartre and Merleau-Ponty on the basis that it represents an outmoded ontology of transcendence, Foucault utilises and radicalises its anti-Cartesian and post-Kantian elements. As is seen in his early *The Order of Things*, by providing a 'pure' phenomenological description of the *episteme* – as in the structure of thoughts that order experience and determine discourse as the system of possibility of knowledge, i.e. what is considered true and false, or relevant, valid, legitimate and valued fields of knowledge, investigation and methodology – Foucault reveals the way the 'subject' is caught in a process of historically contingent signification that precludes any transcendent point of anchorage. Foucault's subsequent *The Archaeology of Knowledge* extends the analysis, by establishing the methodological underpinning of discourse and discursive practice. In so doing, Foucault utilises Merleau-Ponty's concept of the fold – what Foucault refers to as the 'logic of dispersion' – which in turn establishes the basis for his conceptualisation of power and power-knowledge as a *folded* 'micro' force relation and the related principle of double-conditioning.

With regards to folded force, this leads to the identification of practices of resistance that are immanent to 'micro' power-relations by virtue of being no more than the discontinuities of these relations themselves.[1] With regards to the principle of double-conditioning – which in effect is equivalent to Merleau-Ponty's 'great' or 'big' fold – Foucault establishes the fundamental link between micro-powers and macro-strategies: micro (virtual) power relations can sustain or subvert the power of authority, or macro structures, while these very authorities and structures can exercise their powers in ways that strengthen or undermine the microscopic force relations upon which they rely. A change via folded resistance at the micro level, has the potential to effectuate a change at the macro level. I finally move on to Foucault's final works on ethics, which opens up new possibilities for the kind of ethical and political practice prefigured in existentialism. In providing an interiorisation of 'micro' power, in the form of the body and pleasure, and linking this with the principle of double-conditioning, Foucault provides an insight into how seemingly private aesthetical or existential practices of the self and changes in affectivity can serve to animate profound political resistance and change, in the vein of but more perspicacious than Sartre's concept of 'feedback'. I conclude by arguing that, though crucial to the politics of immanence, Foucault's understanding of power and resistance is limited in its understanding of the inside of power/affectivity in terms of pleasure. This signals the limit of Foucault and the relevance of Deleuzian desire as a means of advancing the politics of immanence as a micropolitics.

The Order of Things and Foucault's Relation to Phenomenology

There is usually viewed a veritable abyss between French phenomenology and poststructuralism as personified by Foucault.[2] The prominence of this view is hardly surprising, considering Foucault constantly defined his position against phenomenology. This is first truly made evident in Foucault's *The Order of Things*. In this work, Foucault (2002b: 354) holds that though phenomenology does not constitute a resumption of an old rational goal of the West – the attempt to employ Reason and stable foundations as a transcendent ground to action, morality and thought – it does reflect 'the sensitive and precisely formulated acknowledgment of the great hiatus that occurred in the modern *episteme* at the turn of the eighteenth and nineteenth centuries'. This hiatus refers the dissociation between two types of analysis, one of the 'positive type' and the other of the 'eschatological type' (ibid.: 349). The first type refers to empirical positivities and related contents of knowledge (work, life and language) that are indicative of man's existential finitude. The second type refers to the finitude of the foundational forms of knowledge itself. This is a dissociation, in other words, between the empirical and the transcendental; the unreconciled double-function of man as both the object of knowledge and a subject that knows.

Husserl sought to establish a union between these two estranged analyses, by changing the point of application of transcendental analysis. Actual experience or phenomenological *lived experience* is proffered as the 'third' intermediary space wherein the two finitudes are unified, though without negating their separateness. All empirical content is given to experience, aiming to make the empirical uphold the transcendental, i.e. elucidating the conditions of experience and how these conditions can themselves be experienced. From this also comes a form of reflection concerning 'the relation of man to the unthought, or more precisely, their twin appearance in Western culture' (ibid.: 355). The unthought provides a dialectical relation of intentionality between consciousness and the object, that is given more concreteness in Sartre's 'dialectic of the self' and Merleu-Ponty's 'embodied consciousness'. In both their accounts, an empirical outside of some variety provides the self with positive contents in the form of *personal* experiences (*my* past, and *my* present) that in turn act as foundational forms.

In whichever guise it manifests itself, this particular phenomenological project 'continually resolves itself, before our eyes, into description – empirical despite itself – of actual experience, and into an ontology of the unthought that automatically short-circuits the primacy of the "I think"' (ibid.: 356). Foucault (ibid.: 270) maintains that it is impossible, however, to give empirical contents transcendental value, or to displace them in the direction of a constituent subjectivity,

> without giving rise to, at least silently, an anthropology – that is, to a mode of thought in which the rightful limitations of acquired knowledge (and consequently of all empirical knowledge) are at the same time the concrete forms of existence, precisely as they are given in that same empirical knowledge. (Ibid.)

The mixture between the content and form of knowledge functions through a personalised act of consciousness, intentionality, which is enclosed in lived experience. This results in an *analytic* of finitude, taken in the Kantian sense as a theory of the subject, whereby *man* is the ambiguous mixture of the empirical and transcendental, and thus the constitutive site of reality. By this reading, even Sartre's and Merleau-Ponty's displacement of the ego returns to a practicalised version of it. The functional structure of the transcendental deduction is maintained, even though the entities performing these functions are replaced. In being so heavily associated with the modernist *episteme*, Foucault maintains it was inevitable that phenomenology would revive the problem of the *a priori* and the transcendental motif in this way.

Foucault makes it clear that this relates directly to the problem of transcendence and metaphysics as Platonism. Once transcendence referred to the very meaning of the world, such as the way 'Plato ... opposed essence to appearance, a higher world to this world below, the sun of truth to the shadows of the cave' (ibid.: 345). In modernity, transcendence takes the form of the human as the ground for the world, 'a logic of signification, a grammar of the first person, and a metaphysics of consciousness' (ibid.: 351). Language is reduced to the mere mirror of things, to an order of grammar that grounds the copy of the original, or as the representation of something outside itself such as a fixed Form. It is for such reasons that the history of immanence has been practically inseparable from that of (anti)representation. It is also for such reasons that Plato 'is the excessive and deficient father' (ibid.: 344), and that anthropologism and transcendence are one and the same. The metaphysics of consciousness as lived experience brings transcendence back into the heart of immanence, i.e. immanent to a subject, or tacit cogito via embodiment. Thus for Foucault, phenomenology does not go far enough in overturning metaphysics as Platonism and transcendence, and neo-Kantianism as the modern personification of it.

Foucault never abandoned his reading of French phenomenology as a philosophy of transcendence. As he puts it in his final work, 'Life: Experience and Science', it is important to 'move beyond' a phenomenological notion of 'lived experience', which is expected to supply the originary meaning of every act of knowledge, and look 'for it in the "living" itself', that is, to 'determine the situation of the *concept in life*' (Foucault 2000a: 475). This understanding of life, as Agamben (2000: 221) observes, 'tears the subject away from the terrain of the *cogito* and consciousness', and so 'this experience roots it in life'. Knowledge no longer has as its correlate the opening to a world and to truth, but only life and its errancy, a 'living being who is fated "to err" and "to be mistaken"' (Foucault 2000a: 476). However, Foucault's inclusion of Sartre and Merleau-Ponty in this reading is erroneous in that it ignores, or rather fails to mention, their respective moves beyond Husserlian lived experience and intentionality as a form of transcendence. Whereas Sartre and Merleau-Ponty may have failed to go *far enough* in terms of immanence – due either to restrictions in language or an undertheorisation of politicised force – Foucault overreaches by envisioning them as fully trapped in transcendence. Indeed, Foucault's supposedly new take on life is precisely what Sartre instigated and Merleau-Ponty continued, especially in referring to life as 'an atmosphere' in the 'astronomical sense' or as constantly enshrouded by those mists we call the sensible world or history in the form of the *one*, anonymous, pre-personal subject.

The intimacy between ideas here is, I maintain, far from coincidental. It conveys Foucault's rather convoluted, intricate and self-effaced relationship with phenomenology. Indeed, what is often overlooked is the fact that Foucault's rejection of phenomenology is quite clearly written within its own post-Kantian, and in the case of Merleau-Ponty, anti-Cartesian milieu.[3] Which is also to say that his critique of phenomenology, though based on a simplified reading of it, is an internal one. Foucault holds that by operating within the *Logos* of the modern episteme, phenomenology failed to provide the true and thoroughly immanent conceptualisation of experience as first famously promised – though to varying degrees – by Husserl and Heidegger. A description that is supposed to be beyond *a priori* and external transcendental categories. Thus, I see Foucault's analysis of phenomenology in *The Order of Things* as one that replicates Merleau-Ponty's rejection of his own tacit cogito, i.e. the realisation that his project, and the subsequent bid for the non-dualist lifeworld, cannot be fully realised without investigating, and correcting, its own prejudicative *Logos* to which its expressive style and conceptual apparatus is beholden. Recall that to attend to the presuppositions inherent in one's philosophical *Logos* is at the same time to attend to the 'wild being' that envelopes it, and that, more importantly, it forgets and obscures. For Foucault, this *Logos* is expressed in terms of discourse, and the 'being' that envelops and obscures it, is the *episteme*. In taking up the *episteme* as opposed to the purely philosophical flesh, Foucault's analysis moves beyond Merleau-Ponty to *describe* – and still without reference to a transcendent ground – the *historical* presuppositions of the nineteenth-century system of thought and discourse to which he attaches it, and the regularities that account for its emergence. French phenomenology is taken as the most recent philosophical personification of the said system, but, as indicated, a personification that retains within itself the possibility of overcoming the very same system. Such an overcoming is precisely that which Foucault saw himself providing by revealing how the subject is caught in processes of signification that precludes any 'total history', transcendent Archimedean point, or privileged subject.

Contrary to the dialectical method, which 'is a way of evading the always open and hazardous reality of conflict by reducing it to a Hegelian skeleton' (Foucault 1980b: 114–15), Foucault's historical analysis follows Nietzsche and Bachelard in focusing on discontinuities in the temporal development of *epistemes*, textual and verbal taxonomies, and the actualised expression or visual plane of reality to which they correspond. The modifications and transformations in the rules of formation of statements – not to be understood in terms of some kind of unity of the sentence, the proposition, or the speech act, nor the same kind of unity as a material object, but rather as that which is caught up in a logical, grammatical, locutory nexus, or a functional relation between context and content – fail to correspond to the calm, continuist image normally attributed to them. The choice of objects and methods for analysis are all provided and constituted by historical *chance* (Foucault 2002b: 404–5).[4] Insofar as such a constitution determines the cultural area

– the chronological and geographical boundaries – in which the branch of knowledge can be recognised as having validity, it follows that there is no stable transcendental base or Kantian *a priori*. The appearance of man is not the result of insightful philosophical reflection, the liberation of 'an old anxiety', or 'the transition into luminous consciousness of an age-old concern', nor the 'entry into objectivity of something that had long remained trapped within beliefs and philosophies' (ibid.: 422). Rather, this appearance is the result of a chance change in the fundamental arrangements of knowledge, or a surface effect of more primordial processes, such that if those arrangements were to disappear, then 'man would be erased, like a face drawn in sand at the edge of the sea' (ibid.). It is specifically for this reason that Foucault (2008a: 63), in his earlier *Introduction to Kant's Anthropology*, describes man and the ego as an 'illusion', or even a 'transcendental mirage' – a semblance.

Archaeology and the Logic of Dispersion as Fold

The Order of Things takes up an internal critique of phenomenology akin to Merleau-Ponty's self-criticism, and in this way develops a theory of discourse that displaces the centrality of man. Foucault's subsequent *The Archaeology of Knowledge* advances this project through establishing the inner workings and the formative underpinnings of discourse and discursive practice as that which determines the object of knowledge. The starting point of this investigation is that of regularity. The regularity of the emergence of a discourse is deemed critical in the function of its unity in time, i.e. the more it occurs, the stronger its unity and the more coherent its formation. Consistent with *The Order of Things*, the regularity of discourse and the coherence of the formation are found in statements, making it 'a division that can be located at a certain level of analysis . . . and which enables one to say of a series of signs whether or not they are present in it' (Foucault 2002a: 97). Thus a statement is a function of existence that belongs to signs and on the basis 'of which one may then decide, through analysis or intuition, whether or not they "make sense", according to what rule they follow one another or are juxtaposed' (ibid.). A statement also has a horizontal function in that it always refer to other statements, such that its meaning is determined relationally. It is linked to a 'referential' that 'is made up not of "things", "facts", or "beings", but of laws of possibility' (ibid.: 103). It is the referential of the statement that forms the place, the condition, the field of emergence, the authority to differentiate between individuals or objects, states of things and relations that are brought into play by the statement itself, such that it defines the possibilities or appearance and delimitation of that which gives meaning to the sentence, 'a value as truth to the proposition' (ibid.).

A critical trajectory of Foucault's later thought is prefigured here: the fold. This is evident in the 'logic of dispersion', as the relational logic or synthetic principle of discursive statements. Dispersion, in this instance, is understood as not merely a scattering of elements in an open space, but 'a difference within the convergence of heterogeneous domains', as Widder (2004: 416) puts it. Thus dispersion is inseparable from folded relations, understood as disjunctive syntheses in which differences are not collapsed via negation into a unity or subsumed by a shared logic (as with dialectical thinking), but rather form the intersection where unities can appear. In this instance, however, we are not dealing with the fold of the Outside, as in Merleau-Ponty's 'big' fold, but rather the infinitesimal fold. The folds within the field or intensive space of discourse itself. Foucault dismisses four initial hypotheses that assume internal consistency of discursive statements, on the basis of the logic of dispersion.

The hypothesis that statements different in form and dispersed in time comprise a group if they refer to one and the same object is immediately problematised by the dynamic and shifting nature of the object of knowledge. In terms of madness, for instance, the object presented by seventeenth- and eighteenth-century medical statements is not concomitant or identical with the object that emerges in legal sentences or police action; similarly, 'all the objects of psychopathological discourses were modified from Pinel or Esquirol to Bleuler' (Foucault 2002a: 35). Even if we were to turn our attention to those groups of statements that share the same object, we would soon find that each of these discourses in turn constituted its object and 'worked it to the point of transforming it altogether' (ibid.: 36). Thus we would have to turn not to the eminence and uniqueness of an object, but rather to the intensive space in which various objects emerge and are continuously transformed, the space that allows them to speak. The unity of discourses on madness would be based, then, on the interplay of the rules that make possible the appearance of objects during a given period of time and the interplay of the rules that define the transformations of these different objects. Thus, to 'define a group of statements in terms of its individuality would be to define the dispersion of these objects, to grasp all the interstices that separate them', or, rather, to formulate their law of division (ibid.).

Similar problems arise if we try to define a group of relations between statements, their form and type of connection, as in a style or way of looking at things, or as a series of descriptive statements. For Foucault, it is self-evident that descriptions cannot be abstracted from hypotheses, and, further, that the descriptive statement is only one of the formations present in any discourse. Moreover, the descriptive statement itself is continually displaced. Thus, should there be a unity, its principle would not be a determined form of statements (ibid.: 37). We could seek to establish groups of statements by determining the system of permanent and coherent concepts involved. Yet grammar only appears to form a coherent figure. Instead, we discover a discursive unity not in the coherence of concepts, but in their simultaneous or successive emergence, or the in the interplay of their appearances and dispersion (ibid.: 38). The same obstacle is true of the fourth hypothesis, i.e. the attempt to regroup statements, describe their interconnection and account for the unitary forms under which they are presented.

The unity of statements via the regularity of its emergence, is a fallible and fluctuating one, arising in the intersections of divergent discourses as expressed in statements. It is precisely due to this dispersive nature of discourse, that Foucault (ibid.: 28) encourages us to renounce all those themes whose function is to ensure the infinite continuity of discourse and its secret presence to itself in the interplay of a constantly recurring absence. This serves to restore to discourse its character as a unique *event*, as opposed to a representation of the continuous or total history. The 'subject' is the effect of a self and a society, placed in eventful discursive relations of production and signification. That is to say, there is no a *priori* subject, nor a continuous history to which it could relate (Foucault 2002b: 327). 'Man' is a discourse. This is also to say that there is no single representational condition, merely a number of positive conditions of which the idea of representation is an effect. Thus Foucault once again provides a project akin to phenomenology though in the field of discourse: a *pure description of discursive events* without reference to a transcendent cause or a unity we only pretended to put into question (as Husserl does in his Kantian moments). Foucault restores to the statement the specificity of its occurrence. He describes, quite simply, the interplay of relations within discursive events.

In describing the interplay, we find that a discursive formation is characterised not by privileged objects but by the way it forms objects of investigation and knowledge that are in fact highly dispersed or mutually exclusive without having to modify itself. The remaining question is what puts a statement as a unitary function into action? Why is it is uttered in the first instance? What provokes the unity into actualisation, whereby heterogeneous discursive zones are linked together? By way of a group of relations established between authorities of emergence, delimitation and specification. Unity, principally, is in the practice. It is *forced*. A discursive formation is characterised by both the statement that establishes objects of knowledge and by the relation that is established between objects of knowledge – and in a well-determined form – by discursive *practice* in *non-discursive* environments, or the actual application of a discourse, in, for instance, an institutional setting (Foucault 2002a: 80–1). Here, we find a direct correlation with truth, which later becomes central to Foucault's subsequent works, particularly *The History of Sexuality*. Whereas for the Greek poets of the sixth century BC, the true discourse was that which 'inspired respect and terror', a century later, with Plato in particular, 'the highest truth no longer resides in what discourse was or did, but in what is said' (Foucault 1981: 54). Thus, 'a certain division was established, separating true discourse from false discourse' (ibid.). This forms the basis for a *will to truth*, operating as an internal system of binary exclusion in a dispersed discourse, as established, reinforced and renewed by whole strata of practices by way of institutional support. One is 'in the true' only 'by obeying the rules of a discursive "policing" which one has to reactivate in each of one's discourses' (ibid.: 61).

Nevertheless, though pertinent to the practice of discourse, to remain consistent with the 'radicalised' continuation of phenomenology as a field of immanence proper, the non-discursive environment is bracketed. Recall, Husserl 'brackets out' all the assumptions of the world and the nature of existence and its contents. He suspends judgement of the world though without negating its existence, and instead focuses on experience as an appearance or 'phenomenon'. Foucault opts for the same approach, though with regards to discourse vis-à-vis the non-discursive. Thus *describing* a discursive formation is a question of discovering the regularity of its application. It does not involve a phenomenological description of the non-discursive. It is denied positive status.

From Archaeology to Genealogy

According to Deleuze (2006b: 27), *The Archaeology of Knowledge* marked a turning point in Foucault's thinking. It develops an immanent notion of folded thought in the form of 'dispersion' and relates this to two 'practical formations: the one "discursive", involving statements, the other "non-discursive", involving environment'. As Deleuze goes on to say, however, the 'non-discursive' remains highly ambiguous. Following a Husserlian method of bracketing, it is merely indicated in a negative fashion, such that the connection between the two forms remains partial. Indeed, it is only by virtue of 'bracketing' off the 'non-discursive', that *The Archaeology of Knowledge* was able to posit an immanent theory of thought. And for this reason, the work runs into the same issue Sartre identified in Husserl. Just as consciousness *cannot be bracketed from reality*, for reality plays a fundamental role in its activity, the 'discursive' cannot be bracketed from the 'non-discursive', for the 'non-discursive' plays a fundamental role in its activity. The bracketing amounts to an abstraction.

Nothing provoked Foucault into realising the conceptual futility of such bracketing quite as much as the events in France of May 1968 (see Miller 1993: 175–84). After this point, Foucault went on to give the non-discursive its positive form, developing a link so strong between the two forms that genuine separation becomes problematic and even unnecessary (see Foucault 1981: 198). The 'non-discursive' is translated into power as the true force lying at the centre of a formation, as related to broader institutional, disciplinary and political strategies. The Outside of discourse is thoroughly folded in— though, at least until the incorporation of ethics in Foucault's last works, this Outside fold still designates an exterior relation, i.e. exterior to the interiority of the self. The use of this 'big' fold allowed Foucault to develop an analysis of power and politics that would serve to pervade all his subsequent works and lay the foundation for his understanding of resistance in the form of an ethics of the self.

At its simplest, due to both a theoretical weak point and an historical instance, Foucault (2001c: 327) came to recognise and argue that man is 'equally placed in power relations that are very complex'. In 'The Subject and Power' – which was written towards the end of his life – Foucault retrospectively states that his work is an attempt to illustrate the ways in which human beings are 'made into subjects' through what he calls three forms of objectification (or the three modes that a genealogy can take), determining the conditions of possibility and the limits of subjectivity. First, he says, are the modes of enquiry that try to give themselves the status of science: the objectification of the speaking subject in general grammar, philology and linguistics (the 'truth' axis). These, in turn, define subject positions, which are often accepted as neutral and verifiable facts. Second are 'dividing practices', by which Foucault means the different ways in which 'the subject is objectified by a process of division either within himself or from others' (ibid.: 331) (the 'power' axis), wherein mechanisms of disciplinary and normalising power manage subjects according to discourses of truth and disciplinary regimes. Third are forms of objectification concerning the way in which humans turn themselves into subjects via identification with certain subject positions (the 'ethics' axis), wherein power-relations delineate a form of self-to-self relation upon which, paradoxically, ethical self-formation and resistive creation are possible.

As with his previous work, this transition in Foucault's thought relates back to immanence inasmuch as it accords with the basic principle of immanent causality and transformation that rejects a privileged signifier or subject that would rupture this domain or personify its constitutive negativity. Though Foucault now adds an additional element to his field of immanence: power, as the *folded*, immanent Outside of the discursive field. Discourse is inseparable from power, as the true locus of *force* lying at the heart of the formation, essentially acting as its virtual (inasmuch as it is intensive) double. The one continually affects the other, such that to isolate one as the ultimate cause or to factor in a constitutive negativity within the relation is to enact, as we shall see, a radical abstraction. Indeed, Foucault sees that the

> historical contextualisation needed to be something more than the simple relativisation of the phenomenological subject. One has to dispense with the constituent subject, to get rid of the subject itself, that's to say, to arrive at an analysis that can account for the constitution of the subject within a historical framework, according, once more, to a logic of immanence, an immanent domain accounting for the constitution of knowledge, discourses, domains of objects, and so on, without reference to a subject that is either transcendental in relation to the field of events or runs in its empty sameness throughout the course of history. (Foucault 1980b: 117)

Here, truth is 'linked in a circular relation with systems of power that produce and sustain it, and to effects of power which it induces and which extend it – a "regime" of truth' (ibid.: 132).

Instead of a purely epistemological investigation of pure conceptual construction vis-à-vis the constitution of knowledge as truth, this turn in Foucault's thinking adopts a thoroughly historical and political one. That is, Foucault moves thoroughly within the realm of conceptual materialism. In this way, Foucault became interested in the effects of the centralising powers as linked to 'the institution and functioning of an organized scientific discourse within a society such as ours' (Foucault 2008b: 319). Whereas archaeology would be the 'appropriate methodology of this analysis of local discursivities', genealogy 'would be the tactics whereby, on the basis of the descriptions of these local discursivities, the subjected knowledges which were thus released would be brought into play' (ibid.: 320). The production of knowledge via the Enlightenment-inspired discourses of the human sciences (i.e. knowledge concerning the true nature and liberation of man, moral and ethical deliberation, systems of governance, law and economic exchange and so forth) is not simply the result of accumulated knowledge produced by researchers within a particular historical field. There is an interrelation with power: hence 'power-knowledge'. Insofar as genealogy is a study of discourse within the realm of power-relations, it follows that the logic of discursive formations and its principle of *disjunctive* immanence still applies. Or, to be more precise, the 'knowledge' side of discourse is disjunctive, as is the 'power' side – and the relation between the two is also disjunctive. A disjunction of disjunctions. Thus the 'immanent causality' Foucault aims to explore is not one of perfect harmony.

Power as Force Relation, Knowledge as Segment

We have to be cautious and clear in speaking of power in the context of Foucault. When we think of power, we typically envision something that is possessed and that can be exercised over objects and subjects, i.e. state power, military force or general material capabilities. In this instance, power is represented as domination, a form of saying 'no' or posting limits. It is basically, as Foucault (1998: 85) puts it, 'anti-energy'. It is also centred on nothing more than the statement of the law and the operation of taboos. Thus all the modes of domination, submission and subjugation are, in the end, reduced to an effect of obedience. Foucault notoriously balks against this traditional 'juridico-discursive' notion. In contradistinction, he seeks to present an analytic of 'power without the king' (ibid.: 91), understood as a 'multiplicity of force relations' or 'the moving substrate of relations between forces, which by virtue of their inequality, constantly engender states of power'. Power as force relation, has no subject or object other than force itself, operating between subjects and objects.

On numerous occasions, we find Foucault directly links his idea of power relations with Nietzsche's concept of force, particularly as presented in Deleuze's *Nietzsche and Philosophy*. Here we find, once again, the appearance of Merleau-Ponty's fold, understood as a disjunctive relation, though now in terms of Nietzschean force.[5] Nietzsche's basic contention is that – against mechanistic abstractions of unity and numerical quantity – forces cannot be number, but only relation. There is no 'quantity in itself', but rather 'difference in quantity' that cannot be placed on a fixed numerical scale. What is more, the relation between forces is never equal. Rather, forces are in relations of inequality and continual flux, or, rather, relations of disequilibrium. This presents us with a world of 'dynamic quanta', wherein forces clash with one another in such a way that one will invariably take the superior position and as such subordinate inferior forces (Nietzsche 1968: 46). Thus, as with the logic of dispersion or Merleau-Ponty's infinitesimal folds, heterogeneous forces *vice-dict* rather than contradict one another, they relate without their difference being negated, subsumed or collapsed into a higher unity or a complete non-relation.

By virtue of the disjunctive dynamic (or *disjunctive fold*), it follows that a force must express itself in accordance with the other forces to which it relates, such that the essence of force is its 'quantitative difference from other forces', which is expressed as the force's quality, i.e. if a force dominates over another, if it is quantitatively superior, it will have for itself the quality of being active: it commands, creates, transforms and overcomes (Deleuze 2006d: 46). Hence why Foucault (1998: 94) additionally describes power as the *support* 'which these force relations find in one another', forming a 'chain or a system, or on the contrary, the disjunctions and contradictions which isolate them from one another'.

There is a principle difference between Foucault and Deleuze's respective use of Nietzschean force as related to the fold, however. It regards the type of force relations in question. Initially, for

Deleuze, the force relations in question are psychic or unconscious, in the vein of a Bergsonian virtual multiplicity. Though still virtual, Foucault's use of force here is a socio-political and exterior one. Thus Foucault's later definition of power as a mode of action upon the actions *of others*, as the government of men by other men, which 'includes one important element: freedom' (Foucault 2001c: 342). Power is exercised on free subjects in an environment external to their interiority, and only insofar as they are 'free' to act/react in this environment; it is that which seeks to structure the field of possibilities in which the behaviour of active subjects is able to inscribe itself. Of course the two sides of virtual force (interior and exterior) do not remain mutually exclusive. They are partially, though problematically, unified in Foucault's later turn to ethics, as we shall see, and fully unified in Deleuze's collaborative works with Guattari.[6]

For now, however, Foucault is speaking of an exterior power between selves or 'free' subjects, insofar as they are faced with such a field of possibilities, where several kinds or *qualities of conduct*, active actions and reactions and modes of behavior are available. This should not be taken to mean that there are free subjects of the sort envisioned by liberal theory, but rather to mean the very points of resistance that are engendered by the disjunctive synthesis itself; freedom is power's excess. Indeed, an action upon the actions of others is the *par excellence* of force relations in that it does not refer to domination or total control over the Other, but rather to a set of actions that always allows room for counter-actions, the *process* of 'ceaseless struggles and confrontations', by which power 'transforms, strengthens, or reverses' the multiplicity of force relations as actions/reactions (Foucault 1998: 92). That is to say, one can employ a number of active actions (to incite, to seduce, to make difficult) or reactive actions (to be incited or seduced, and so on), techniques to determine another person's field of possibilities, e.g. through a panoptic gaze or the disciplinary tactics of the school room, which instantly engender an excess or simply opportunities for their reversal and inversion, setting up a complex set of ever-changing relations and a multiplicity of points of resistance.

The relation between a student and a teacher, for instance, is always one of force understood in terms of actions/reactions, in which either side can respond to the action of the other through inversion, subversion, reversal, etc. Does not the arrangement of the classroom give a sense of permanent visibility? Every pupil can be seen by the teacher at the front of the class. Furthermore, it is often the case that the seating arrangement of the class is designed to reflect a regimented and hierarchical order, usually pertaining to a set of norms and moral evaluations, or a series of unwritten codes. Disruptive students are sent to a particular section of the classroom for punishment (usually to the back of the room or sometimes right at the front). In conjunction with these actions, the teacher can use a reward system to encourage or incite good behaviour or hard work or to pit students against each other. On the flip side, however, as well as being incited, the students can interact with each other to construct a collective gaze that serves to intimidate, undermine, devalue and embarrass the teacher, alongside tactics of mockery and humour (such as putting a pin on the teacher's chair), disobedience and non-compliance (collectively refusing a demand) or apathy (collectively refusing to take an active and visible interest); the seating system can be used to set up formidable zones of disruption or alliance, where students empower one another through mutual encouragement and camaraderie. In addition to this, the students can completely invert the hierarchy so that being sent to the back of the room becomes a marker of respect among sections of the student cohort; and the students may also use the reward system to extrapolate an advantage from the teacher by currying favour, even using it as a counterbalance to anticipated violations or accusations. All these resistances, again, are actions and reactions not directly upon the teacher and other students but upon the range of future actions and reactions the teacher and other students can take.

Power as force relation, then, is not a form (as in a state-form), such that it cannot be found in the existence of a central point, nor is it that which lies between two forms – it is a *virtual non-place*, real without being actual. *A relational non-place*. It is seemingly obvious as to why Foucault abstains from developing a *theory* of power. If we are to move from concept to praxis, we can only but provide an *analytic*: in viewing power in relational terms, the central issue is to provide oneself with a grid of analysis which makes possible an account of such relations, as well as their playful (re)configuration. And given, as already stated, that power so defined is the true locus of *force* lying at the heart of a discursive formation, any analytical account of power will inevitably entail the question of knowledge. Where there is power, there is knowledge, and where there is knowledge, there is power.

The relation between power and knowledge is one that precedes Foucault. Indeed, lurking beneath the traditional notion of power is an unquestioned reverence for the purity of knowledge and truth, i.e. knowledge can be utilised either to strengthen power or to undermine it. Thus the old and tiresome adage: *knowledge is power*. In liberal democracies the concern among political groups (the intelligentsia, the press, politically active citizens, and so on) sitting outside of the state apparatus is always with keeping knowledge and information free from the manipulations of power, either through false press, omission of fact, political spin, or outright political lies, so as to strengthen democratic procedure and scrutiny. In classical Marxist terms, this concerns the power of ideology, in which our intersubjective understandings of our material reality are obscured, inculcating a false 'sense' (*sens*) of self. An intricate part of class struggle, and therefore emancipation, once more concerns the capturing of knowledge. In either case, there is a loose Platonic vision of knowledge – loose, for though not grounded in a supposed ideal realm 'beyond', there is belief in its stability, permanence and objective representation, such that it can be said to exist in a pure or at least untarnished form. In contradistinction to this model, Foucault maintains that knowledge is always already in a dance with power— power *as force relation*. The notion of untarnished knowledge is a mere fantasy of transcendence. Thought and the knowledge to which it corresponds, is immanent to the real that provokes it.

To return to the classroom example provided earlier, we can see how pedagogical knowledge and institutional and moral rules underpin tactics of force, but also allow for the force to be exercised in the first instance. Quite simply, the idea of the school and the classroom – along with its institutional rules and structures – is precisely that which allows the relation between the student and the teacher to be established in the first place. There are other ways in which knowledge is central. For instance, the student *knows* the teacher is not allowed to hit him/her or even touch him/her (in school systems that prohibit corporal punishment), and thus disobedience can have a trying effect. S/he *knows* that s/he can turn the teacher's code of conduct against him/her by, for instance, accusing the teacher of indecent behaviour or complaining to his/her parents that the teacher is failing to address disruptive behaviour in the class (even if it is the student him-/herself that is the cause of the disruption). The teacher, in turn, may justify his/her actions by reference to educational and personal expectations, moral duty or institutional and societal rules encapsulating ideas of civility and practicality. Even the idea of the 'good citizen' or the pervading notion of the norm can be put to effective use in making the student scared and anxious of his/her future ('if you don't listen to me, you will amount to nothing'), which is often reinforced through the use of his/her parents (employing the discourse of the family as the ultimate responsible unit, which will itself feel a moral and social duty to produce a functioning member of society).

Thus, where power can be considered diagrammatic as Deleuze (2006b: 61) aptly puts it – in that it is detached from any specific use, mobilising non-stratified matter and functions – knowledge is archival, concerning formed matters or substances and formalised functions. The difference in nature, however, does not foreclose a mutual immanence. We are not just dealing with the surface of projection of a power mechanism, but with a complex of power and knowledge. The diagram and the archive are tied together through discourse, articulated on the basis of their difference in nature (Foucault 1998: 100).[7] More specifically, the two domains remain intricately linked in that if something is 'constituted as an area of investigation', it is because 'relations of power had established it as a possible object; and conversely, if power was able to take it as a target, this was because techniques of knowledge and procedures of discourse were capable of investing it' (ibid.: 98). Thus, between techniques of knowledge and strategies of power, there is no exteriority, only 'local centres' of power-knowledge, e.g. between the students and teachers.

It is precisely for this reason that Foucault calls for the abandonment of the 'whole tradition that allows us to imagine that knowledge can exist only where the power relations are suspended and that knowledge can develop about its injunctions, its demands and its interests' (Foucault 1991a: 27). It is of conceptual and political necessity to come to terms with how power and knowledge directly imply one another; 'that there is no power relation without the correlative constitution of a field of knowledge, nor any knowledge that does not presuppose and constitute at the same time power relations' (ibid.). The relationship is reciprocal, but the reciprocity itself is ambiguous, forming a Gordian knot that, by virtue of that fact, is difficult if not impossible to unravel, to the point that we are incapable of isolating the primary cause in analysis.[8] If discourse is understood as the result and interplay of power-knowledge – both sides of which are comprised of disjunctive relations between and within – then it must be conceptualised 'as a series of discontinuous segments whose tactical function is neither uniform nor stable' (ibid.: 100). There is no division between the dominant discourse and the dominated one (as with ideology) or between accepted and excluded. We are dealing, instead, with a core-periphery relation on a flat plane, made up of 'a multiplicity of discursive elements that can come into play in various strategies' (ibid.).

We are faced with a complex and unstable process whereby discourse can be both an instrument and an effect of power, 'but also a hindrance, a stumbling-block, a point of resistance and a starting point for opposing strategy' (ibid.: 101). Discourse, which is now understood as being made up of power-knowledge, may transmit and produce power, but it also undermines and exposes it. The appearance of psychiatry, jurisprudence and fictional/non-fictional literature on homosexuality, perversion, pederasty, and so forth, may have made it possible to exercise a degree of control and regulation of homosexuality but it also made possible the formation of a reverse discourse: 'homosexuality began to speak on its own behalf, to demand that its legitimacy or "naturality" be acknowledged, often in the same vocabulary, using the same categories by which it was medically disqualified' (Foucault 1998: 101). That is to say, homosexuality was once normatively treated and institutionally managed as a medical perversion, and in this odd sense, natural, at least insofar as it was the flip side of the medical norm. Today, its 'natural' status allows for its liberalisation, with gay marriage often supported on the premise that homosexuality is not a choice but a result of genetics. Such a 'naturalist' discourse clearly runs contrary to the very progressive-style politics that attaches itself to it, in that this politics tends to resist such 'naturalist' arguments in other domains (for instance regarding intelligence and G-factor analysis, and the social Darwinist concept of the 'deserving poor') lest it be employed as a way to rationalise and justify social stratification and socio-economic division. Such a contradictory element points to the fact that the 'truth', in the grand sense of the word, is not what matters. Rather, it is the 'games of truth' employed that are to be considered. And such games are possible precisely because discursive domains are linked together by disjunction, and so remain unstable, dynamic and open to alteration. Put differently, it is by virtue of its disjunctive or dispersive nature (of power, of knowledge and of the relation between the two) that the entire power-knowledge network continually creates the conditions of its own resistance.[9]

Double-Conditioning

As it is, Foucault's concept of power-knowledge seems largely concerned with micro-powers, or relationships that though social and institutional are cut off from the broader political realm of experience. Such a view would certainly lend credence to the idea that Foucault opts for an insular and individualist 'politics'— an idea that, as we saw in the introduction, has been attached to micropolitics more generally. However, from Foucault's conceptualisation of power-knowledge, comes the principle of 'double-conditioning', which directly concerns the connection between micro-powers and broader political movements: the broader, bigger, 'big' fold of the Outside. As we will see, this connection to the 'bigger outside' is essential to understanding micropolitical resistance, or rather how seemingly aesthetic practices of the self can animate broader political movements of resistance.

In speaking of a 'bigger Outside', I envision a direct, though formal, correspondence between the principle of double-conditioning and Sartre's concept of 'scarcity' as the socio-historical substratum of the 'de-totalised totality'; though, in adopting Merleau-Ponty's fold, beyond the Sartrean restrictions of dualistic language. That is, all three concepts concern the interaction between the macro/'exterior' and the micro/'interior', between and within which operates the infinitesimal, to form – especially when connected to a socio-historical substratum – an assemblage or *dispositif*: 'a thoroughly heterogeneous ensemble consisting of discourses, institutions, architectural forms, regulatory decisions, laws, administrative measures, scientific statements, philosophical, moral and philanthropic propositions', and so forth (Foucault 1980a: 194). That is, there is no discontinuity between the multiplicities, yet neither is there homogeneity. Instead, 'one must conceive of the double conditioning of a strategy by the specificity of possible tactics, and of tactics by the strategic envelope that makes them work' (Foucault 1998: 100). Thus the principle presents us with the same sort of immanent and disjunctive relation that we found present in the power-knowledge network itself, wherein the two domains reinforce and undermine each other, albeit now in the form of the microscopic and macroscopic as major elements, or the multiplicity of a multiplicity forming an assemblage.

This leads us to Foucault's idea that the fostering of and power over life, as in sustaining and continuing the biological existence of a population for the sake of the social body, has since the seventeenth century become the overall strategy encapsulating power as force, but also as interlacing with knowledge insofar as it concerns discourses on life. This provides a more historical and tangible account of the earlier description of genealogy as a power concerning, primarily, the body. A power where the 'death that was based on the right of the sovereign is now manifested as simply the reverse of the right of the social body to ensure, maintain, or develop its life' (ibid.: 136), primarily proceeding down two routes: (1) the *anatomic*; and (2) the *biological*.

The first (anatomic) focused on the body as a machine, its 'disciplining, the optimization of its capabilities, the extortion of its forces, the parallel increase of its usefulness and its docility, its integration into systems of efficient and economic controls' (ibid.: 139). Referring in particular to the way in which the Classical age 'discovered' the body as object and target of power, as something that may be subjected, used, transformed and improved, this attention to the body clearly differed from medieval techniques of punishment (Foucault 1991a: 136). The concern of penal justice shifted from the general defence of society through techniques of declaration, exclusion, forced labour and retaliation to the control and psychological reform of the attitudes and behaviour of individuals. The entire penal regime of the nineteenth century became a matter of control not so much over what individuals did 'as over what they might do, what they were capable of doing, what they were liable to do, what they were imminently about to do' (Foucault 2001b: 67). This, in turn, was accompanied by the idea of dangerousness, the idea that the 'individual must be considered by society at the level of his potentialities, and not at the level of his actions' (ibid.: 57).

By the start of the nineteenth century, the great spectacle of physical punishment disappeared and the 'theatrical representation of pain was excluded from punishment' (Foucault 1991a: 14). The body conceived as a site of the sovereign's power was no longer the target; it was the body conceived as a path to the soul. Therefore, the question was no longer only, 'Has the act been established and is it punishable?', but also, 'What is this act? What is this act of violence or this murder? To what level or to what field of reality does it belong? Is it a phantasy, a psychotic reaction, a delusional episode, a perverse action?' It is no longer simply, 'Who committed it?', but, 'How can we assign the causal proofs that produced it? Where did it originate in the author himself? Instinct, unconscious, environment, heredity?' It is no longer simply, 'What law punishes this offence?', but, 'What would be the best way of rehabilitating him?'

From this, a whole set of assessments or rather diagnostic, prognostic and normative judgements concerning the criminal were lodged in the framework of penal judgment (see ibid.: 19–20). There formed methods, a kind of social orthopaedics, through which the meticulous control of the operations of the body were made possible, 'which assured the constant subjection of its forces and imposed upon them a relation of docility-utility' (ibid.: 137) up to and including: the art of distribution (ibid.: 141–9); the control of activity (ibid.: 149–56); the organisation of geneses (ibid.: 156–62); and the composition of forces (ibid.: 162–9). Their instruments included: hierarchical observation (ibid.: 170–7); normalising judgement (ibid.: 177–84); and their combination in a procedure that is specific to it: the examination (ibid.: 184–94).

Combined with the gaze of the panoptic society – constant surveillance and supervision – these methods and instruments, dispersed across the political plane, aimed at constituting the *docile subject*. Such a practice, Foucault highlights, did not stay within the penal system, but spread throughout society, for the control of individuals at the level of their potentialities could not be performed by the judiciary itself: 'it was to be done by a series of authorities other than the judiciary, such as the police and a whole network of institutions of surveillance and correction – the police for surveillance, the psychological, psychiatric, criminological, medical, and pedagogical institutions for correction' (Foucault 2001b: 57). Indeed, education came to be designed to prepare the child '"for a future in some mechanical work", to give him "an observant eye, a sure hand and prompt habits"'. Truly, the disciplines function as techniques for making individuals useful. Unlike the soul of Christian theology, it is not born in sin as much as it is born out of methods of punishment, supervision and constraint. Power and knowledge relations invest human bodies and subjugate them by turning them into objects of knowledge.

The second route down which the power over life proceeded focused on the 'body as imbued with the machines of life and serving as the basis of the biological processes' (Foucault 1998: 139). Such a strategy was an indispensable element in the development of industrialised capitalism, insofar as capitalism 'would not have been possible without the controlled insertion of bodies into the machinery of production and the adjustment of the phenomena of population to economic processes' (ibid.: 141). A fine balance was required between optimising forces and maintaining life in general, without for all that making life more difficult to govern and manage. Sex, inasmuch as it presented a means of access both to the life of the body and the life of the species, was employed as a 'standard for the disciplines and as a basis for regulations' (ibid.: 146).

Foucault (ibid.: 37) describes the nineteenth century as an age of 'multiplication', an epoch that had initiated sexual heterogeneities, wherein elements of repression or, better, prohibition regarding sex played a subservient role, one that was microscopic and even local to the transformation of sex into a discourse. The prohibition of sex was, if anything, an indication that it had been produced as a something universally in our minds, a universal concern, included in the body as a mode of specification of individuals. This was not the discovery of some new form or rationality or fundamental truth. It was rather the progressive formation of that interplay of truth and sex. As such, sex became something not only produced and judged, but also administered. And though creating a discourse on sexuality, the eighteenth century did not find a truth of the human or a hidden secret of his or her identity. The aim was not to suppress sexuality, but rather to provide it with an analytical, visible and permanent reality.

Recourse to liberation through sexuality is thus an illusion, as 'where there is desire the power relation is already present', vanity, then, 'to go questioning after a desire that is beyond the reach of power' (ibid.: 151). In this way (and only this way), despite identifying the respective roles of government and the state insofar as these concern macro-strategies, Foucault (2008b: 324–5) holds that recourse to sovereignty as a tool against discipline is misguided, for sovereignty and disciplinary mechanisms 'are two absolutely integral constituents of the general mechanisms of power'. If one wants to look for a non-disciplinary form of power or struggle against discipline and disciplinary power, it is not towards the ancient right of sovereignty that one should turn, but towards the possibility of a new form of right, one which must indeed be anti-disciplinarian but at the same time liberated from the principle of sovereignty. We are obliged to turn away from the typical approach of analysing power from the point of view of its internal rationality in order to analyse power relations through the antagonism of strategies.

Not only is productive modern power inevitably ignored by

humanist theorists, but humanism itself emerges as an agent of productive power/micro-fascism, as a stratagem of the new growing mode of control. The 'conventional histories' of the human sciences provide illusions that function, as Foucault (2003: 154) defines it, as a 'retrospective justification'. In this vein, power is justified if it is exercised under the veneer of scientific truth. Attempts to liberate or rehabilitate 'man', to bring about his reason or his 'true' nature based on a predefined finitude or a perceived normality, exclude otherness and commit us to an oppositional or binary logic on the level of semblance. That is to say, conventional histories take the identities that are thrown up by virtual processes or force relations – identities that are in essence mere surface effects of primordial transformations of power-knowledge – as given truths upon which to effectively classify subjects. Such classifications lead to the categorisation, identification and exclusion of subjects who are not in tune with this 'true' essence of man's being.

Nevertheless, the fixing of identities was never part of the disciplinary society. As Foucault (1991a: 271) makes clear, if the 'law is supposed to define offences, if the function of the penal apparatus is to reduce them and if the prison is the instrument of this repression, then failure has to be admitted'. Instead, disciplines are 'techniques for assuring the ordering of human multiplicities' (ibid.: 218) and nothing more. They seek to reduce the inefficiency of mass phenomena, to make a multiplicity more manageable. Any apparent failures only serve to further justify and intensify penal and disciplinary practices, and to support the spread of such practices into non-penal systems. Thus the failure of the prison 'has always been accompanied by its maintenance' (ibid.: 272). This seems to suggest, then, that there is no fixing of identities, for identities are not 'real' (or representations of what is 'real'). Rather, identities are constructed surface effects.

The Subject and Ethics

In addition to the truth and power axes of genealogy, Foucault sought after a third: ethics. This refers to the way in which the individual constitutes and recognises him-/herself as a subject (self-subjection), in particular a subject of sexuality, 'how men have learned to recognize themselves as subjects of "sexuality"' (Foucault 2001c: 327). Such a formation speaks to a person's retroactive consumption of the very identities and norms produced and thrown up by (micro) virtual processes of power-knowledge relations in conjunction with strategies of (macro) bio-power. The identities and norms are used as coordinates by which a person my plot their 'identity' and thus their sense of self. This is retroactive in the sense of providing an identity narrative by which the 'subject' may come to understand all *past* – and ergo present and future – action, thought and feeling; an instance where exterior micro-macro relations of disjunctive folds by way of the power-knowledge network are themselves folded into the self, acting on the body (via sex and desire) as the 'inscribed surface of events', so as to create an interior, a crease and an Inside that exceeds that interior (a multiple self) (Foucault 1991a: 70). That is, once more taking his cue from Merleau-Ponty, specifically his emphasis on the body as the pivot point between interiority and exteriority. Genealogy, as Foucault tells us, 'is thus situated within the articulation of the body and history. Its task is to expose a body totally imprinted by history and the process of history's destruction' (ibid.), so as to disrupt all that has previously been imagined or presupposed permanent and secure, revealing the heterogeneity that lurks beneath all that was and is assumed cohesive and consistent with itself (ibid.: 82). Its purpose, bluntly put, is not to 'discover the roots of our identity', but rather to 'commit itself to its dissipation' (ibid.: 95). Indeed, according to Foucault, it was by this particular focus on the body that 'sex' and 'desire' were established as discourses, in turn creating a permanent and visible reality that effectively served to – and arguably still does – regulate self-to-self relations.[10] *A fold of a fold.* It is by virtue of this conclusion of the interior self, the inside, that the concept of the immanent Outside is extended to its fullest point.

In order for the recognition or identification with a subject position to remain somewhat stable, for the fold to function or at least to take effect, practices of the self that serve to reinforce it are required, such that ethics involves 'technologies of the self'. Thus, when in 'The Subject and Power' Foucault (2001c: 327) declares that 'it is not power, but the subject, that is the general theme of my research', he is in fact referring to the immanent double-conditioning process by which the subject and the identities by which it attempts to plot and sustain itself are generated. Once more, there is no privileged subject as the precondition of thought, meaning and action, but rather a subject now with its very own, seemingly private interiority, as an immanent effect of a folded Outside.

Sexuality and bio-power are clearly critical to this third axis, yet, as Simons (1995: 34) notes, when Foucault analyses sexuality and bio-power in the first volume of *The History of Sexuality*, 'he had not yet formulated his notion of ethics. However, it is possible to reconstruct his discussion of sexuality along the lines of his later analyses of ethics.' It can be said that the first volume of *The History of Sexuality* represents the vital pivot point from the second to the third axis, ambiguously sitting between the two. Indeed, what prompts this shift to ethics, according to Deleuze (2006b: 78–9), is the impasse of the movement of liberation as the return to repression outlined in this first volume, which is precisely why the first volume ended on a doubt:

> If at the end of it Foucault finds himself in an impasse, this is not because of his conception of power but rather because he found the impasse to be where power itself places us, in both our lives and our thoughts, as we run up against it in our smallest truths . . . How can we 'cross the line'. (Ibid.: 79)

How can we, in other words, envision an addition to power-knowledge or a way out/through it while remaining true to the immanence of genealogy?

Recall that the discourse of 'liberation' runs the risk of falling back on the idea that there exists a human nature; one merely returns to a constructed and alienated truth. Freedom cannot be understood as the liberation of desire, as the liberation of an essential self, nor is it simple negation. Indeed, if immanence is taken seriously, we are left to conclude that there is no transcendent outside, either as a positive Body or a negative self, to which we can to refer, 'no single locus of great Refusal, no soul of revolt, source of all rebellions, or pure law of the revolutionary' (Foucault 1998: 95–6). And given the omnipotence of power, it would seem that there is no scope for resistance. However, as we are dealing with an immanent and *disjunctive* network of relations, a fold of folds, then we are by necessity also dealing with a multiplicity of points of resistance present, as they are, everywhere in the network, and everywhere in the self as the interior of that network, each one of them unique unto themselves. We have already seen this with respect to the student-teacher relationship, and the discourse of homosexuality.

The question now is how this relates to ethical self-practice, or, rather, to embodied existence. Through strategically codifying these points of resistance and thus through harnessing the excesses

– the *folded disjunctions* – built into the network, certain practices of the self, *modes of being*, can be turned around so as to propel and subvert the condition, to re-/un-/infold a self-identified subject position which reverberates across the dispositif. Practices of the self can affect institutional micro-powers, which in turn can affect the macro-strategies upon which they rely. In this way, resistance becomes sort of 'practice of freedom' as opposed to a 'process of liberation' that can subvert an entire *dispositif*.[11]

Foucault turns to the Classical Greeks as, for him, their notion of life as material for a work of art contains the seeds for the conceptual growth of such a practice. The first point, in this respect, is that ethical substance ran in conjunction with a particular *mode d'assujettissement*, 'to build our existence as a beautiful existence' (Foucault 1991c: 356). The ethical question is not: which desires? which acts? which pleasures? But rather: 'with what force is one transported "by the pleasures and desires?"' (ibid.: 343), in what way was one's existence made beautiful? In this case, the *object* for moral reflection is not the act itself, nor desire, nor even pleasure, but 'more the dynamics that joined all three in a circular fashion' (ibid.). The dynamics were analysed in terms of two major variables: quantitative, as in the intensity of the practice; and qualitative, as in the subject of the activity or its object. Though we may still find moral codes here, particularly concerning the body, married life, sex with boys, the Ancient Greeks are said to 'accept those obligations in a conscious way for the beauty or glory of existence' (ibid.: 356).

Such an ethical practice relates back to immanence in that we are separated from the language of moral codes and dialectical thought, where, through an appeal to a transcendent Law, the self takes the form of a moral subject, a self-reflexive 'I' or ego, standing apart from what it is not and quelling in its own 'self-responsibility'. Such an ego proves critical in Christian and Enlightenment ethics and their mutual inclusion of internal alienation or a hierarchical opposition between a 'true' and 'false' self. In Christianity, internal alienation takes the form of the devil and devilish base instincts; the reason one is compelled to gain knowledge and insight is in order to gain self-mastery for the sake of keeping 'pure', or realising one's 'higher' self. Advancing a distinctly Nietzschean view, Foucault adds that though it may be tempting to praise the Enlightenment for the demise of religious hegemony, the fact remains that only the form differs. The ethical substance (*substance éthique*) and the mode of adjustment (*mode d'assujettissement*) of the theo-juridical element remain relatively intact. Self-examination and confession are no longer utilised as a means of tracking down the devil as such, but are nevertheless still utilised as a means of tracking down an internal alienation, a base-self in the form of, for instance, the 'pervert', the 'mad', the 'abnormal' essence within, and realising in turn the hither-side, 'true' or 'pure' self. It is a form of self-deciphering relative to the ideal bio-social norm, coinciding with the shift since the Classical age in the mechanism of power, from the sovereign's right of death to the power over life (bio-power), as per above.

The ego and morality as the corollaries of conceptual transcendence, then, are necessary complements of each other, such that the separation from moral language as personified in the immanent ethics of the Classical Greeks, is tantamount to the rejection of the subject as a homogenous substance. Indeed, the Classical Greeks envisioned the subject as a form that 'is not primarily or always identical with itself' (Foucault 1996: 440). One does not always have the same relationship with oneself, there is a perennial excess, 'there are relationships and interferences between these different forms of the subject; but we are not dealing with the same type of subject' (ibid.). It is by virtue of tending to this excess, in treating oneself as a malleable form, that we are able to 'play games of truth otherwise' (Foucault 1988: 15), to self-create and practise life as a work of art that can disrupt an already existing subjectification of the self and loosen the threads of genealogical power as associated to such subjectification.

The conceptual principle here is no different to that underpinning the teacher-student example, in that it is possible to subvert the very techniques and tactics used to discipline subjects through utilising the points of disjunction within them. However, as already suggested, Foucault is not only concerned with self-to-Other relations as they are related to macro-strategies but also with self-to-self relations that in turn affect self-to-Other relations and thus macro-strategies. As Foucault (1992: 43) puts it, the ethical substance in Ancient Greece – aphrodisia – is a nexus of forces that *links together* rules, techniques and institutions, along with 'acts, pleasures, and desires', operating '"beneath the codes and rules" of knowledge and power'. In this case, the interior crease of the folded Outside creates an Inside that is recomposed and contorted within and folded back out in the form of exterior actions/reactions on forces, so as to create a new folding, a new doubling; a relation that ultimately exploits the paradoxical yet positive content of dispersion and disjunction that exceeds the terms of identity and opposition referred to previously, allowing a new relation to oneself to emerge, constituting an inside which is hollowed out. Thus why Deleuze (2006b: 86), in reference to Foucault's ethics, identifies 'four folds of subjectivation: the body and its pleasures, the fold of the relation between forces, the fold of knowledge, and finally the fold of the outside itself, or "the ultimate fold"' (ibid.). Thus contrary to the temptation to view Foucault's previous work as anathema to the conception of interiority, it remains that the inside is of the outside, the crease of the fold that, as we have seen, was always, albeit latently, present in the conceptual mosaic.[12]

This means, at its most basic, that ethical practices not only change the relation to oneself; in changing the relation to oneself, the mode of behaviour changes. The change in the mode of behaviour, if substantial, will affect the micro-powers circulating the institution within which the self is operating. In accordance with the principle of double-conditioning, affecting the micro-powers upon which macro-strategies rely has the potential to subvert macro-strategies and thus change the entire dispositif. The body, via sex and desire but also through the various techniques of institutional discipline (focusing on posture, handwriting, walking and marching), forms the central pivot point of this relation. It is the interface.

In linking the interior Inside with a folded resistance, Foucault makes a link between resistance and affectivity. This is a body and therefore an interior, with affectivity. Of course! It is only insofar as there are potentially threatening pleasures and desires that the body is acted upon. In an eagerness to avoid carrying the metaphysical weight of psychoanalytic idealism, and thus the reinstatement of the repressive hypotheses and the Christian-like idea of a 'true' self, Foucault (1998: 44) speaks in terms of pleasures, of a 'sensualization of power and a gain of pleasure', in which the pleasure discovered feeds back to the power that encircled it. There is a certain 'pleasure that comes of exercising a power that questions, monitors, watches, spies, searches out, palpates, brings to light' (ibid.). He also speaks of a 'pleasure that kindles at having to evade this power, flee from it, fool it, or travesty it ... power asserting itself in the pleasure of showing off, scandalizing, or resisting' (ibid.: 45). Thus, even though power captures pleasure, and finds pleasure in its capturing, pleasure also offers the 'possibility of resistance' (ibid.: 156), which is to say that there are *'perpetual spirals of power and pleasure'*, offering an affective and agentic site that need not refer to an essentialist factor sitting outside of the immanent process of subjectivity (ibid.: 45). This seems to imply that pleasure has its reactive and active moments; when of the former, it is the most effective method of re-folding: *acts* of pleasure over *analyses* of desire.

From Pleasure to Desire

Despite his own statements, Foucault has not abandoned but instead further radicalised Sartre's ethico-politics of authenticity, moving it beyond the confines of abstraction towards a recognition of force and an overt theorisation of political power that was lacking in both Sartre and Merleau-Ponty. Hence, we still have with Foucault the theme of ethics as the reflective part of freedom, or as the primordial starting point for politics, but now embedded into broader socio-political strategies.[13] At this point, however, it is typically objected that Foucault deprives political theory of any normative criterion by which to differentiate between different struggles – the good versus the bad, and acceptable versus unacceptable forms of power.[14] This objection has undoubtedly continued to plague Foucauldian political theory, and in this sense has had a significant impact on our understanding of political normativity. The objection, however, is rooted in a profound misreading of Foucault and a neglect of the implications of the ontology of immanence he advances. There is an ethical and to a certain degree normative dimension to Foucault's thought that is entirely consistent with his ontology of immanence. My view is that the real issue lies with how this immanent ethics is construed. I believe that the affective/agentic dimension it relies on (bodies and pleaure) lacks the conceptual perspicacity required for an effective political praxis. My ultimate point is that Foucault is missing one critical element in his political theory: desire, or more specifically, Deleuzian *immanent* desire, as that which underpins and determines pleasure.

In asking how we differentiate between good and bad, legitimate and illegitimate, we must observe that, insofar as power is relational and omnipresent we are not differentiating between powers.[15] It is not as if, at the constitutive or micro level, some forms of power are repressive and others productive, or that it is contained in some places and possessed by some people but not in and by others. As we saw, this is not Foucault's thesis. What is more, Foucault's ethics concerns ways to cultivate care of the self *through* relations of genealogical power, in a manner reminiscent of Spinoza's ethics, i.e. it is a matter of what a body *can* do as opposed to what it *should* do. For from genealogy it follows that there is no epistemic vantage point by which we can form moral diktats; knowledge, after all, is a surface effect. Indeed, the true irony of those who charge Foucault with relativism is that their reproaches are informed by the very desire for a 'fixed origin' that Foucault highlights as merely a discursive habit of modernity. The reproach is reliant on a pre-philosophical notion of rationality or a metahistorical deployment of ideal signification and indefinite teleologies. This is to merely reassert, in a conceited case of *circulus in probando*, modernist values premised on a transcendent critique in the guise of a neo-Kantian 'practical reason', as a method of justifying modernist values.

Against this we are left with an ethics that must, by metaphysical necessity, be grounded in the immanent *modes* of existence themselves, with reference to processes of subjectivation and stratification, i.e. what mode of existence does a particular thought, action or feeling imply? From where does it derive and what does it express? How is a mode determined? Or rather, what criterion – and upon what basis – do we use to differentiate between different ethical struggles or forms of resistance, i.e. the good versus the bad, and acceptable versus unacceptable forms of power?

It may be said that Foucault does account for such modes or agentic capacities (which need not evoke a self-conscious subject) through his emphasis on 'bodies and pleasures' as the rallying point for the counter-attack against the deployment of sexuality. Certainly there is a case to be made here. As we saw, pleasure is taken as the central affect in understanding bodily forces and how they can be resisted. Conversely, it would also be misleading to say that this account is in any way substantial or indeed that pleasure, as he presents it, is a satisfactory model, for the question as to how or rather what causes pleasure to be configured in different ways, how it can come to take on a different character (pleasure found here, but not there), and how it can serve to animate resistance, is abundantly unclear. The concept of the disjunctive linkages and folds can at least account for the possibility of a pleasure configured through power possibly serving to resist it – this pleasure being the fold, refold or infold of another pleasure and power, and so forth – but what of the affective motive? Without the motive, which again needs not invoke a self-conscious subjective motivation, there is no indication as to whether the pleasure in question is a real resistance or simply one floating on the surface of strata or organisation. That is, with Foucault we know conceptually where to locate resistance and how to construe it, but not what compels or drives it and its opposite, or what decides whether one finds pleasure in resistance or in exercising powers of observation. What gets pleasure going?

Now, it may be the case that with a degree of creative effort we could devise a consistent answer of sorts; but if there is one, it certainly is not present in Foucault's work. His use of pleasure remains so under-theorised that we are left with a rather ambiguous or at least generic understanding of it, ultimately undermining the reference to 'reactive' and 'active' pleasures. This may partly be the result of Foucault's rather late retroactive application of pleasure to his analytics of power, and also, as previously suggested, his allergy to psychoanalytical concepts. Whatever the case, pleasure as it stands in Foucault is problematic, and opens the way for Deleuze's chief criticism that pleasure so (un)defined, is always an *effect* or secondary to a process in which desire is assembled; that pleasure marks the (mostly failed or unfulfilled) satisfaction that is born out of the negative of a fictitious lack, short-circuiting desire's positivity or blocking its flows, taking form in accordance with or in reaction to it through a socially invested assemblage. That is, there is an absence of a third and fourth form pleasure can take: pleasure in one's own repression and pleasure in the punishment of others by way *ressentiment.* In which case, as Deleuze (2007: 131) puts it, pleasure is 'a re-territorialisation', it sits 'on the side of strata and organization . . . it is in the same breath that desire is presented as internally submitting to the law and outwardly regulated by pleasures'.

The question here is: 'Why are some troubled people, more than others, more vulnerable to, and perhaps dependent on, shame?' (ibid.: 126). Or, rather, why are some in bad conscience and others not? Why do they vary in degree? As I will argue in the next chapter, this question of agency or motive comes down to the assemblage of desire in conjunction with its social dimension. *Desire disseminates power formations.* This is still in keeping with Foucault's contention that the objectives and aims of power are not the result of the choice or decision of an individual or collective subject, but nevertheless it identifies a headquarters of sorts in desire. Where Marxism speaks of class interest, however, we are speaking here of unconscious libidinal interests, in accordance with a given assemblage. In this case, love and sexuality 'are the exponents or the indicators, this time unconscious, of the libidinal investments of the social field', which oscillate between reactionary and revolutionary investments (Deleuze and Guattari 2004a: 386–7). This also still continues the thesis that the inside is a fold of the Outside and vice versa, but it reads the inside in terms of desire.

There is a resemblance here to Freud's (2005: 235) *pleasure principle*, in that Deleuze is speaking to the existence of motivations and forces beyond pleasure. However – again as we will see in the following chapter – Deleuze moves firmly beyond Freud's solipsistic unconscious and his psychoanalytic idealism. Indeed, whereas Foucault avoids the language of desire precisely because it seems to evoke lack and repression (contra his reversal of the repression hypothesis), and in the same vein some sort of discursive fiction or essentialism, Deleuze, alongside Guattari, construes desire as something productive and machinic, in a way that is reminiscent of Nietzsche's will to power and concurrent with Foucault's immanent ontology. Desire does not lack anything and it has no set nature. Desire is an affective force, part of a functioning heterogeneous assemblage, and therefore also a process that is connected, productive and produced.

Fundamentally, desire so understood explicitly employs the Nietzschean ethic of affirmation in conjunction with that of agonism/difference, simultaneously providing a substantial conceptualisation of subjective inside of power. Where Foucault politicises the fold through the addition of force, which speaks to a topological relationship in which the inside is formed by a crease in the outside, Deleuze (2007: 264) makes desire the inside in general, or 'the mobile connection between the inside and the two other features, the outside and strata'. From this, it follows that Deleuze's recourse to desire as the ground or criterion of ethical judgement presents a wholly consistent and, more importantly, immanent solution of sorts. Of course, this doesn't immediately settle the issue. At the very least, it gives an indication as to why we should turn to Deleuze's systematisation of immanence.

Notes

1. Many interpreters of Foucault have failed to recognise the importance of the incorporation of the disjunctive fold in this respect. This has resulted in a number of misreadings and obscurations by a number of Foucault's interpreters (as evidenced in the introduction), who

generally envision an inconsistency in Foucault's genealogy with respect to power and resistance. Interpretations of Foucault, provided by Giles Deleuze (2006b) and Nathan Widder (2004) are notable exceptions. Both systematise Foucault through the concept of the 'disjunctive fold'. Clearly, my reading takes its cue from them, though it provides a unique interpretation by virtue of linking the fold and micropolitics to Sartre and Merleau-Ponty.
2. See for instance Allen (1998: 192), Dreyfus and Rabinow (1983: 112), Duncan (2005: 101), Flynn (2005a: 2), Jay (1986: 178–9), McCumber (2011: 328-9) Moss (1998: 5) and Paras (2006: 27–9). On numerous occasions, Foucault commits himself to this reading (i.e. 1991c: 351, 2000a: 466, 2000b: 351, 2001a: 248), and certainly the public spat between Sartre and Foucault serves to reinforce it (see Paras 2006: 32).
3. Foucault was in fact trained in phenomenology and his first few works were phenomenological (such as his work on Binswanger). See May (2003).
4. As Foucault (1991b: 88) makes clear(er) when turning to his genealogical studies, the forces operating in history do not accord with a single regulative mechanism, but rather are the result of *haphazard conflicts*.
5. As Foucault puts it in 'Truth and Juridical Forms', knowledge is the 'spark between two swords'; there is no form of 'congruence, love, unity, and pacification', but rather 'hatred, struggle, power relations' (Foucault 2001b: 12). More significant is Foucault's acknowledgment of the influence of Deleuze's 'superb book about Nietzsche', in the construction of his understanding of power (Foucault 2000a: 445).
6. On this point, it is interesting to note, albeit briefly, how Foucault develops his concept of power through Deleuze's interior notion of force relation, while Deleuze in turn develops his theory of political power through the incorporation of Foucault's exterior re-conceptualisation.
7. Contra Hoy (1986: 129), May (1993: 72), Rorty (1986: 47), who each maintain that genealogy has no proper epistemological grounding, it is evident that the addition of force is part and parcel of a broader epistemologically and ontologically engaged project, one that elucidates their mutual implication. In showing that thought is immanent to the real that provokes it, Foucault effectively reworks the Kantian transcendental field, accounting for the conditions of experience in a way that links it directly with the empirical as opposed to the representational. A central part of this reworking necessitates a reworking of Kant's immanent critique. Foucault, then, follows the Kantian Enlightenment tradition, so long as it is understood not in terms of 'faithfulness to doctrinal elements, but rather the permanent

reactivation of an attitude – that is, of a philosophical ethos that could be described as a permanent critique of our historical era' (Foucault 1991e: 43). Such a critique is read via Nietzsche's genealogy, which figures as the genetic underpinning of thought or speaks to its contact with the Outside that provokes it, the double affirmation as per above (Foucault 1991b: 81).
8. This stands in contrast to readings provided by Dews (2007: 211–13) and May (1993: 77). Foucault's (1981: 201) central point is that power can only be exercised over something that techniques of knowledge and procedures of discourse are capable of investing. Its legitimacy is based precisely on a form of knowledge, which its function serves to reinforce. A strict demarcation between cause and effect is not possible. Is that not the entire point of the ambiguous immanent network?
9. This should put to rest the tired and unrecognisable caricature of Foucault as an heir to Althusser, wherein he is interpreted as utilising concepts concerned with the way in which power serves to fix social identities through individualising practices that are both discursive and institutional, as if Foucault abides by some sort of historical materialism or variant of interpellation. We saw already that Žižek, Butler (in the introduction) and May (see note 7 above) are all guilty of providing a variation of this argument. Other examples include McCumber (2011: 328–9), Olssen (2006: 30), Racevskis (1991: 23) and Wolin (2004: 13).
10. Despite this network containing a micro- or intensive-multiplicity in the form of power relations, it is still exterior, whereas with Deleuze, following Bergson by way of Sartre, it is intricately tied in with the interior of the unconscious. Thus though power relations and segments of knowledge form each other's Outside-Inside, they are still both Outside of the self. It is only in his turn to ethics that the interior, by way of the bodily practices, is added, or that the Outside is folded into the self to create the absent interior, albeit in a convoluted manner, as we shall see.
11. Poulantzas (2014: 78) maintains that this notion of power neglects the role of state repression and violence, or rather domination. However, domination, on the standard interpretation of political power, does exist, as Foucault concedes (1996: 434). The point is, however, that supplanting domination, though plausibly opening avenues for new relations to emerge, guarantees nothing in terms of freedom, as these are two different types of power. Though intersecting, they remain distinct. This links back up with the *rule of double-conditioning* laid out in volume 1 of *The History of Sexuality* (see Foucault 1998: 99).
12. Although Foucault does not employ the word, such folding is found in *The Order of Things*, where the unthought is not external to thought

but lies at its very heart as that impossibility of thinking which doubles or hollows out the inside, and it is evident in *The Archaeology of Knowledge* in terms of dispersion. As Deleuze (2006b: 81) puts it, 'the theme which has always haunted Foucault is that of the double'. And though locating it in the Ancient Greeks, it is undeniable that the concept of doubling is inspired by Merleau-Ponty's fleshism.
13. Though Foucault (1991c: 351) rejects Sartrean authenticity for its moral underpinning, it is evident that his interpretation conflates authenticity with a static state of Being or an identity as opposed to a practice of continuous negation, creation and becoming. As argued in the first chapter, it is evident that Sartrean authenticity is of the latter.
14. I.e. Habermas (1987: 284), Norris (1993: 50), Putnam (1983: 288) and Taylor (1986: 34).
15. As Fraser (1989: 32–3) erroneously suggests.

Chapter 4
Deleuze and the Micropolitics of Desire

'Desire' is an undoubtedly slippery concept, and one that seems constantly weighed down, as it were, by metaphysical, essentialist and discursive baggage. As we saw in the last chapter, it was for this reason that Foucault felt uncomfortable with Deleuze's use of desire, albeit subverted. A number of interpreters – Žižek chief among them – have since made this the basis of their critique of Deleuze and the micropolitics of immanence. It is essentially argued that by virtue of retaining desire as a primordial 'micro' essence or pre-social multiplicity, Deleuze ends up viewing power as a negative force concomitant with the macro level or macropolitical.[1] It follows from this that ethical resistance (becoming a BwO, a Body without Organs) concerns liberating desire from the repressive effects of the macropolitical. With such a reading, Deleuze is said to be led right back into the very Marxian-Freudian repression hypothesis that Foucault painstakingly dissected as a production of modern power itself. Inasmuch as this vision speaks to the political theory of old, in which power is 'anti-energy' and freedom the negation of this energy, we would have to reject Deleuzian desire as a suitable contender for accounting for the agentic interiority of immanent/relational power.[2] As we know from the introduction, Žižek goes so far as to argue that an inherent impasse over the nature of Deleuze's transcendental empiricism – specifically the virtual as a surface effect versus a productive power – caused an otherwise apolitical Deleuze to turn towards Guattari and this 'old' idealist politics of desire which, while masquerading as radical chic, effectively transforms Deleuze into an ideologist of today's digital capitalism. Thus, not only is Deleuzian desire under question but also the very basis of 'pure' immanence and the philosophical thinking that precedes and informs it (i.e. Sartre, Merleau-Ponty and Foucault).

Whereas it might be believed that 'Deleuze proper' faces an ontological deadlock that ultimately fails to account for the Outside/Other, I begin this chapter by arguing that Deleuze's transcendental empiricism follows and draws on the previous three thinkers to construe the transcendental field – the 'micro' virtual multiplicity – in terms of a spatio-temporal folded depth derived and informed by a dynamic and forceful encounter with the folded Outside/Other – a 'macro' actual multiplicity. In so doing, Deleuze provides conceptual clarification on the nature of the fold, both interior (micro) and exterior (macro) and the fold between the two, as a disjunctive synthesis of force relations. Spatio-temporal folds are a set of disjunctive force relations within and between micro and macro multiplicities, forming a univocity of Being. From this, immanence is construed as the regulative ideal of philosophy precisely because univocal 'pure' immanence itself is real, or is reality itself in the making.[3]

I then argue that this in fact has a reciprocal and consistent relation to Deleuze and Guattari's micropolitics of desire. On the one hand, it serves to challenge morality and its corollary form of subject-centred politics in favour of an a-subjective ethics grounded in the notion of immanent modes of existence (as opposed to a transcendent ground, be that the subject or a form of the Good). In the vein of existential ethics, the exploration of this ethical dimension with the aim of returning to and experiencing the transcendental field in order to establish the conditions for new, creative, abundant or affirming modes of existence (how to become a BwO) is, I maintain, the central driving factor behind the political works. The 'Guattari' encounter as the personification of said political works, then, does not arise from an impasse, but rather is a logical extension of Deleuze's transcendental empiricism. On the other hand, in striving for this, Deleuze and Guattari employ the conceptual schema of transcendental empiricism. The virtual multiplicity is recomposed in terms of an *affective* spatio-temporal depth (desiring-machines/production), and actual multiplicity in terms of a socio-political extensivity (social machines/production), underpinned by the axiomatic of capital, through which is formed an assemblage or a micropolitics of desire. It is only in obscuring this connection that one will be invariably led to overlook the way in which desire is (coherently) immanent and therefore relative to the real that provokes it, such that it can only have for itself a productive 'nature'.

More importantly, such an ontogenetic and *immanent* analysis is precisely that which enables the identification and differentiation between destructive negative (lack) desire/modes of being that are conducive to the functioning of capitalism and upon which capitalism relies (i.e. neurotic subjects of lack and *ressentiment*), and affirmative (abundance) desires of creativity that challenge and subvert capitalism. Desire presents both the site of social production of subjectivity or repression, and creative productivity or resistance. I end the chapter with an analysis of how the abundant and life-affirming energies of desire – returning to the transcendental field or BwO – can be harnessed through self-experimentations that operate through relations of power. This is to again follow Sartre, Merleau-Ponty and Foucault in stressing that resistance starts with a transformative ethic of the self that, in accordance with the principle of double-conditioning between multiplicities forming an assemblage, can serve to problematise and radically subvert macro powers. Though in framing the transcendental in terms of desire, Deleuze construes what I believe to be a more nuanced take on this politico-ethic. Desire is the penultimate site for a post-capitalist emancipatory project.

Transcendental Empiricism

We turn first to transcendental empiricism. Keeping with the general theme of the study, we can see that Deleuze develops his theory of multiplicities and thus his account for the genetic and immanent conditions of existence by working through and drawing on critical elements in the previous three thinkers. The difference is, Deleuze does this in a systematic and perspicacious manner foreign to the very thinkers on which he draws. Even the name of his metaphysical system – 'transcendental empiricism' – clarifies a latent motif in the previous three thinkers. For although the system eschews the transcendental idealism of both Kant and Husserl, it is nevertheless still transcendental insofar as it concerns itself with the conditions of experience, and yet still empirical insofar it concerns itself with the real to which it is immanent. Contra Husserl, in particular, who modelled the transcendental field after the empirical, with the relation between the two being that of resemblance; Deleuze posits their separability. The transcendental field can be distinguished from experience 'in that it doesn't refer to an object or belong to a subject (empirical representation)' (Deleuze 2001: 25). As a consequence, philosophy must explore the transcendental field for itself, and not as a Kantian redoubling of the empirical that still precludes the transcendental from being posited as an object of experience. This duality does not amount to an ontological dualism. Rather, it establishes a philosophy of univocity, of folding.

In following the tradition of thought forged by Sartre and Merleau-Ponty (and their respective reworking of Husserl and Bergson), it is perhaps unsurprising that Deleuze's initial account of the transcendental field – as conveyed in *Difference and Repetition* – is construed in terms of a temporal dynamic, or more specifically, through three syntheses of time, *'which must be understood as constitutive of the unconscious,'* and which in turn reveal selves to be 'larval subjects' or 'dissolved' (Deleuze 2004a: 140). The incorporation of time is once more central in showing that beings are not represented by analogy or in comparison with a higher being or separate plane of existence (as in Plato's Forms), but rather only ever become. Indeed, the discontinuous structure of time conditions time's passage and the passage of the things that exist within it, ungrounding movement in chronological time such that neither past (in terms of conditioning) nor future (in terms of destiny) can imprint an enduring mark. Expression is of central importance here, as we move beyond representation to express the sense of the *untimely*, in which each event in time always only repeats difference. Congruent with the view that *Difference and Repetition* is an anti-Hegel book,[4] this results in a rethinking also of difference, wherein repetition is, for itself, 'difference in-itself': a pure difference or virtual force, which is not defined in relation to identity or to the negation of an identity, but which underpins and transforms identities.

The first synthesis accounts for the constitution of the linear, chronological form of time (what Heidegger calls the 'vulgar' conception), on the basis of a living present that makes the past and the future two asymmetrical elements of that present. Following Sartre's criticism of Kant's invocation of a non-temporal permanence, Deleuze holds that this synthesis speaks to a static line of time only, and as such cannot account for the passage of the present. It follows, then, that we must further constitute time as a present, 'but a present which passes' (ibid.: 100). So although it is originary, the first synthesis of time must be considered no less intratemporal. It needs to be shown why the present passes and what prevents the present from being co-extensive with time.

Deleuze turns to a second, passive synthesis of memory or Bergsonian duration, which 'constitutes the pure past in time, and makes the former and the present present . . . two asymmetrical elements of this past as such' (ibid.: 103). Following Bergson, this is to locate the conditions of real experience in virtual (as opposed to actual) multiplicities of the past, which, though not a 'negative' in the typical sense, essentially function as non-being, in that it is real but not actual: it gives the actual present its sense and direction, embedding the past unconsciously in habits and consciously in recollections, by virtue of which it allows the present to pass without dissolving into nothingness. Immanence is already evident, in that duration will continually record only that which is within its own plane or experience, as in the immediate real of experience, and it will only explicate within that plane or reality of experience. Thus there is no real distinction between virtual and actual multiplicities, or between the One and the many, as much as there is a continuum of a multiplicity of a multiplicity. The difference between pure duration and the extensive is, as far as the psyche is concerned, one of degree: between dilation and contraction.

However, the 'second synthesis of time points beyond itself in the direction of a third which denounces the illusion of time in-itself as still a correlate of representation' (ibid.: 111). As we saw in the first chapter, the inclusion of time as the form under which undetermined existence is determinable (the dissolving force of duration and diaspora of nihilation) already displaces the Cartesian myth of the unified self, the 'I think, therefore I am', or of a personal, individual self.[5] Insofar as this formula provides an image of resemblance, identity, analogy and opposition as nothing more than effects or the products of a primary difference, a virtual differential or system of difference, it follows that difference must be articulation and connection itself, without any meditation whatsoever by the identical, the similar, the analogous or the opposed. A mediated difference would present a paradox. You cannot rely on that which has already be shown to be a semblance or illusory effect, as the basis of constitution of the real. Indeed, one of Deleuze's most fundamental of points is that one cannot think of the transcendental in the image of, and in the resemblance to, that which it is supposed to ground (in this case, empirical time and actual experience), for this will only uncover the conditions of possibility of knowledge and experience as opposed to the genetic conditions of thought itself or the way phenomena are actually generated.

This relates to the question of transcendental unity and, subsequently, individuation. As I noted in the first chapter, there must be some principle of unity *in duration* if the continual stream of consciousness is able to posit transcendent objects outside itself. That is, there must be an enduring stable identity of myself that consciousness can refer to as a basis for differentiating 'myself' from the objects of consciousness, i.e. 'I' am not the table, 'I' and not John, 'I' shot the sheriff, but 'I' did not shoot the deputy. It was made evident in the first chapter that, for Sartre, the for-itself is at the centre of a unifying act – nihilation – that unifies by individuating. The flux of consciousness itself participates in this unity by an interplay of 'transversal' intentionalities which provide concrete and real retentions of past consciousness to which consciousness can continually refer. Thus though Deleuze commends Sartre's restoration of the rights of immanence via repudiating Husserl's latent Kantianism, he in turn maintains – though problematically, inasmuch as he ignores the flesh as encapsulating the Other of the situation – that the thesis is hindered precisely because the transcendental field is still determined as the field of consciousness, as the site of individuation and unity, and thus is caught within the paradox of mediated difference.

Similarly, for Bergson (1998: 3) the unity and individuation is performed via the past's retention in the present, becoming the form of an ego that, though in flux, *endures* or changes without passing. As Deleuze (2004a: 105) puts it, 'however strong the incoherence or possible opposition between successive presents, we have the impression that each of them plays out "the same life" at different levels'. Though temporality is a dissolving force and despite its fallibility, Bergson places it in the unifying act of the ego; it is retained as a unity and centre of action, wherein consciousness remains the ground for such temporality, in turn excluding incompossibles and undecidabilities from the self and its past.[6] It endures enough to create at least a modicum of permanence to retroactively spatialise time through quantifying our feelings of succession, by which thetic attention places clean-cut states side by side, as well as to thread the undifferentiated abyss of artificial independent psychic states and the disparity of matter (or our experience of it) together. The ego, here, simply refers to a unity created after a unity destroyed, and in order to function in this way it is imagined as formless, unchangeable and individual (Bergson 1998: 2).

According to this reading, both Bergson and Sartre posit an

artificial though *practical* ego, whereby the functional structure of the transcendental deduction is maintained, even though the entities performing these functions are replaced. Hence the retention of the paradox of difference. Against both, Deleuze (2004a: 105) seeks 'a differenciation of difference, an in-itself which is like a *differenciator* . . . by virtue of which the different is gathered all at once rather than represented on the condition of a prior resemblance, identity, analogy or opposition'. As we will see, in this instance a virtual multiplicity of the past is related to consciousness through the disjunctive syntheses of incompossibles related and folded into one another through a 'dark precursor', *in and through the unconscious*, which is in effect an immanent connection with the Outside in terms of folding. This is the time of the 'aborted cogito', (ibid.: 135) – as linked to Nietzsche's notion of the eternal return of difference itself or of the *untimely* – of a self that is not progressively fractured through chronological time, but rather typified by a fundamental discontinuity, inasmuch as it is assembled in non-chronological order from different periods of time, each referring to different subjectivities or existential states. Signifying a shift towards an entirely pre-personal and pre-individual, or simply unconscious transcendental field, this, to be sure, is a process in which unity and individuation are taken out of the hands of the subject completely. And though a germinal version of this zone can be located in Sartre's and Merleau-Ponty's thought, as we have seen, there is a case to be made that Deleuze does in fact go further in his elaboration and perspicacity, accounting for it beyond the actualised differenciations it underpins, including that of consciousness of dualistic/dialectical discourse, and in terms of force.

The Will to Power as Disjunctive Fold

What exactly is a dark precursor, and how does it function so as to secure a difference in-itself? The *dark precursor* is the differenciator, the agency of force – the will to power – ensuring communication between differences, or the communication of peripheral temporal series, relating heterogeneous systems and even completely disparate things: 'Thunderbolts explode between different intensities, but they are preceded by an invisible, imperceptible *dark precursor*, which determines their path in advance but in reverse, as though intagliated' (ibid.: 145). It is primarily at this point where much confusion arises, specifically insofar as this drive or agency of force is related to an essentialist or at least asocial image of Deleuzian desire: it is either taken in the anthropomorphic sense as known by psychology or, relatedly, in the mechanic sense of a strict relation of cause and effect as known by classical physics. It is neither. The 'willing' of the will to power is the virtual aspect of force by which it differentiates (or 'makes the difference' between incommensurable perspectives) and differenciates itself (or differenciates intensive and differential relations of forces into distinct actual types), involving and explicating itself in a repetition of difference, *immanent* and thus relative to the real that provokes it. The will to power, in other words, is simply the genetic and differential element of force relations. This relates back to what was said in the second chapter, vis-à-vis Merleau-Ponty's fleshism, i.e. that force is the transcendental condition of sensation. Relating the virtual to force is far from arbitrary or coincidental, given that in Latin force is *virtus*, and thus the etymological root of virtual. That said, Deleuze has a very particular concept of force in mind, which, given the name accredited to it 'will to power', is evidently traceable to Nietzsche.

As we previously noted, Nietzsche's basic contention, at least according to Deleuze (and Foucault), is that force is relational. A force must express itself in accordance with the other forces to which it relates, and the 'essential relation of one force to another is never conceived of as a negative element in the essence' (Deleuze 2006d: 8). The quantitative differential determines difference in kind (quality). As with Foucault's logic of dispersion, forces *vice-dict* here, rather than contradict one another, precisely because the synthetic nature of this differential relation of forces is one of disjunction. Heterogeneous forces relate to one another without their difference being negated, subsumed or collapsed into a higher unity or a complete non-relation, establishing an intersection where unities may arise; as with the folded paper example provided in the second chapter, in which two points can relate without ideal coincidence or without negating each other. At this stage, however, Deleuze is referring to psychic forces of the unconscious. It is a conceptualisation pitted against Hegel's *Dialectic of Consciousness*, where the thing of sense certainty and object of perception are subsumed by a relation of equal forces that oppose or negate each other.[7]

Evoking the Outside fold as we identified it in Foucault, Deleuze adds that the will to power itself, or rather the synthesis of forces, must have qualities, something such as a moral diktat, compelling the evaluation and differentiations of forces so as to affect their means of expression or differenciated becoming; something underpinning the impetus and the stuff of interpretation itself, less it fall into a problematic essentialism and linear causality. This is the primordial qualitative element underpinning interpretation, and in turn determining the qualities of force. Crucially, 'these fluent, primordial and seminal qualitative elements', Deleuze warns, 'must not be confused with the qualities of force' (ibid.: 50). Whereas the quality of a force is determined by the differential of quantities, designated in terms of active and reactive forms of expression, the quality of the will to power itself is designated in terms of affirmative and negative, i.e. affirming or negating via a moral or discursive system, the expression of a particular active or reactive force. This means one type of force will be encouraged at the expense of the other, affecting its chance and opportunity for expression on the level of the actual, and, relatedly, once it is negated (or as anticipated negation) and thus forced to return to itself, its relation to the other forces at the level of the virtual (pre-expression).

Immanence is operative here, inasmuch as the will to power relates and synthesises differences in degree of the intensive world (virtual multiplicities) to produce differences in kind in the extensive (actual multiplicities). Crucially, though it is only by virtue of already relating to and *folding* this Outside extensive world, via chance encounters and primordial qualities or Outside moral diktats, those differences will be related *and* expressed/unfolded in a particular manner, as we will come to see in our imminent discussion on repression. Or, if you prefer, the *will to power* represents an exogenetic (as in a genetic force from all aspects of the Outside) fold of the endoconsistent (as in the virtual or immanent field itself) through which differences are derived, related and folded into one another, resembling a 'sheet of paper divided into infinite folds or separated into bending movements, each one determined by the consistent or conspiring surroundings' (Deleuze 2006b: 6). It is specifically in this sense that the third synthesis is understood as the eternal return of 'difference in itself', as in the continual return of the enigmatic differenciator (disjunctive fold) that always differs from itself.

Like Merleau-Ponty's flesh, then, it is evident that the will to power is manifested as a capacity for affecting and being affected. It is the space between the virtual and the actual where everything happens, and out of which perspective and points of view are constituted and expressed.[8] Thus, to be actualised 'is also to be *expressed*'

(Deleuze 2004b: 127), and every level of expression is simultaneously a process of stratification and organisation, as in giving form via qualities to force relations. Alas, in terms of the will to power, or disjunctive folding, as construed in *Nietzsche and Philosophy*, it is related primarily to *affective* forces. What is crucial to note, however, is that in *Difference and Repetition* Deleuze (2004a: 214) additionally applies disjunctive folding and its immanent relation to the Outside, to the temporal and to space, forming a 'spatio-temporal dynamism', much in the same way that Merleau-Ponty's concept of depth connects time with inextensive space.

In terms of time, it signifies its purest form, prior to its expression in habit or memory. In this instance, it follows that the virtual is more extensive than that of a past retained within the present. To argue this point, Deleuze (ibid.: 151) turns to Freud's thesis that phantasy is constituted on the basis of at least two time series as related to an existential or subjective state, one infantile and pregenital, the other genital and post-pubescent, wherein 'the series succeed one another in time from the point of view of the solipsistic unconscious of the subject in question'. The question here is how to explain the phenomenon of delay, as in the time it takes for the supposedly original infantile scene to produce its neurotic effects, in an adult scene that resembles it. Though Deleuze concurs with Freud that the problem concerns a resonance between two series, he departs from the notion that they are distributed within the same subject across a space of chronological time. The childhood event is not one of two real series, but rather the dark precursor which establishes communication between the basic series, 'that of the adults we know as a child and that of the adult we are among other adults and other children' (ibid.: 152). Phantasy, then, is the manifestation of the childhood, such that what is originary in the phantasy is not one series in relation to another but 'the difference between series insofar as this relates one series of differences to another series of differences, in abstraction from their empirical succession in time' (ibid.). That is to say that phantasy relates to external reality or the Outside at and through the differenciator, beyond any condition under which one would enjoy the identity of a model and the other the resemblance of a copy. One series, quite simply, does not produce the other for they themselves, as differentitated and actualised, are the result of a primary difference or differenciator. Any resemblance or identity is strictly a functional effect of this difference that is originary within the system.

This brings about a renewed take on the death instinct, one that supplants it with the eternal return of 'difference in-itself' as in the continual return of the enigmatic differenciator that always differs from itself. Each series itself returns, not only in the others which imply it, but for-itself, insofar as it cannot be implied by the other without itself becoming that which implies them. Thus, temporal disjunction becomes the groundless ground or law of a system that never resorts to the return of the same and the similar precisely because it relates to and is derived from a world of pure difference. Each time the 'I' arises – i.e. I feel angry – one is merely actualising a variant, and new configuration, of the relation of forces as found in the spatio-temporal virtual. Thus each arrival of the 'I' is different to the one that preceded it. This serves to break the self into multiple subjectivities, as in a fractured *I* that is not only the basis of the superego, but 'the correlative of the passive and wounded narcissistic ego, thereby forming a complex whole that Paul Ricoeur aptly named an "aborted cogito"' (ibid.: 135). In fact, it is precisely because there is no negative in the virtual (only vice-diction), that the virtual unconscious is a real realm full of a number of seemingly contradictory possibilities, housing a resonance between different selves or between different series that co-exist without in fact succeeding each other in empirical time.

In terms of space, Deleuze initially follows Merleau-Ponty's notion of non-extensive primordial depth as the ultimate and original 'heterogeneous dimension', or as the 'matrix of all extensity, including its third dimension considered to be homogeneous with the other two' (ibid.: 229). This expression of primordial depth in the form of qualities and extensive localised intensities presupposed by thermodynamics (wherein, as Carnot showed, difference in input and output energies of an engine, or a difference between the temperature entering and leaving a system, is essential for anything to happen), makes up what Deleuze deems the second spatial synthesis (the first being the synthesis of habit, or the vulgar and immediate experience of space). A primary non-extensive spatial differentiation of intensive properties and individuation, in the same vein as the second Bergsonian synthesis of time as explicated in *Difference and Repetition*. By doing this, Deleuze makes a more resolute link between depth so defined and the intensive-virtual, arguing that the ground, or unground, is the projection of something 'deeper', a deeper depth, the pure, intensive *spatium:* intensity 'is developed and explicated by means of an extension [*extension*] which relates it to the extensity [*extensum*] in which it appears outside itself and hidden beneath quality' (ibid.: 287). If extensity does not account for the individuations which occur within it, or if the figure and ground are individuating factors that take place within an already developed extensity, then 'their value is only relative'. From this, however, Deleuze goes further, linking this notion of depth with another third synthesis of space, which like its temporal counterpart, is linked to Nietzsche's eternal return, and thus the notion of *disjunctive force*. This displays a significant advance, in overcoming what I previously claimed to be an ambiguity in Merleau-Ponty's infinitesimal folds (the notion of pluri-dimensional 'non-superposibility' only gestures toward disjunction), signifying a non-striated 'pure space', related to though distinguishable from the 'intensive properties' that compose it. It is a virtual continuum formed by multiplicities, or the plane upon which the dissolution of the actual occurs. This 'pure space' is also deemed a 'smooth space' or a 'plane of consistency', in that it is a space where differences or quantitative intensities are not marked by a transcendent identity that would place them into a hierarchical order. Just as with Gauss's differential or Riemannian space, there is no extrinsic global dimensional embedding, but instead folded relations (or n-dimensional curvature) of disjunction.

Deleuze significantly expands this idea in his monograph on Leibniz. Indeed, it is here that Deleuze truly connects the spatio-temporal dynamic – as personified by disjunction – with Merleau-Ponty's fold, to establish the 'disjunctive fold', in turn relating it Merleau-Ponty's depth and the virtual-actual structure of the Real as derived from Bergson: depth being the result of folds *and* the dimension where folds occur.[9] As with the book itself, in making this connection, it is best to start with the allegory of the Baroque house. The Baroque house is primarily composed of two levels (read: multiplicities): the pleats of matter (the lower level of the extensive) and the folds in the soul (the upper level of the intensive), which correspond via the large, or 'great fold' that cuts across these levels (Deleuze 2006b: 106). The one is the double of the other: 'the soul is the expression of the world (actuality), but because the world is what the soul expresses (virtuality)' (ibid.: 28). This follows the Baroque conception of an interior without an exterior, in that the Outside is expressed in the Inside by the monad (what Leibniz ascribes to the soul or to the subject as a metaphysical point), and an exterior without an interior, in that the 'subject' is nothing more than this folded Outside or the provisional site of a virtual surface preceding it. The 'non-relation' between the two is much like the split between the façade and the inside of the building, as is typical of Baroque architecture. Immanence and its corollary, the double-condition – whose conceptual origin in this instance Deleuze ascribes to Leibniz – is still central. The microscopic (as in the virtual multiplicity of perception) and the macroscopic (as in the actual multiplicity of perception) form a circuit, a continuum, or a reciprocal determination, 'the being-for the world of unconscious or minute perceptions, and the differential relations that hold for conscious perceptions' (ibid.: 107); 'Folds over folds: such is the status of the two modes of perception' (ibid.: 106).

Taking the allegory further, Deleuze (ibid.: 33–4) is able to clarify his point regarding the smooth or consistent surface, stressing that it is not designed to invoke an epigenesism, in which the organic fold is produced from a solely pre-given undifferentiated, but rather something akin to performism, 'to a Difference that endlessly unfolds and folds over each of its two sides, and that unfolds the one only while refolding the other, in a coextensive unveiling and veiling of Being'. Every fold originates from a fold, 'plica ex plica', or the Heideggerian *Zweifalt*/'fold-of-two, an entre-deux, something "between" in the sense that a difference is being differentiated' (ibid.: 11). As for the temporal dimension, it is referred to as a sort of resource pool containing the 'dark depths' (thus spatio-temporal) of the monad by virtue of also being surface, or *space* (the upper floor) of reception and inscription of a variety of differential relations pertaining to individual existential states, with each one living out a different time series in co-existence with others, without being subsumed into a higher unity (ibid.: 102).

Deleuze (ibid.: 112) adds that together this dynamism between space and time creates, and relies on, perception; this is once more related back to Merleau-Ponty via the organic body, as the 'sum of the theory of the fold'. This is not a return to a Husserlian (or early Merleau-Pontian) body in the form of a transcendent Other or tacit cogito, but a body composed of an alter ego, springing from an earlier stage of phenomenological deduction, or from a pre-given appurtenance, as a variant of what Merleau-Ponty would refer to as primordial flesh (ibid.: 124). Indeed, as with Merleau-Ponty's flesh, the Other is already presupposed in the forces that make up the virtual self. The Other, as with the Outside vis-à-vis the will to power, is a disjunctive fold or a 'vinculum' fixed to an individual monad with a body (where the parts of this body have crowds of monads of Others, each one of which has a body itself) that dominates the others, where, just like the will to power, a relation of quanta determines the quality and differenciated expression.[10]

All this means is that the body has a virtual-actual structure composed of multiple selves or monads that are actualised into a specific zone of clarity, that are then organised into a possible-real structure. (This is not a relation of the part to the whole, however, as much as one from the ordinary to what is notable or remarkable.) The possible is always thought of and carried out under the form of extension, and thus presupposes the actualisation of the virtual. Thus it is 'not the body that realises, but it is in the body that something is realised, through which the body itself becomes real or substantial' (ibid.: 120). The process of actualisation operates through distribution, while the process of realisation operates through resemblance. One actualises the world, the other realises it, denoting two floors of the *same* Baroque house. It is in 'depth or this material fabric between the two levels, that the upper is folded over the lower, such that we can no longer tell where one ends and the other begins, or where the sensible ends and the intelligible begins' (ibid.: 137).

Aside from providing an image of subjectivity in terms of a fold (as opposed to a Hegelian hole), as in a forceful and disjunctive spatio-temporal or virtual-intensive dynamism by which the Inside is created through a crease in the folded Outside, without, for all that, evoking negativity or a naive harmony between the conditions of experience and the experience itself; the fold so construed, particularly this last point concerning the two floors, more or less relates back to what is perhaps the fundamental point made by Deleuze in *Difference and Repetition*: negative difference is an effect of a disjunctive process, as opposed to a constitutive cause. There are no breaks of this kind at the level of Being. It is in this way that it is said all modalities and differences, or all individuals and substances, are expressions of a single ontological substance: "Being is said in a single and same sense, of all its individuating differences or intrinsic modalities" (Deleuze 2004a: 45). Infinite substance (Being) and finite modes (beings) are in immanence, as opposed to modes being immanent to substance, so that it is not akin to a predicate that belongs to a subject. That is to say, there is no difference of category, of substance and of form, between the senses of the word 'Being', e.g. for-itself and in-itself.

Such an idea would, on the face of it, seem to lend itself to the vision of a world of a monotonous and complete inclusivity of differences. A world that, when taken to its ultimate conclusion, negates any *qualitative* (rational, pure, good), *analogical* (rational, pure and good measured in proportion to a focal analogate, i.e. God: God possess eminent goodness and his beings, or creatures, derivatively and varyingly so) and thus *hierarchical* (some creatures are analogically 'closer' to the light of God, i.e. have a higher level of reality) distinction among beings and with it, the breaks and ruptures, and moral distinctions that are taken to define the political. A naive harmony akin to new ageism, would reign supreme. There would be no difference, and thus nothing by which to make judgements of thought, meaning and action. But Deleuze is quick to add that though Being is the same for all modalities, these modalities *are not the same*. Though with univocity we are barred from distinguishing beings by their qualitative essence (analogy of Being), they can nevertheless be differentiated and distinguished according to their quantifiable degree of power, or their expressed magnitudes that realise one and the same Being. Each finite expression of Being incarnates a particular degree of actualisation. And it actualises, lest it be forgotten, the difference in-itself of Being, such that not even repetition would yield the same actualisation and nomadic distribution in the extensive world. There is still a qualitative difference in kind to be had (i.e. the active and reactive qualities of the will to power), but this, as we saw, arises as an after-effect of a virtual quantitative differential of forces, the *pure spatium*. It is not constitutive, in other words. Thus univocity is a problem of the virtual: how a multiplicity goes from a virtual incompossible existence to an actualised expression of it. The monad, the finite mode of a being, expresses the same world as the others, in one and the same sense of which everything is said, but owns an *exclusive zone of clear expression* of the said/the difference in-itself that distinguishes it from every other monad, and that relates directly to its will to power.

In more practical terms, this means that we cannot understand or categorise a being according to its essence, or how 'rational' it is – according to a fixed and prime analogate – which would speak to a latent potentiality on the part of the being in question (the being's essence of rational may not always be realised to its full, requiring a moral effort to provoke fullness). Rather, we understand and define a being according to a qualitatively anarchical existence: the power of a being's affective capacities or will to power, i.e. its ability to affect and be affected. This provokes a very particular way of approaching the topic of ethics and politics, which we shall come to shortly. For now, however, we can note, and this is certainly a significant point, that Deleuze does not misunderstand Hegel in ignoring the gap of/in immanence. It is precisely the nature of this gap that he disputes and seeks to subvert via the fold. Thus it is not the 'gap in the immanence', as Žižek contends, that 'Deleuze cannot accept' and that is responsible for the 'spectre of transcendence'. Rather, it is the fold. Which means we need not choose between the virtual as a surface effect and a productive power. It is both. But what relevance does this bare to ethics, let alone politics, beyond the repudiation of the central 'I' of subjectivity?

The Double-Axiom of Thought and Immanent Ethics

Deleuze 'proper' does not face a deadlock by virtue of the ontogenetic concept of the fold. That being the case, what can be said of the Guattari encounter? It surely cannot now be viewed as an escape route, for there is nothing from which to escape. It is my contention that we may understand this encounter as representing a logical consequence and continuation of transcendental empiricism. It is a consequence, in that transcendental empiricism provokes the immanent concept of the ethico-politics of this encounter, while providing the conceptual schema for the very *active destruction* (as in destruction of reactive forces themselves, related to a power of affirming) on which such an ethico-politics relies. Whereas what we have explored of Deleuze thus far speaks to a subjective and ontological conceptual dimension of transcendental empiricism and the disjunctive fold, we now stumble across the related third and fourth conceptual dimension: the former is epistemological and the latter ethical.

First, provocation. Immanent univocity makes the concept of morality – as a transcendent, external and analogical ground for a trans-historical system of good and evil and its corollary imperatives – unthinkable and metaphysically untenable. There is no fixed or higher essence of man, nor a prime, external analogate by which this essence can be figured and hierarchised and thus by which man's actions and thoughts may be judged and directed for the purpose of realising the alleged higher or true essence, i.e. to fully realise the potential of an alleged purity, or to realise the image of God we are alleged to be. It is thanks to the alleged that we have the language of good and evil, i.e. 'What must I do?' The outright ontological negation of a higher essence analogous to the transcendent ground of the pure Being of the One notwithstanding, to sustain or construct this ground, and with it an external point of reference for moral judgement, is to also obscure the genetic force that gives *thought* form or sense. That is to say, even were there an external truth of this kind, the assumption that it can be accessed through reason or sound thought alone is highly specious. Following Sartre in seeking to philosophise the concrete as that which grounds the abstract-epistemological, the fold serves to radically challenge transcendence not just of the subject and of Being, but also in the conceptual form of a dogmatic image of thought that maintains the existence of a direct correspondence between thought and an imagined 'higher' truth, as if thought were concomitant with the 'higher', as if it 'were endowed with a talent for truth and an affinity with the true, under the double aspect of a *good will on the part of the thinker* and an *upright nature of the part of thought*' (ibid.: 166).[11] But thoughts and reason, as Deleuze (2006a: 18) later adds, evidently do not 'originate in a good nature and a good will', but rather 'come from a violence suffered by thought . . . as a function of an Outside'.

Even our most apparently intuitive and pragmatic sense of right and wrong – that felt (*senti*) virtual resonance between the inside and outside, that is so often mistaken for good sense, or even something of ethereal profundity – is the product of our immersion in the world, and therefore contingent. Such a sense cannot be relied upon as the basis of critique. Thus Deleuze, echoing Foucault's Nietzschean addendum to our understanding of Enlightenment, proposes an alternative image of thought by which to address and radically critique the critique, its dangerous naiveté and the postulates it implies. An image that can be said to contain a double requirement, or double-axiom: the thought of critique must be exo-endo. *Exo*, following the Greek, refers to the need for thought to be mindful of its *Outside* genetic conditions, or rather the exo(onto) genetic condition of transcendental empiricism.[12] *Endo*, again following the Greek, refers to the *inside*, or in this case, the notion of the *fold*, and thus the way in which thought is not only external to what it thinks (exogenetic), as per above, but also *immanent* to what it thinks— the real that provokes it (endoconsistent). It is precisely with this double-axiom in mind, that Deleuze and Guattari

(2004b: 415) come to conclude that the notion of the 'private thinker' is unsatisfactory, at least inasmuch as it 'exaggerates interiority, when it is a question of *outside thought*'.

No objective, 'higher' analogical vantage point/no transcendent Outside to which we can refer and no stable vantage point of thought = no morality with a universal ontological or epistemic basis. What then? To remain consistent and logical, Deleuze suggests we follow Nietzsche's genealogy, but also Spinoza's *Ethics* (the two are sewn together in a way that makes for a partly indiscernible union), to overturn moral questions that imply essence via potentiality and in reference to external primary analogates (i.e. what *should* I do?) in favour of ethical ones that refer to Being in terms of existence and its capability and the power of effectuation (i.e. what *can* I do?). That is, the consistency between univocal immanence and ethics so conceived is found in the fact that such ethical questions are grounded in the immanent *modes* of existence themselves, with reference to the degree of power, the processes of actualisation, subjectivation and stratification, i.e. what mode of existence does a particular thought, action or feeling imply? From where does it derive and what does it express? How is a mode determined? Modes of existence or expressions of the virtual, in other words, should be evaluated according to the intensive criteria of power (in its qualitative and typological senses) – that is, its dark precursor or its determining will to power in terms of active and reactive wills to power (and capacities), with one ultimately affirming life in its difference of creative becoming and the other negating it.

As well as provoking this turn to ethics, we can now catch a glimpse of how this ethical system – as with the double-axiom – relies on the ontogenetic basis of transcendental empiricism. It is necessary in accounting for the ontogenesis of multiplicities and subsequently the way they are related to given a mode of existence (or the way the virtual is expressed in a process of stratification and organisation); as we shall see, this forms the metaphysical basis for Deleuzian desire. But for all that, transcendental empiricism, at least as it is construed in *Difference and Repetition* and *The Logic of Sense*, does not make any kind of overt valuative distinction between different modes, which is necessary for the very immanent ethics it provokes as a logical consequence of its image of thought. This distinction is what Deleuze sees Spinoza and Nietzsche as contributing through an affective dimension in the form of conatus (Spinoza) and/or the will to power (Nietzsche). It precisely this affective dimension that underpins their turn away from moral questions to ethical ones, insofar as such an affectivity is – congruent with the double-axiom – immanent to the real that provokes it or the immanent condition of that which gives rise to thought. Thoughts are the shadows of our affectivity.

Underpinning all this is a certain veneration of life itself – a veneration also found in Sartre – such that any requirement or demand for a transcendent justification for it is immediately deemed to negate its intrinsic value. In contrast, affirmation proper 'enjoys its own difference in life instead of suffering the pains of the opposition to this life that it has itself inspired. *To affirm is not to take responsibility for, to take on the burden of what is, but to release, to set free what lives*' (Deleuze 2006d: 174). That is, to affirm life is to affirm eternal becoming and the difference in-itself which defines it. We are not speaking, then, of freedom for freedom's sake, but of a type of existence concerning a way of, and attitude to, life. Whereas the general focus in Deleuze's earlier metaphysical works is pure philosophy, concerning itself primarily with the genesis of thought, the direction of the ethical works as presented in the monographs on Spinoza and Nietzsche by contrast is concerned with reversing this operation. Rather than accounting for the genetic conditions of thought as such, it is concerned with *becoming*, or rather with bringing virtual intensities – the eternal return of difference in-itself and thus creative becoming – back into life, such that it is possible to affirm difference beyond its own tendency to negate itself in identity and repetition of the same. Thus the ethical question concerns how to attain active affections, abundance, where affirmation of life relates directly to the ability of the power of action of a mode of existence, or an active will to power: 'Hence the properly ethical question is linked to the methodological question of how we can become active. How can we come to produce adequate ideas?' (Deleuze 1992: 221). Through this engagement with Nietzsche and Spinoza comes a fundamental addition to transcendental empiricism.

The entire impetus of Deleuze's political works with Guattari regards this ethic of affirmation, in accordance – following the events of May '68 – with the fundamental realisation that there is a deeply socio-economic and political dimension to the ontogenesis of force relations, or the Outside fold (Deleuze 2007: 234). This is personified in the notion of 'becoming a Body without Organs

(BwO)', i.e. a body, in other words, without social *organisation* and *stratification*, which itself is political repression in the form of imprisoning intensities, or demarcating the virtual plane of immanence with lines of force. The BwO is itself the field of virtual intensities, the plane of immanence itself, prior to actualisation. To become active and creative is to overcome these vicissitudes of transcendence by working through the intensive, through movements of folding, refolding and infolding, all of which personifies *active destruction*:

> Active destruction means: the point, the moment of transmutation in the will to nothingness. Destruction becomes *active* at the moment when, with the alliance between reactive forces and the will to nothingness broken, the will to nothingness is converted and crosses over to the side of *affirmation* which destroys reactive forces themselves. Destruction becomes active to the extent that the negative is transmuted and converted into an affirming power. (Deleuze 2006d: 164)

Active destruction, as the prerequisite to and process of becoming active, is realised in micropolitical analysis itself.

This micro-ethico-political project is initially fleshed out in Deleuze and Guattari's first collaborative work, *Anti-Oedipus* (2004a). At first glance, *Anti-Oedipus* presents an alternative to Freudian psychoanalysis in the guise of what Deleuze and Guattari call 'schizoanalysis'. Whereas psychoanalysis privileges the neurotic pole of delirium in its analysis, schizoanalysis privileges the 'schizophrenic pole', which presents 'a state of desire at its most critical and acute' (Guattari in Deleuze 2002: 266). The true purpose of schizoanalysis here is to realise *active destruction*. Indeed, the schizophrenic as Deleuze and Guattari understand the term, is a person of an actively destructive *dis*organisation, hence its usefulness as an analytical pole. With this intention in mind, *Anti-Oedipus* embarks on a politicised ontogenetic, or a genealogical analysis not of pre-conscious interest but of unconscious libidinal investment in association with the capitalist world order as the abstract machine. Whereas Marxism typically poses the problem of power in terms of the interests of the ruling class, Deleuze and Guattari turn to the interests of desire. Or, rather, where Spinoza speaks of modes and conatus, and Nietzsche of will to power, Deleuze and Guattari speak of desiring-machines. Given that conatus is determined by an affection or feeling we actually experience, it is best understood in such terms (see Deleuze 1992: 231).

That is to say, fundamentally, that Deleuze and Guattari's *Anti-Oedipus* takes up the will to power as conceived through Deleuze's metaphysics and ethics, and applies it to desire and politics, or social production. Here, the two sides of the will to power (the differential interpretation and exogenetic evaluation; or the two multiplicities as they are construed in *Difference and Repetition*) are construed instead in terms of desiring-production (micropolitical) and social production (macropolitical), or desiring-machines and social machines. The principle of syntheses in this case – as in that which connects these two multiplicities in immanence (and the series there within), as per the will to power – is construed through the BwO. Congruent with the two multiplicities (virtual/actual), desiring-production is relative to social machines (hence social production), such that the distinction between the two modes of production/multiplicities (desiring- and social) does not amount to an ontological dualism, such as the dualism between the One and the Many, 'but on the contrary, of distinguishing two types of multiplicities', or rather two types of production that form a continuum (Deleuze 1991: 39). The molecular and molar share the same machinic nature, differing only in regime (univocity). Further, the difference in regime does not exclude the immanence of each to the other, for there are 'only multiplicities of multiplicities forming a single assemblage, operating in the same assemblage: packs in masses and masses in packs. Trees have rhizome lines, and the rhizome points of arborescence.'

This forms an assemblage of desire – in fact, desire is always already assembled – that has elements or multiplicities of several kinds, interpenetrating one another. For this reason, Deleuze and Guattari claim it is the assemblage of both the micro and the macro that is the province of the unconscious, 'the way in which the former condition the latter, and the latter prepare the way for the former or elude them or return to them'. Indeed, they are unequivocal in stressing that there are 'no desiring-machines that exist outside the social machines that they form on a large scale; and no social machines without desiring-machines that inhabit them on a small scale' (Deleuze and Guattari 2004a: 373). The elements of an assemblage can be of a different type, consequently engendering contradictions and tensions, while at the same time producing consistencies and parts that cohere – this concerns once more the very folding of the exogenetic on the endoconsistent, as the twofold requirement of Deleuze's image of thought.

Desiring-Production (*Micro*political)

In the case of desiring-production (the virtual multiplicity/unconscious), the impersonal and pre-individual element of the transcendental field, is accounted for through three non-chronological syntheses of drives and partial objects as opposed to the syntheses of time; though of course there is still a spatio-temporal dimension. The first synthesis is productive and concerns desiring-production as the production of production (as production without telos and without distinction between producer and product). It is inherently connective in nature: 'and ...', 'and then ...', and so on, connecting the continuous flow of libidinal drives with partial objects of satisfaction, all of which are by nature fragmentary and fragmented. Such is the case with the Mother's breast and the infant's mouth. The breast and the mouth are only partial objects, parts of wholes that have not yet been constituted.[13] The drives too are partial insofar as they are invested with erotic value. In addition to the connective synthesis, there is the inclusive disjunctive synthesis of anti-production, in which the productive energy of the connective synthesis is disrupted and counteracted, but this anti-production is also formed by and within the connective synthesis itself. There are two modes of inclusive anti-production, and a third mode of exclusive anti-production which is tantamount to the kind of repression enacted by social machines. As the third regards social production, we will deal with only the first two here.

In the first case, the mouth is connected to the breast and some valuable energy is produced (nutritionally and erotically), achieving satiation. At some point sucking stops and the connection is broken (in fact the nipple does not guarantee its presence when demanded), and production produces anti-production while simultaneously recording the image of the nipple as an object of satisfaction on the recording surface – recording the trace of an excitation – of the BwO (see ibid.: 1, 50–1, 303). Thus the nipple takes on a bivocal character, becoming both an object of love and hate. In the second case, the connection can also be broken by distraction, whereupon the nipple-mouth is replaced with another connection. Thus, 'a connection with another machine is always established, along a transverse path, so that one machine interrupts the current of the other or "sees" its own current interrupted' (ibid.: 6). The connection is never merely a choice between one thing and another, 'this or that', but a momentary choice among a multitude of possibilities. In this way, it is inclusive, i.e. 'either . . . or . . . or', as opposed to 'either/or'.[14]

Insofar as this is recorded on the BwO for future reference, the BwO is the non-productive component, but nevertheless 'it is produced, at a certain place and a certain time in the connective synthesis, as the identity of producing and the product' (ibid.: 9). In accordance with its broader definition as the plane of immanence, the BwO in this context marks the zero point of virtual intensities. It differs drastically from Freud's death instinct, which implies a kind of thermodynamic reference or a process of repetitive compulsion to seek satisfaction from the same object, matching a particular memory trace of previous satisfaction (i.e. nipple-mouth). In contrast, the BwO, alike with the *dark precursor* of the will to power, represents an interruption in this process, wherein the subject is open to a virtual past that contains a limitless variety of modes of satisfaction. This is a repetition of difference as opposed to identity, afforded by intelligence and institutions functioning with but outside instinct; it interrupts flows and 'sets up a counterflow of amorphous undifferentiated fluid' (ibid.: 10).

For this reason an apparent 'conflict arises between desiring-machines and the body without organs. Every coupling of machines, every production of a machine, every second of a machine running, becomes unbearable to the body without organs' (ibid.: 9). The disjunctive synthesis works in tandem with the connective synthesis (in a process of attraction, differentiation and repulsion of drive-partial object relations), which together, depending on their particular configuration alongside social production, give rise to a particular figure of the ego. Indeed, Deleuze and Guattari argue that 'desiring-machines work only when they break down, and by continually breaking down' (ibid.) – anti-production coupled with production. If we were to go to extremes of this relation, say for instance the extreme of connection without disjunction, we would be presented with total fixation with a predetermined object, or what Freud identifies as neurosis (ibid.: 133). The other extreme, that of the disjunction without connection, presents us with psychosis, a complete withdrawal from reality. Thus, the cause of the disorder, neurosis or psychosis, is always in desiring-production, but, as we will see, 'in its relation to social production, in their different or conflicting regimes, and modes of investment that desiring-production performs in the system of social production' (ibid.: 140).

The 'subject' emerges as an after-effect of this interplay between production and anti-production (relative of course to social production, to which we shall come shortly), in which the particular networks of relations and states of intense experience they generate are recognised and consummated *ex post facto* by a subject of that experience, leading to the third and final synthesis: 'a conjunctive synthesis of consummation in the form of a wonderstruck "So *that's* what it was!" and "So it's *me*!"' (ibid.: 21). The subject is produced as a residuum alongside the machine, or as an appendix, and passes through all the degrees of the circle formed by the points of disjunction on the BwO, which converge on the desiring-machines – the *eggo rather than the ego* (insofar as the BwO is like the full biological egg before extension). The subject 'is not at the centre, which is occupied by the machine, but on the periphery, with no fixed identity, forever decentered, *defined* by the states through which it passes' (ibid.: 22). Such states can be identified with particular personages, or, rather, one can identify such personages with zones of intensity on the BwO. Thus the Nietzschean subject who passes through a series of states and who identifies these states with the names of history (i.e. 'The crucified one', 'Caesar', 'Dionysus'). It is clear that these states are not chosen, but rather the subject is driven to them. Once more following transcendental empiricism, the formation of the ego or the subject is retroactive, and thus becomes a particular actualisation via differen*c*iation of a virtual unconscious process of differen*t*iation.

Social Production (*Macro*political)

As with desiring-machines, social machines are constituted by connective, disjunctive and conjunctive syntheses, organising productive flows at a molar level. And just as desiring-machines 'involve an unengendered non-productive attitude, an element of antiproduction coupled with the process', so too do forms of social production, coupled with 'a full body that functions as a *socius*' (ibid.: 11). Social production has its own Body without Organs, its own differenciator, its own *dark precursor* – capital is 'the body without organs of the capitalist' (ibid.). But what is truly important for our purposes, in that it underpins an understanding of desire outside of any asocial or ahistorical essentialist category, is the way in which desiring-production is relative to socialproductive, or rather how desiring-machines form a continuum with social machines.

Given that the BwO is in effect a continuation of the will to power as dark precursor, it is unsurprising that it is critical in understanding this continuum. We noted earlier how the BwO is a recording surface, registering multifarious images of objects of satisfaction as reminders of potential future satisfaction. However, in the third mode of anti-production, which is where and how the social machine is truly connected to the desiring-machine, some are captured, coded and as such repressed and territorialised (as in a subjectification closed in on itself), but in a way distinct from Freudian primary repression. Instead of an inclusive disjunction, desire is subjected to an exclusive one, as in 'this and not that', good and bad. Such is the case with the Oedipus complex. Such repression finds its *raison d'être* in the fact that desire, in constantly seeking new connections, is revolutionary. That is to say, schizophrenia is 'the *absolute limit* of every society, inasmuch as it sets in motion decoded and deterritorialized flows that it restores to desiring-production, "at the bounds" of all social production' (ibid.: 288). Thus, the 'prime function incumbent upon the socius has always been to codify the flows of desire' (ibid.: 35).

The social machine stands as an apparatus of repression, for it stands opposed to the creative potential of desire's schizophrenic processes of inclusive syntheses. Within this rubric there are three forms of molar repression: savage-territorial; barbarian-despotic; and civilised-capitalist. Each of these stages relates its flows to certain codes – this 'is the business of the socius' (ibid.: 153), where the socius 'may be the body of the Earth, the body of the Despot, the body of Money' (ibid.: 35), which correspond to the segmented lines that lie in the heart of an assemblage, interpenetrating with the molecular lines of connection, or even cutting off lines of flight. Whereas the first social machine, the pre-capitalist territorial machine, is one 'of primitive inscription' (ibid.: 155), and the second despotic social machine merely overcodes, establishing the transcendent position of the despot, the capitalist machine is characterised by a curious *double-movement*: on the one hand, it can proceed only by continually developing the subjective essence of abstract wealth for the sake of production, operating via the axiomatic of capital, 'as a worldwide enterprise of subjectification by constituting an axiomatic of decoded flows' (Deleuze and Guattari 2004b: 505); and, on the other hand, it can do so only in the framework of its own limited purpose as a determinate mode of production, in which at the molecular it enacts vicious reterritorialisation.

Under the first aspect of its double-movement, where it replaces qualitative or evaluative codes of pre-industrial society (good versus evil), with the abstract quantities of the axiomatic of capital (the value of exchange), capitalism displays a 'cosmopolitan, universal energy which overthrows every restriction and bond' (Marx in Deleuze and Guattari 2004a: 281). According to Deleuze and Guattari, this movement initially arises from the conjunction of two relatively new deterritorialised flows: that of production in the form of money-capital and that of labour in the form of the worker. These two seemingly contradictory decoded flows are not excluded, but are brought together, conjoined into the social machine's centre, in the form of an *inclusive disjunction* or differential relation (in the mathematical sense: Dy/Dx; Dy = the fluctuation of variable capital and Dx = the fluctuation of constant capital) unified by the principle of quantitative value, i.e. primarily determined by what they can be bought and sold for on the market. Whereas pre-capitalist societies entail the extraction of a code surplus, the capitalist machines extracts a surplus of flux or 'flow' surplus', deriving from the conjunction of constant and variable capital, or money as credit and as a form of payment, as reflected in the twofold function of the banking system, i.e. investment and retail. The conjunction amounts to a generalisation of flow surplus to include surplus that derives from the flows of intellectual, scientific and technological codes, such that knowledge, 'information, and specialized education are just as much part of capital ("knowledge capital") as the most elementary labour of the worker' (Deleuze and Guattari 2004a: 255). In the same vein, conjunction opens the path for further de-coding of values and deterritorialisation of all flows (familial, social, institutional, economic material, consumptional, and so forth). Thus, through deterritorialising, capitalism ends up creating its own interior limit. It creates the space for the rise of what Deleuze and Guattari are fond of referring to as the 'schizo' who is open to multiple modes of libidinal connection. Take for instance the increasing number of sexual acts, habits, desires and behaviours that, having previously been discursively produced as deviant, abnormal or even deranged, are now partially accepted or at the very least tolerated enough to be granted a given space in society, and, more importantly, in the global market, i.e. the explosion of internet-based pornography, and the ease with which a large variety of extreme, explicit and hard-core material and genres are accessed and distributed.

Alas! Schizo desire, as Deleuze and Guattari call it, is one that is always seeking new and divergent libidinal connections and investments, and poses a threat to a post-industrial, consumer-based growth society that is increasingly reliant on specific and reliable forms of subjectivity for its continued existence. If subjects no longer felt any kind of lack and thus ceased to partake in fetishised consumption; if subjects ceased to buy things they do not need, with money they do not have, to impress people they do not like, to ultimately fill the void of the 'something missing', the constructed lack; if subjects no longer felt a sense of guilt regarding debts or pride in having a good credit history; if subjects did not valorise entrepreneurship or fetishise profit; if they did not feel a sense of responsibility to work hard for the social body or the company, willingly submitting to discipline on the basis of guilt and humbling themselves before figures of authority; and if subjects no longer felt an emotional need to satisfy and please authority figures, clamouring for positive recognition from the teacher, the police officer and the doctor; in short, if subjects did not strive to be the 'good' Hegelian citizen – the entire socio-economic system would collapse. Thus capitalism, without any real or initial planning or thought, embarks on its second movement: reterritorialisation.

Reterritorialisation concerns restoring all sorts of residual and artificial, imaginary or symbolic territorialities or values, in a bid to recode and rechannel persons who have been defined in terms of capitalist abstract quantities so as to insulate itself from its interior limit. This is primarily achieved through the privatisation of organs and the family, in which it is 'placed outside of the field, the form of the material or the form of human reproduction begets people whom one can readily assume to be all equal in relation to one another' (ibid.: 285–6). It is the condition under which the entire social field can be applied to the family, through which the very neuroticism central for such reterritorialisation is created. For it is one thing to recode social values, it is quite another to garner a libidinal investment or an emotional support for them. Specifically, through such a move, capitalism is able to employ the Oedipal complex as a way to truly internalise its limit and reterritorialise the flows of desire, 'where desire lets itself be caught' (ibid.: 288). Thus reproduction process, though not directly economic, passes by way of the non-economic factors of kinship.

The way this is achieved is seemingly convoluted and dynamic, but it is mostly reliant upon *ressentiment* and bad conscience. This brings us back to the Nietzschean notion of *will to power*, and

Deleuze's account in *Nietzsche and Philosophy* of the two kinds of reactive forces operating in a double structure. According to this account, the system that receives an excitation is not the system that retains a lasting trace of an excitation – what is considered the Freudian schema of life (whose origins are found in Nietzsche's *internalisation of man*). These two systems correspond to the distinction between the conscious – as that which acts on the reactions of present excitations or the direct image of the object – and the unconscious – as that which retains and reacts to mnemonic traces and lasting imprints of excitations. In acting on a reaction to a present or actual excitation, the active force is actualised and thus the will to power discharged. Indeed, consciousness is born at the point the mnemonic trace stops, i.e. consciousness is consciousness *of* something outside itself. It is at the boundary between the Inside and Outside, arising from, as it were, and serving an evolutionary expediency.

Crucially, Deleuze maintains that the two systems must be kept separate so as to prevent confusion and hesitation in the exercise of the will to power. That is, certain active forces are given the job of supporting consciousness in its required renewal and freshness; to keep it moving, to prevent it from being bogged down by doubtful hesitation or a perceptual confusion. Should a mnemonic trace invade consciousness as its object, it will forestall consciousness's immediacy of action, it will distract it from acting on and reacting to the actual and present excitation. Forgetfulness, then, has a positive function as a guard, or supervisor, preventing the two systems from becoming confused, and allowing the self to continue to act without hesitation (Deleuze 2006d: 106). When there is a lapse in the faculty of forgetting, reaction to the trace of the excitation becomes perceptible, and consciousness is bogged down. Thus at the same time as reaction to traces becomes perceptible, '*reaction ceases to be acted*' (ibid.: 107). The reactive force blames its object, whatever it is, as responsible for the powerlessness to invest anything but the trace – the infinite delay – against which revenge must be exacted (*ressentiment*). But even this reactive sense of revenge itself is not acted. It is endless, it is felt (*senti*).

More deeply, the memory of the trace itself is full of hatred, in that it blames the object in order to compensate for its own inability to escape from the traces of the corresponding excitation. Thus ressentiment's revenge, even when realised, has a spiritualised, imaginary and thus symbolic power. Out of this symbolism is born a typology, or more specifically a dialectical ideology of slave morality, where the triumph of the reactive is given a primordial affirmative quality, an Outside fold (the reactive is affirmed). Here, we find a reversal or inversion of good and bad. As Deleuze (ibid.: 113) says, in the Nietzschean master, everything positive is in the premises, and the negative is the conclusion of the premises ('I am good, therefore you are evil'), whereas in the slave reversal, the negative passes to the premises; premises of reaction and negation, of *ressentiment* and nihilism ('you are evil, therefore I am good'). Thus the values of good and evil are not created by acting, but by holding out on acting, which is to abide by a fiction that the master, the strong, is able not to manifest its force or exercise its will to power and thus separate itself from *what it can do* (thus the moral language: *what you should do*). *Ressentiment* is given form and type. Thus the birth of the Judaic priest: 'it is *your* fault!'

Though active force is fictitiously separated from what it can do, Deleuze (ibid.: 119) argues that in this scenario something real still happens to it as a result of this fiction. Being deprived of its material conditions of operation, separated from what it can do, active force is turned back inside, turned back against the self. The active does not simply dissipate, it produces pain. The internalisation or introjection of active forces is not the opposite of reactive projection (*ressentiment*). It is the consequence and continuation of projection, inasmuch as the reactive is able to project by virtue of its triumph, which is permitted by the displacement of active forces in the first instance. Where one goes out, the other must go in. As with the *ressentiment* it arises from, bad conscience too has a typology. The resultant pain is conceived as the consequence of an inward fault, an act of sin or injustice against another (guilt before God). Thus is born the Christian priest: 'it is *my* fault!' Whereas pain was first multiplied by the redirection or internalisation of force (topological), *pain itself is now internalised*. Both result from the change of direction of *ressentiment*. Indeed, for *ressentiment* to be fully appeased, it must spread its contagion, and make the whole of life reactive. Thus it is not enough to accuse Others; man must accuse himself as the cause of his own suffering (ibid.: 123). Even typologically, then, bad conscience is the consequence and continuation of *ressentiment*.

At last, as Deleuze (ibid.: 125) states, the priest provides us with the ascetic ideal, and the analogate world beyond according to which it relates. Both are designed by the priest to make this nasty, nihilistic world *bearable*. The priestly type makes it possible to live with the culpability which he introduces: there is a solution to the pain, to the gap, to our infinite debt to the God we have wronged, to the lack of harmony we feel. It is out there, beyond us, in God himself! The internal nihilism of life. The semblance of affirmation. What is more, such redemption does not relieve debt, it confounds it, for now one is in debt to the redeemer (ibid.: 132). Suffering merely serves to pay off the interest. Hence debt's infinity.

Deleuze's point via Nietzsche is that moral diktats of good and evil, as tied to an entire mnemotechnics, or the training of reactive forces via methods of discipline and punishment (Foucault's second genealogical axis), endows man with a faculty of memory. This is not a memory of traces, but an acted and active memory of words or promises— memory as commitment to the future. Once such memory is seized upon by the reactive priestly type, shifting from responsibility-debt to guilt-debt, it effectuates something akin to the very lapse in forgetfulness that was provisionally posited as instigating this sorry affair. It forecloses the options of immediate action available to one by making it both socially and personally illegitimate, and inconsistent with the promise to the future. This does not negate active desire outright, but rather redirects it down the path of displacement, projection and introjection.

In terms of macropolitical social production, Deleuze and Guattari contend that the coded territories and discourse of society act as active memory, and so effectively deprive active forces of desire from being discharged. An exclusive disjunction – morals, discourse – on the BwO, as we saw, is designed to prevent certain thoughts, behaviours and actions; to prevent an excitation from being acted upon. What is more, in terms of the Oedipus complex, and at least insofar as Westernised societies are concerned, the psychoanalyst – though this can be generalised to include any figure – takes on the Judaic priest's role in locating blame for the resultant neuroses in our parents, and the Christian priest's role in compelling us to blame ourselves through a fictionalised guilt-ridden narrative or the Oedipal discourse, i.e. 'I truly and wrongly wanted to sleep with my Mother', internalising and spiritualising the guilt of 'infinite debt', and replacing Oedipus-the-despot with Oedipuses-as-subject (Deleuze and Guattari 2004a: 130). This further adds to the exclusive disjunctions of the socius, by which the active forces of desire are deprived of their means of discharge, and thus redirected. There is, then, a 'double direction' given to reactive desire: the turning back against oneself, and the projection against the Other (ibid.: 291). The double direction forces us to recognise, contra Foucault, that there is an absence of a third and fourth form that pleasure can take: the pleasure in submitting to power, or, for Deleuze, the desire for one's repression (bad conscience); and the pleasure of repressing the Other (*ressentiment*). In this way, too, pleasure marks the (mostly failed or unfulfilled) satisfaction that is born out of the negative of a fictitious lack – to lack the ideal purity that guilt implies or the impossible harmony and satisfaction that the evil Other, or even the enigmatic Father supposedly disrupts – short-circuiting desire's positivity or blocking its flows, taking form in accordance with or in reaction to it through a socially invested assemblage.

Socio-politically and in terms of the turning back against oneself, wherein pain is taken as salvation or the appeasement of guilt, I believe this means that one will find pleasure in, for instance, paying back a debt, in sacrificing various activities in order to obtain a good credit history, suffering through gruelling work as a way of paying off spiritualised interest of a debt to society, or consuming a certain product so as to fill the perceived lack or achieve satisfaction. It is precisely this guilt-pleasure dyad that a post-industrial society, as we said, comes to rely on. In this case, Oedipus and related discourses and neuroticism aids capitalism via indirect means, insofar as it is harnessed and employed by seemingly apolitical institutions: marketing groups, the advertising industry, educational institutions, training programmes, the military, the film industry, the music industry, institutional human resources, party political communications, and so forth.

In terms of turning against the Other, a certain *pleasure* is attained when a reactive body of desire is augmented or empowered. Thus it follows that libidinal investment is attracted to the degree of development of productive forces or power. I believe the political import of this affective zone is made evident on a regular basis in the way that, for instance, discussion on the European Union or immigration proceeds not by way of a presentation of facts or arguments about practicalities – statistics 'proving' the financial benefits of foreign labour seldom win over a xenophobe – and is driven more by viscerally emotive forms of resentment or other affective discharges. A resentful political discourse resonates only with a resentfully assembled desiring-machine, which it serves to reinforce. The same undoubtedly rings true of anti-welfare sentiments, which are constantly accompanied by highly emotive slogans and terms (i.e. 'benefit scroungers') and tabloid articles. That said, the affective dimension is no less present in more 'high-brow' political debates and discussions. Even a socialist notion of justice is often derived from a spiteful reaction! In all these cases, subtle affective tactics of hatred, fear, patriotism and more are employed to harness an always already assembled desire and set presumptive agendas for macropolitics. In addition to setting agendas, the use of *ressentiment* can even be said to benefit capitalism once again, inasmuch as it can be seized upon to localise a perceived evil or at least the structural inefficiencies of capitalism to one group, leaving the true cause of social disintegration untouched.

In both cases, one is guided and ruled by real abstraction on the one hand and new territorialities that recode in order to displace the internal limit on the other. Clearly this engenders a *split* at the centre of the subject between his abstract ideal, preceded by the potential of the axiomatic, and the codes by which he lives (ibid.: 334). Thus, failure to engage on this micropolitical level is also a failure to engage with that which shapes our lives, attitudes and thoughts, and therefore that which is truly political. Though the particulars of each form of bad conscience and *ressentiment* and the interaction between the two will change from institution to institution, society to society and age to age, the need for a (re)territorialised and neurotic and manageable subject of convenience remains.

How to Become a Body without Organs/What Can a Body Do?

Subverting the micro-macro powers of capitalism, and the reactive assemblages of desire the micro-macro dynamic constitutes, is not a mere question of freedom, as we have already seen. It is a question of ethics and life, a question of affirmation, a question of returning to or becoming a BwO understood as the plane of immanence, the plane without reactive stratification and *organ*isation. But how precisely is reactive organisation to be subverted? Not only is desire always already assembled and directed by political forms of organisation; it also, by virtue of being the agentic and affective pivot point of such forms, has the capability to surmount them, and, indeed, to surmount the general categories of standard politics all together. That is to say, if we are constituted on an intensive level, albeit in disjunction and immanent causality with the actual/macro, then it is to the intensive level, first and foremost, that we must seek political subversion. But this is so only on a theoretical level. Practically speaking, we can never reach the intensive directly, and to suggest it as a possibility would obscure the immanence of the two domains (micro-macro); or the way in which micro-power relations of the intensive sustain and/or subvert macropolitical powers of authority, and how in turn these authorities can exercise their powers in ways that sustain, reify and/or subvert the microscopic intensive upon which they rely.

What then? If, as Deleuze and Guattari's ontogenetic analysis indicates, thought is immanent to the real that provokes it and is instigated by its encounters with this real, then in order to have thoughts that we can be worthy of – which means enacting a reversal of the relation of forces so as to deny the reactive and release active intensities back into life – we must have the right type of encounters, the right type of real. In other words, though we can never reach this intensive level directly, as we continually operate at the actual level, we must engage in various methods and tactics of the self, that, though indirect in their own right, directly affect the intensive and the related processes of differentiation and differenciation, so as to release intensities and/or that allow active forces of desire to express themselves, i.e. to act on reaction. As Deleuze and Guattari (2004b: 166) put it, to become a BwO is to engage with 'a set of practices', concerning the transmutation of the reactive into the active, a conversion and a crossing over to the hither side of affirmation, as opposed to sublimation. As with Foucault's relational take on power, then, it is only by virtue of lodging yourself on a stratum or the actual, refolding yourself through techniques and practices of the self, experimenting with the opportunities that the actual or given segments offer, that we have any chance of playing the game otherwise, of disarticulating, disorganising and expressing. We must tend to the intensive, but in a manner that accords with immanent causality.

Simply understood, this is to say that certain techniques or tactics, which act on the body so as to instigate and titillate microperceptions, alter thinking in its direction, speed, intensity and sensibility. Is it not precisely to instigate new patterns, or to subvert cyclical ones, that we 'go for a walk' or spend time relaxing, either out with friends and family or on selected hobbies? Even the simple act of relaxing in a warm bath, with your favourite music playing in the background, while entertaining nostalgic or romantic thoughts, can instigate new patterns of thinking or actualise different intensive states. Nietzsche speaks to such thinking in a section in *Ecce Homo* where he details how his dietary habits, preferential climates, and daily routines and practices aid him in his thinking – the 'choice of nutrition; the choice of climate and place: the third point at which one must not commit a blunder at any price is the choice of *one's own kind of recreation*' (Nietzsche 2000a: 698) and the 'slightest sluggishness of the intestines is entirely sufficient, once it has become a bad habit, to turn a genius into something mediocre' (ibid.: 696). Now, taken at face value, such activities are akin to those that the advertising industry, the well-being cult and the 'lean in' school of capitalist self-help rely upon, endorse and commodify. To a certain extent, as I argue in the next chapter, that is the point: to utilise the opportunities and material that capitalist production offers, as a way to exceed its reterritorialising grip. Though of course, some practices are more 'radical' in their affirmative potential than others. One must locate and engage in practices – any practice whatsoever – which release the active, or affirmative mode of becoming, as per the differential ethic of life affirmation. Of course, such practices of the self are always open to an overpowering axiomatic reterritorialisation and commodification, in which case the line of flight they entail would simply turn in on itself. When this happens, it is imperative either to change the practice from within (there is difference in repetition after all) or to simply change it for another.[15] That is to say, resistance via practices of the self must be dynamic, in the vein of Sartre's ethic of authenticity. The only 'right' type of practice is the affirmative one and this is subject to constant change in accordance with the dynamic nature of social production and de-/reterritorialisation. The authentic attitude, in this case, concerns a constant questioning and judgement as to the affirmative outcome of one's practices and a willingness to 'change it up' when a practice fails to yield results or becomes too axiomatic and therefore redundant.

Mimicking Foucault even further, the disjunctive fold – the differenciator, dark precursor or BwO – through which the virtual is related to a plane of organisation (either in the case of virtual interior psychic forces or the exterior substrate of force relations underpinning disciplinary practices and power-knowledge), creates the very excess through which this surmounting can be technically realised, or through which codes and lines can be reshuffled and renegotiated. In terms of the micro or virtual unconscious, it is by virtue of the disjunctive connection of the affective and psychic forces that comprise it that there are a variety of virtual intensities and thus ego forms, waiting at any given time to be actualised, reshaped and added to, through various techniques that create new encounters and opportunities for expression, across a range of personal, social and political strata. That is, a new and radically different configuration or relation of the virtual incompossibility can always be provoked into actualisation, either through practices that alter the make-up of the virtual unconscious relation of forces and/or through practices that allow otherwise negated active forces to express and discharge themselves, which will in turn affect the virtual unconscious. Both activities presuppose a certain form, however: the transmutation of values, or the conversation of the primordial quality of negative evaluation into affirmation. One must affirm all that is different in their life, or indeed their own difference, their own becoming, if the active force of desire is to be properly permitted and discharged. This correlates with the destruction of the ego – or the social *superego-like* demand for a unified, organised, consistent, predictable and officially recognisable identity, with its own discursive confines and structural constraints (exclusive disjunctions) – and the coordinates of identity and identifiable action and behaviour, by which such an ego is plotted, judged and made to make promises. The promise of consistency. The promise of sameness. The promise of identity. Indeed, such an ego is more often than not the prerequisite of axiomatised practices of the self. Thus the meaning of *active destruction* as a transmutation, destroying all that is necessary to allow reactions to be acted, for the discharge of the active, and thereby overcoming of all that is *human, all too human*: bad conscience, *ressentiment* and the like.

And so an ethics of becoming a BwO, as with the ethics of the care of the self, feeds into politics and acts as a strategy of political engagement, entailing political questions concerning, as Foucault (2004: xiv–xv) puts it in the preface to *Anti-Oedipus*, how to tackle 'the fascism in us all, in our heads and in our everyday behavior, the fascism that causes us to love power, to desire the very thing that dominates and exploits us', and therefore the fascism that sustains capitalism. In this sense, tending to the intensive certainly does not mean returning to a primordial or essentialist self that has been repressed by social forms. For Deleuze and Guattari, repression, as we saw, is meant in a way vastly distinct from Freudian repression or the negative of the Law, referring instead to the redirection or re-routing of the flows of desire, which in turn codifies them. In redirecting the forces of desire, as opposed to negating them outright, repression or the macropolitical *produces* new assemblages of desire. That is its critical power, the power to produce modes of subjectivation. What is more, as we saw, this production always already involves the intensive and virtual level as that which gives the given. That is why to refer to the actual or given alone when discussing emancipation or political struggle is to come in too late. There is even a correspondence here with Sartre's idea of 'feedback mechanisms' in processes of totalisation, wherein practices of authenticity alter the feedback or change its resonance. The broader political point is that given that the assemblage is a complex system interacting with all levels of social reality, the slightest change can have a significant and unpredictable effect. Or, concordant with Foucault's concept of double-conditioning, a change to the self changes the macropolitical. Desire is the pivot point.

Notes

1. Butler (2012: 214–20), Grace (2009: 71–3) and Žižek (2012a: 28).
2. Butler (2012: 220) claims that in replacing Deleuze's 'precultural ontology' of desire within a theory of power-knowledge, Foucault brings to light the discursive limits of Deleuze's position, thereby sharpening his 'challenge to psychoanalysis'.
3. As Beistegui (2010: 12) notes, the fact the immanence becomes an ideal, as opposed to a reality, signifies a paradox in wanting to 'extract the pre-conceptual conditions of thought by way of *concepts*'. The concept is an attempt to draw a plane, to bring out its own image, yet it can never be fully reached given this paradox.
4. See for instance, Baugh (2003: 148), Malabou (1996: 115), Patton (2000: 30) and Žižek (2012a: 44).
5. It was the Kantian critique which first showed that, contra Descartes, it is 'impossible for determination to bear directly upon the determined' (Deleuze 2004a: 108). However, 'Kant did not pursue this initiative: both God and the I underwent a practical resurrection' (ibid.: 109) in the form of a transcendental subject.
6. See Widder (2012: 138) for a more detailed discussion on this point.
7. Deleuze does not at any point wholeheartedly reject the 'dialectic' as such, only particular realisations of it. For instance, in *Difference and Repetition*, Deleuze concedes that the dialectic is 'the art of prob-

lems and questions, the combinatory or calculus of problems as such' (2004a: 196).
8. This relates directly back, then, to Deleuze's (1992: 180) main book on Spinoza.
9. To be sure, Deleuze (2006c: 91) gives clear credit to Merleau-Ponty for the creation of the fold.
10. Like the will to power, Deleuze (2006b: 111) refers to the vinculum as a mechanism of communication on the side of the monad (the virtual) and the propagation of extrinsic movement. Indeed, viniculum, as taken from mathematics, denotes a grouped together expression.
11. Such is the case, for instance, with Descartes's *cogito*, in which 'everyone knows' what thinking is, wherein it is said the *I* is predisposed towards truth, such that the *cogito* is taken as the unquestionable point of departure for thought, or the pre-philosophical plane for the construction of moral concepts and imperatives. Similarly, Kant discovers in his transcendental philosophy conditions that remain external to the conditioned, namely in the form of practical reason.
12. Deleuze (2006d: 85) initially proposes the Nietzschean will to power as 'a genetic and genealogical principle, as legislative principle', holding it to be 'capable of realising internal critique' insofar as the will to power replaces the transcendental principle with genealogy. Even the end of Nietzsche's critique is vastly different, in that the point is not justification but a different way of feeling, 'another sensibility' (ibid.: 88). This legislative principle speaks to the Deleuzian invention of concepts on a plane of immanence, in that it breaks with the 'self-evidence' of the dogmatic image of thought in favour of the actualisation of a given pure event in a specific context. The creation of concepts acts as a 'counter-effectuation' (Deleuze and Guattari 1994: 158).
13. For Klein, the 'part-object' refers to the 'part of' a lost unity or totality (molar), such as the mother's breast. This can be identified as either good or bad, depending on the function the part-object serves. Deleuze and Guattari rework this concept through their *object partiels*, which is translated as 'partial objects'. Partial replaces part, in that it refers to bias, as in evaluating intensities that know no lack and are capable of selecting organs (see translator's note in Deleuze and Guattari 2004a: 340*n*).
14. As Holland (2012: 322) notes, this resembles Freud's 'polymorphous perversity' of the infantile (pre-ego) unconscious in that 'anything goes; before being fixated on specific organs, erogenous zones, or activities, pleasure can be found or taken almost anywhere; it is not instinctually determined'.
15. It is often assumed that one repetitively turns to the same kind of practices (i.e. listening to the same music, or playing the same instrument) as a way to 'relive' the initial abundant feeling it provided (nostalgia).

But it certainly can be the case that one turns to the same practice insofar as it represents an efficacious and consistent means by which to release the affirmative, or 'difference in-itself'. In such an instance, one is not trying nostalgically to relive a feeling, but is rather repeating the same practice so as to create a new one.

Conclusion
From Immanence to Micropolitics

I stated in the introduction that my primary aim was to offer the conceptual answer to the question of capitalism's survival. As is evident, I took subjectivity as my starting premise, in the vein of Marx. Moving beyond the pre-conscious interests of ideology, however, I have sought to provide the conceptual basis for micropolitical unconscious investments of desire. That is, the way in which desire is, though productive, socially produced and managed such that it comes to desire its own repression (capitalism) and/or comes to be shaped in a manner conducive to the continual functioning of capitalism. Conceptually speaking, this notion of desire is a 'pure' immanent one, defined primarily in terms of a seemingly simple idea: the fold. A 'pure' immanence is a folded immanence. Indeed, the fold also allows us to conceptualise and ultimately articulate immanent resistance to the social contortion and productive repression of desire.

How are we to understand the fold? In tracing the thought of Sartre, Merleau-Ponty, Foucault and Deleuze, I have conceptualised the fold in terms that pit it against Hegel's idea of 'holes' or negativity as the constituting factor of being. The Outside extensive multiplicity is folded into the Inside intensive multiplicity, and an Inside is folded back out or into the Outside, in what is a seemingly circular process of folding. Metaphysically, this equates to saying that the seemingly purely philosophical (the plane of the virtual multiplicity) is deeply related to the seemingly purely socio-political (plane of the actual multiplicity), forming a continuum. One cannot be separated from the other, if we are to reach the Absolute. Any philosophical account of the subject and subjectivity must, by necessity, deal with the concrete socio-political Outside and vice versa; any theoretical account of the concrete must, by necessity, deal with the philosophical. There is no truly public-private distinction to be had, no matter or action that is truly beyond the marriage of the philosophical and socio-political, no ultimate stable point of departure, no transcendent outside, nothing truly beyond that which we live in ultimate flux that can be relied on as a pre-socio-political or extra-socio-political ground, and certainly no subject – be that as a positive Body or a negative Being – as an external precondition of thought, meaning and action. The 'I' of the subject and the identities by which it marks itself, are the surface effects of folding; and all that makes up and defines our life consists of the political functioning of the society in which we find ourselves enclosed. The 'subject' is a fold. And desire is the inside of the fold, its crease.

'Pure' immanence – or folded immanent desire – is precisely that which, as seen in the introduction, is obscured and in cases rejected by contemporary post-Marxist thought. This is somewhat unsurprising, given that 'pure' immanence offers a position that is both radical it its counterintuitiveness and counterintuitive in its radicalness. There is no subject of emancipation from capitalism, and to construct one is to paradoxically obscure the real path to emancipation, if by that we understand the release of the chaotic multitude of the self and vitalistic life forces. Instead, one must seek an a-subjective and a-systematic emancipatory praxis. Pure immanence is also radical, in that its rejection of the subject is at one and the same time a lively refusal to engage in the chronic practice of seeking yet another ingeniously conclusive theoretical and philosophical path to reinforce and endorse that which has already been pre-philosophically supposed and intuitively taken as supreme or as the correct and morally superior image of thought. What is 'intuition', after all, if not the sibling of a dogmatic image of thought? Indeed, 'pure' immanence ultimately questions the interests and desires of those betrothed with such practices. Interests and desires that are not only multiple and contradictory, but so well concealed, so unconscious, as to be only truly explicable in our choice of sexual lovers (Deleuze and Guattari 2004a: 386).

In any case, it is proclaimed, particularly by thinkers of 'lack' such as Žižek and Badiou, that immanence leads to some kind of deadlocked harmonious unity, denying the very ruptures and breaks – between the relation of interior and exterior life – that supposedly define desire, subjectivity, politics and, more importantly, resistance. However, as we saw, folded circularity or the double-condition is, at best, a useful shorthand for a rather involved process, with a rich genealogical lineage of its own. The fold is far from self-coincidental, the circle is far from perfect, and there is never an exact correspondence. The fold is *disjunctive* and so contains a series of excesses, though of a different kind to that of the dialectical tradition. As I indicated in the introduction – and argued in Chapters 2, 3 and 4 – *disjunction* refers to a kind of connection, relation or synthesis of differences, of contradictory and heterogeneous elements, singularities and forces that, as opposed to being collapsed into a higher unity or assimilated and thus compromised by having to share a singular and same logic, maintain their difference or their disparity. That is to say, these heterogeneous elements *vice-dict* as opposed to contradict one another. All contradictions exist at once, without contradicting each other. And herein lies the excess: any one of these elements may be exaggerated, or seized upon, at the expense of the others, so as to recompose the relation, the apparent unity, or rather to exceed it, so as to compose a new one. The entire process knows no true ontological negativity.

What is more, this great fold – the big fold – is punctuated by a series of infinitesimal n-dimensional folds, circles of circles, a variety of modalities of folds and seemingly folds of/in folds; much in the same way that Riemann envisions sub-curvatures along all possible orthogonal directions within a continuous manifold. This is also to say that there are disjunctions of disjunctions, paralleling the Bergsonian idea of a multiplicity of a multiplicity, which makes perfect sense if we understand that disjunction is the relational logic operative within and between multiplicities. Thus the fold not only refers to the Outside extensive multiplicity that is folded over into an Inside intensive multiplicity, which is folded back out or into the Outside, but also to the multiple folds that take place within/without this folding, between which is a mutual reliance, again in the form of a double-conditioning. At its simplest, the n-dimensional *is* the disjunctive fold(s) of the spatio-temporal-libidinal-bio-social, i.e. the assemblage. The disjunctive fold and the excesses therein, is crucial to a nuanced understanding of the relation between 'pure' immanence and the (micro)politics of desire, and, more importantly, resistance and emancipatory praxis. For the sake of expediency, we can retroactively identify three levels of disjunction and thus three levels of immanent micropolitics.

The Three Disjunctions of Micropolitics

The first disjunction concerns that of the intensive multiplicity. Following what we saw as Deleuze's reworking of this Bergsonian concept via Sartre, Merleu-Ponty and schizoanalysis, this can be understood as our pre-personal and pre-individual transcendental condition or the virtual and unconscious affective-spatio-temporal self: a self that precedes and determines the conscious 'subject' in the form of an ego, as alluded to above. When the synthetic concept of disjunction is applied, it follows that the virtual unconscious is a spatio-temporal-affective depth, full of a number of seemingly contradictory possibilities, affective forces, existential traces, subjective states and physic elements. Insofar as these elements compose a self, we can say that the unconscious houses a resonance between different selves or between different series that co-exist without being subsumed by each other. Each lives a different spatio-affective-time series in abstraction from its empirical succession in time. Thus we not only reject the idea of the self as defined by negativity, but also as progressively fractured through chronological time via duration (as per Bergson's thesis). We come to conceptualise and embrace, instead, the self as typified by a fundamental discontinuity and an eternal return of difference itself: a *Body without Organ*(isation)*s*. The self is always becoming *Other* and any sense of continuity or sameness is a contrived simulacrum,[1] an unstable after-effect that requires various ritualistic practices, acts of reconstitutive recognition via Others ('Chris, you don't seem yourself today') and an unyielding discursive support, in order for at least some semblance of it to be retained, *should that be desired*.

The threat this type of raw Being poses to a codified society, or at least the political functioning of a society and in fact all forms of organisation, is clear. Our true disjunctive self, when taken to the ultimate extreme, is the figure of the chaotic, unpredictable and creative multiple self, forever wandering about, forever evading and straddling rigid structures of identities, rigid structures of thought, action and behaviour. In a series of convoluted moves, social machines – as in socialised and organised force relations designated by some elusive, fluctuating and at times unrealised sociopolitical and economic interest[2] – are established in order to tame, if not neutralise, the socially dangerous and unpredictable creative energy of human rebel-becoming. In order to tame and neutralise, social machines tactically manipulate drives, thoughts, feelings and actions by way of discourses that operate on the virtual transcendental self, that *etch, burn the rules of society on the proverbial soul* – the BwO – as the immanent forceful Outside of it. Enculturating processes and cruel forms of inscriptive mnemotechnics, this serves to transform biological bodies into social bodies of identity (biosocial bodies), with the ultimate aim of creating a reliable and useful variable. When such taming fails to constitute and fix the perfect identity on the BwO, when desire cannot be totally reterritorialised, social machines settle on utilising discourse as a means to manage disorganised BwOs and mitigate their effects, i.e. the discourse of sex, the discourse on public health, the prison and the entire penal system, a whole array of bio-power strategies and disciplinary operations that emerged in Westernised societies in the eighteenth and nineteenth centuries (and solidified in the twentieth century) that create a permanent and visible reality by which to categorise and regulate individuals within the institution (the school, the prison, the hospital, etc.). In both cases – tactical manipulation and bio-disciplinary procedures – there is a reliance on discourse, as in what Foucault conceptualised as the amalgamation and mutual constitution of relational social forces with constructed segments of knowledge, i.e. power-knowledge.

It is through discourse that we come to the *second disjunction* of micropolitics. What is important to note regarding any discourse, above all else, is that it will never be exclusively exclusionary. A discourse is comprised of heterogeneous elements (dispersion/disjunction), unifying a variety of contradictory epistemic and concrete elements in a didactic practice, without subsuming their singular difference. Put simply, Foucault did to the socio-political or exterior social force relations as that which lies at the heart of a discourse, what Deluze did to the interior unconscious: applied Merleau-Ponty's concept of the *fold*, in conjunction with Nietzschean genealogy. It follows from this, once again, that any one of these singular differences can be harnessed and exaggerated so as to exceed the initial disjunctive relation of the discourse. Thus though it is exclusive and binary in its application as social repression, discursive practices rely on non-binary formations, or a series of *inclusive* disjunctions that in turn exceed and undermine its binary or exclusive applicatory procedures or its unity as formed in its practice. This engenders a constant battle and dynamism on the social level, in part accounting for the fluctuating and evolving nature of social repression.

What connects the first disjunction to the second (i.e. how precisely does the first threaten the second, and how precisely does the second tame the first), is the *third* and final *disjunction* of micropolitics, which in effect is the coming together of the first two: the ultimate fold, the big fold of the Outside, a disjunction acting on a disjunction, via disjunction. Indeed, the first disjunction – that which makes up the nature of the BwO or the virtual self – is a disjunctive connection, or rather comprised of singularities, experiences, traces and forces, as derived and folded in from the Outside second disjunction of discourse, that are then folded back Out through actualised expressions. This leads to the idea mentioned at the start of this chapter of folded circularity, though now it can be expressed also in terms of a double-conditioning whereby the micro (virtual) life of thought and desire can sustain or subvert the power of authority, or macro structures, while these very authorities and structures can exercise their powers in ways that strengthen or undermine the microscopic desires upon which they rely. The third disjunction also constitutes what Deleuze and Guattari conceptualise as the assemblage, i.e. the holistic means by which the sociopolitical is managed and controlled, but even possibly subverted.

How does this all figure in our present age?[3] It is perhaps not so controversial to state that, for better or for worse, we live in an age of advanced global (post-industrial consumerist) capitalism. What is curious and notable about capitalism – at least according to Deleuze and Guattari – spanning from its early industrialist stage to its current consumerist stage, is that its first movement of decoding qualitative values and deterritorialising flows of social production and activity caters to our interior excess or our virtual inclusive disjunction. Capitalism unleashes free-form desire and thought on the BwO, namely by slowly disrupting and in some cases outright destroying primordial qualities of evaluation that seek to limit it: the harsh moral values and diktats, exclusive disjunctions, friend/enemy distinctions and filiations of old. As we saw in the last chapter, though decoding is evident in pre-capitalism via the expansion of private property, commodity production, markets and the accumulation of money, capitalism proper is defined by the generalised decoding of flows. It achieves this by conjoining all decoded or deterritorialised flows under the auspices of an economic and social system underpinned by the axiomatic of capital or abstract exchange.

Instead of a systematic correspondence between the elements of different signifying systems, the axiomatic is defined by purely syntactic rules for the formation of a-signifying discursive practices, in which multiple, foreign, disparate and contradictory elements and domains, acts and types of Being are allowed to exist simultaneously, unified only in principle by abstract quantities and in practice by production and consumption: thus a disjunctive synthesis of the second order. And where there is a disjunctive synthesis, there is, by logical necessity, an excess, as in the points of disjunctive connection themselves. Indeed, it would seem that post-industrial capitalism has, via an ever-expanding consumerist market, provided the discursive, mental and physical space, as well as the technical and material means, by which subjects can engage in personal and thus politically transformative practices of the self, which have the potential to provoke the actualisation of new intensities on the BwO, or a radical change in the speed and direction of thought; practices that tend to the intensive and to the disjunctive excess in us; practices that the decoding of flows carries forth as an element that exceeds the axiomatic and by which subjects can become, in effect, *active*, though socio-economically *unproductive* and *unmanageable* subjects of *inconvenience.*

I can take advantage of, for instance, the opening of sexual space or sub-culture within the consumer market (i.e. attend bars and clubs that allow me to discharge active desire, or perform and engage with certain transformative acts; to purchase specifically designed clothing and equipment that assist sexual transgression or experimental 'limit-experiences' that alter the unconscious relation of forces; join forums and websites that connect me with other people interested in such pursuits so as to establish a collective micropolitics or *subject group*), in order to subvert, question, alter and experiment with my sexual identity and thus – insofar as sexual identity is related to other identity-segments, including my gender identity – my sense of self. The experimentation and release of active desire may take on a life of its own, to the point that it can exceed and outgrow its origin, i.e. de-commodifying my identity, and destroying the *bad conscience* of lack upon which it relies, so as to generate an active refusal to purchase and consume products that feast on a configured phantasy of gender-related beauty or reified sexuality. I may become gender neutral (agender or neutrios), or at least find ways to play with my identity outside of the market. That is to say, I can escape consumerism, through consumerism. This is to say also that capitalism produces unproductive surpluses that represent the outer limits of its productivity, in a similar vein to the way unemployment and dead labour present the unproductive hither side of labour-intensive production. Such was the case, albeit in a different guise, with the drug-fuelled elements of the 1960s' hippie movement, inasmuch as it sprang from and exceeded the culture industry.

What is crucial here, however, is that such decodification is accepted to flow, to exist on the macro level, granted it is *productive*. That is, free form desire is allowed insomuch as it is financially prudent, insomuch as there is a market for it. For production is the *raison d'être* of capitalism. Unproductive domains have to be reassimilated. And herein lies a pertinent danger. The master stroke of capitalism is to internalise such outer limits by inventing new axioms so as to turn anything unproductive into a commodity, a source of profit and thus a source of production: the presence of anti-prodution within production itself. The unproductive element of anti-production, in other words, is in truth the unrealised value of flux, as embodied in the outer limits: subversive sub-cultures, unemployment and stagnation. The outer limits are absorbed into capitalist production in spheres of consumption and investment, but also outside these spheres, i.e. advertising, civil government, militarism and imperialism. As soon as a non-commodified and/or subversive space is found it is commodified and/or converted.

That one can purchase 'hippie wigs', vindicates the above point. And when considered in specific situations and from a certain point of view, a person assigned with male sex, adopting the gender identity of a 'woman', for instance, is less subversive than may at first seem. There is a tendency in such movements and flows to reinstate the repressive – though seemingly 'repressed'— identity, where recourse to the liberation of the 'true' self is merely recourse to yet another commodified and well-organised identity/bio-social desiring-machine. A case of 'transgender essentialism'. Though such a 'gender swap' would certainly make the old conservative blush with discomfort and remonstrate in hectoring ire, it holds that the person in question is essentially transitioning from one well-configured and established gender identity – with its own reality, codes, rules, discursive structures and socio-economic market place – to another. Nothing is truly put 'in play', shown up or transformed. Even where the transition is imperfect, inasmuch as it fails to meet the exact discursive coordinates of the gender it has transitioned to, there is the opportunity of creating yet another lucrative industry, another site of capture whereby one is swallowed up once more in an endless routine of mindless and shallow consumerism, propped up by an ever-expanding credit industry, all the while feigning personal liberation, authenticity and even left-wing radicalism. In this case, the line of flight immanent to consumerism (i.e. by which one may escape consumerism by going through it) is reterritorialised, muted, turned inwards, rerouted, and so condemned to return to its cause. Similarly, the apparent 'anti-establishment'/'anti-capitalist' lyrical content and artistic form of the music of, say, Rage Against the Machine can, and often is, marketed towards angst-ridden individuals who are seeking an outlet or discharge for their psychic dissonance or ressentiment. Once again, the political content is muted or at least overridden by the immediate, self-indulgent, narcissistic and ultimately neurotic needs of a 'subject of lack', while also sustaining and in this case even commodifying the rebellious indentity to which such music is often associated (in the case of fashion: Che Guevara T-shirts, Converse trainers, and so forth). Thus, commodification not only provides the dangerous illusion of subversive left-wing or anti-capitalist radicalism, but also the intense feeling of it. In lieu of any genuinely resistive work on the self or on society, we are given a self-satisfying impression of it, a cultural chic which by virtue of that fact forestalls any authentically subversive acts. Is this not the truly gruesome joke of capitalism: selling rebellion, while simultaneously shredding a space of its rebellious content?

This is not just true of consumptional flows. The stagnancy of knowledge capital, as in the rise of computer viruses, illegal internet downloading and content sharing, unregulated financial and trade markets (the dark web – arguably the only true free market in existence), alternative e-currencies (Bitcoin), 'illegal' data sharing (WikiLeaks), and so forth – all seemingly undermining domestic and international laws, the political system and, the ultimate sin, the productivity of particular industries (film, music, etc.) – is made productive via the use of anti-virus software, and fraud prevention/cyber-security companies, reactive and pre-emptive government funded research and development programmes. This also applies to more traditional types of unproductive surpluses, such as unemployment and dead labour, either by serving to sustain a downward pressure on wages and thus increasing the surplus value of certain industries (thus why European financial centres tend to be pro-European Union/free movement); or by offering a constant reserve army of workers to be absorbed by, for example, benefit-related job schemes, whereby large companies gain a work force at a quarter of the minimum wage and without any real contractual obligation; and expansionary military endeavours (weapons and military vehicle contracts, infrastructural investments and projects, conscription and enlistment), boosting employment so as to instigate a bastardised Keynesian fiscal stimulus process, thereby serving to bring the economy closer to full output within the given limits, and by widening these limits in turn. As Deleuze and Guattari (2004a: 255) put it: 'it took a war to accomplish what the New Deal had failed to accomplish'.

This process by which capitalism seeks to quell its excesses and make productive that which is unproductive is partly reliant upon – and at times the result and cause of – the reterritorialisation of desire on a micro level, or the BwO. As stated previously, capitalism still requires a reified form of subjectivity, or rather a stable and predictable or even manageable subject that must feel lack in order to consume and sustain growth, and so in this sense be more susceptible to market capture when engaged in subversive sub-cultures and consumer markets. Ressentiment too, can be utilised to misdirect desire and libidinal investment, i.e. by provoking one to *identify* with political music merely for the sake of discharge (as noted), or by provoking one to direct their ressentiment toward, and *identify* all hardship and pain in the localised Other (the immigrant, the benefit-scrounger, the inefficient public sector, the unions, etc.), serving to localise the structural inefficiencies of capitalism and justify a politically motivated austerity agenda. Beyond this, the repressive processes of capitalist social machines produce subjects that feel a perennial sense of guilt and therefore a sense of duty in paying back a debt and providing surplus labour for the benefit of the organisation, institution and therefore social body. Such a guilt is efficacious in compelling one to internalise, psychologise and individualise all structural faults. To achieve all this, capitalism 'institutes or restores all sorts of residual and artificial, imaginary, or symbolic territorialities, thereby attempting, as best it can, to recode, to rechannel persons who have been defined in terms of abstract quantities' (Deleuze and Guattari 2004a: 281), reusing for itself codes, overcodes and rules, strictures of thought, action and behaviour, or simply discourses that attack the BwO, creating new assemblages of desire, i.e. the discourse of the Oedipus complex. Even where the reterritorialisation of desire fails, discourse is still employed in a disciplinary manner, so as to mitigate and manage revolutionary or subversive tendencies, as Foucault effectively argued.

The point is that capitalism finds ways to displace, absorb, limit and discipline what Deleuze and Guattari would describe as the subversive 'schizophrenic' content or disjunctive excesses that exist on both a micro and macro level, where, specifically, discursive arrangements are employed to inscribe and assemble desire and social machines, or merely to manage and mitigate the effects of said content. The state, here, acts as an immanent model of realisation for an axiomatic of decoded flows and the supreme institutional arbiter of disciplinary processes. Whereas under its first movement capitalism employs an *inclusive disjunction*, under its second movement capitalism employs an *exclusive disjunction* (though it still depends on inclusion) – either on the BwO itself, or on the macro level via disciplinary procedures (though the two are clearly intertwined) – precisely to mitigate the excess of the first. As said, it is the connection of the social machine with the desiring-machine that constitutes the third disjunction of micropolitics: the assemblage.

The Three Disjunctions of Resistance

We have been given three disjunctions: the micro, the macro and the assemblage. As we saw, where there is disjunction there is excess, as in the points of disjunctive connection themselves, or the a-signifying points of rupture that are always present. And where there is excess, there is the opportunity to resist. Thus there are three levels to resistance, each corresponding to the three levels of micropolitical subjectivation. This is also to say that, if we are constituted in immanence – internally or from within – then resistance to this constitution must be immanent, internal or from within the power of constitution. Then, and only then, will we be capable of instigating something akin to Gramsci's *war of position* and *passive revolution*, and thus the basis for the creation of the new.

The first level of resistance concerns the BwO or virtual self, which guarantees and condemns us to a continual and active Becoming Other, an eternal return of difference in-itself. We are freedom, if by that we understand it in intensive terms, or as our being in disjointed spatio-time, the fact that there is no permanence to the self or to the ego we identify with. This is also to say, in the language of Deleuze and Guattari, that we are multiple, incompossible and schizomatic. We are always exceeding ourselves, such that there is no-self, per se. The second concerns the macro level, the discursive arrangements as attached to capitalist social machines, the disjunctive excess of which establishes discursive spaces of thought and activity. As the example of the teacher-student relation in the third chapter demonstrates, where there is discursive institutional- or bio-power, there is an ability to *play it otherwise*, or to put in play, show up, transform and reverse. It was in this way, too, that homosexuality began to speak on its own behalf, utilising the same categories that sought to 'medically' disqualify it, whereby the very 'naturalism' that was previously used as a measure of its deviancy was in turn used as its very justification. What is more, such resistance is not only immanent to capitalist social machines, it is constantly being actualised by the activities of capitalism, despite itself. Capitalism is forever opening up new spaces of activity through production and consumption (such as sexual, digital), thought and creativity (TV, cinema and music), allowing one to engage in practices of the self that tend to the intensive, or tend to our own disjunctive nature. It is through such practice, as I have argued throughout, that we may activate an affirmative and creative becoming Other that can serve to implode micro-repression and the macropolitical forms that intersect with and rely on micro-repression. This leads us onto the third level of resistance, or disjunctive excess, which is, as with the third level of micropolitical subjectivation, the coming together of the first two, the double-conditioning; employing the second excess to release the first excess, in turn altering and further releasing the second, and so on in an endless though ever-expanding circle. That which can be folded, can be unfolded. By changing one level, we change the other, we change the entire resonance, and release and set forth a creative becoming that can exceed even itself. That is to say, the second excess can be utilised to create the discursive spaces of thought and activity required for practices of the self that can be employed to push for and find new domains by which such practices can be expanded and by which, more importantly, capitalist social machines can be utterly subverted.

Remembering that the micro is not tiny but constitutive and relational, permeating all levels of the macro, it follows that the subversive potential can be expanded through *socialising* and *collectivising* practices of the self. Even the simple act of altering one's outward appearance in a non-conventional manner (long greasy hair, an untrimmed beard, playfully and ironically synergising feminine and masculine attire, dressing down when one's authoritative status suggests dressing up as a matter of etiquette) is enough to provoke the release of new intensities in Others, and to challenge existentially satisfying though politically questionable rules, assumptions and convictions. One can imagine how effective and expansive a non-conventional (as in those experiences that have been rejected by civilisation) social movement or protest can be. Thus, though the bringing together of heterogeneous decoded familial, social, cultural and political domains in a series of disjunctive syntheses according to the axiomatic establishes capitalism's ability to adapt and live off its contradictions, it also establishes its own eventual, albeit slow, downfall.

Given that this guarantees a certain inevitability in the failure of reterritorialising and disciplinary strategies, capitalism and its adjacent forms of power is always mutating, and finding new ways of axiomatising (employing *brute force* when pushed into a corner—though this will be the last recourse, given that brute force exposes social machines). All the more reason that resistive work must be a continual process of creativity that seeks to find the ever-changing and dynamic points of resistance, heightening or radicalising capitalism's deterritorialising tendency, at least enough to outpace the second movement of capitalism, reterritorialisation. Resistance must retain a certain mobility, in which it is constantly and always renewed and re-imagined. Indeed, as outright opposition can be so easily engulfed and utilised by capitalism, the crucial lesson is that it must be done from within, and that it must continually adapt. That is also to say that there is no one formal method or means of resistance. As with the BwO, resistance as excess is multiple and dynamic. And if the excess is most evident in those domains where we may engage in experimental practices, then it is those domains and those practices that we must be engaged with. If those domains become commodified, then they too must be transmutated from within, or exceeded so as to create a new domain; finding, tracing and following a line of flight, an excess. This goes back to Nietzsche's idea, as adopted by Deleuze and Guattari (ibid.: 239–40) of *accelerating the process*.

The principle lesson in all this is quite simple: we must change ourselves before we can change our 'politics'. This is a politics that demands that you risk 'yourself', as in the unified and reified ego and the identities by which it is plotted, and to partially forego all that belongs to it. Any system-structure-institutional arrangement, or revolutionary struggle, is likely to perpetuate a hierarchical, repressive and stifling existence, as long as the desiring-machines of which it is comprised are reactive and of bad conscience, without edge, without creative explosive energy, without vitality. This is not to deny the efficaciousness – strategic or otherwise – of utilising micropolitical insights, such as normatively embedding the concept of primordial difference in-itself as a principle, into democratic-based identity politics, as some recommend.[4] Such efforts can and do serve to open up space for practices of the self, or the social re-evaluation of values necessary for transmutational release of the active and the pursuit of pluralism. But one must at the same time recognise that elevating and situating micropolitics within identities and democratic institutions – at least insofar as this is taken to be primary and/or sufficient – is to effectively domesticate and obscure the conceptual point. The intensive-micro level of the unconscious virtual life speaks to a 'profound game of difference and repetition', that permeates, constitutes and more importantly *exceeds* identity (Deleuze 2004a: xix). To start with identity and institutions is to operate at a secondary level, and thus to come in too late.[5]

What is more, micropolitical resistance and the immanent ethics it is necessarily attached to regards an ethic that exceeds that of (re)producing a pluralist and democratic society, though that is most certainly an element of it. It is an ethic primarily concerned with harnessing the fertile and affirmative forces of life, enabling the conditions for a creative explosion of thought that cannot be entirely captured by present institutions, and intuitions, or presupposed in concepts and current practices, by virtue of birthing the 'new'— that which ruptures and exceeds the discursive confines of the thought of past and present and the telos of the future as calculated from and thereby restricted to the logical coordinates of past and present. This is also to say that experimenting with molecular fluxes and creative deterritorialisations is not a mere matter of freedom for freedom's sake, the reawakening of a turgid and outmoded liberal dream tenuously perched on false allusions of grandeur and loosely supported by an inconspicuous theological hangover. It is a matter of life itself, of returning to life those very intensities that affirm difference beyond their own tendency to negate and cancel themselves out in identity or extensities, the release of affirmative modes that seek no divine or metaphysical justification nor explanation for suffering, for existence or for Being. It is a matter, in other words, of creating a new notion and practice of life, and of the political that avoids the seductive trap of transcendence and identity, the nostalgia for binaries and fixed oppositions, and desire for the status quo or its simple negation, its inverted image. Unpredictable though it may be, revolutionary in both method and promise it most certainly is.

This is not to deny, of course, that there are a great many other reasons as to why one should overthrow capitalism and its repressive effects, most of which concern its blatant unsustainability, namely from an environmental and a human perspective (as in extreme exploitation of natural resources and living organisms, the organised enclaves of underdevelopment in exterior [underdeveloped countries] and interior peripheries [ghettoes and council estates] and thus apartheid structures of transnational-class). But, as far as 'pure' immanence is concerned, it is primarily a matter of life-affirmation— though this certainly bears a relation to the issue of unsustainability. Capitalism, either as a form of material exploitation and generator of poverty or as a form of immanent repression, is inherently life-negating. It depends on both organised enclaves of exploitation and underdevelopment and a society of neurotic subjects of lack, guilt and ressentiment. It is a calculative, technical and 'rational' world inconsistent with the expressive vitality of immanent being-as-becoming.

A Dangerous Opportunity

The politics of immanence, which is a micropolitics of post-capitalist emancipation, clearly sides with 'radical' or loosely left-wing post-Marxist thought and action, and locates opportunities to that effect. Where there is opportunity, however, there is also danger, and the ethico-politics being proposed is no less dangerous than a more traditional, or visceral revolutionary politics. There are no guarantees as to the direction a line of flight, and the form an explosion of creative thought, will take. Deleuze and Guattari's (2004b: 305) principle advice in this regard is that we should not operate on either extreme, or either side of abstract poles/planes – the Dionysian chaos of the absolute BwO and the Apollonian form of absolute segments – but rather between them, in the intermezzo. What this means is that the process of actualisation/expression/stratification is in part beneficial, for it provides life with a minimum identity structure and stability suitable to the task of self-to-self and self-to-Other navigation. It provides the very stuff out of which we can transform and guide our selves – an idea first truly formulated by Sartre, i.e. the 'practical ego' – even though, on the other hand, it obscures the true genesis of forms and formation (organisation) and thus the real realm of difference and transformation that operates beyond identity. To go to the extreme of complete disorganisation, or de-stratification, in an act of overt mass destruction of self and Other, is, according to Deleuze and Guattari, highly risky and indeed entirely misguided. For instead of connecting with other lines and each time augmenting their valence, the lines of flight may well spin off into a void, turning to destruction and the passion for abolition: 'like suicide, double suicide, a way out that turns the line of flight into a line of death' (ibid.: 253). This does not refer to any kind of death drive, for, as we know, desire is always assembled; it is what the assemblage determines it to be. It simply refers to an over-accelerated line of flight, one that is too chaotic, and thus too destructive.

There are other ways 'of botching the BwO' (ibid.: 178), the most dangerous, other than that of over-accelerating, is that of existential fear, a kind of bad faith premised on a reactively configured desiring-machine. The more rigid the segmentarity is, the more reassuring it is for us. Thus, though we may engage with subversive practices and enter subversive spaces, it does not take much for us to betray the subversion, and utilise the practice and space, especially where already commodified, as a means to generate a new segment of identity, i.e. *I am* the progressive or radical student; *I am* the punk rocker; *I am* the hippie free-lover; *I am* the moderate and sensible social democrat. We will always have identities, but the point is not to take any of them as permanent, set and destined. In fact, one must be cautious not to overstate the first caution (acceleration) on this basis. It is all too easy for the second caution to become, as it often does, an apology for the adoption of a stable identity and a more traditional academic-liberal mindset, where any revolutionary plunge is too easily denounced as unnecessary or dangerous, without any critical interrogation.

In any case, and with any danger, the practice of authenticity as initially proposed by Sartre is of practical necessity. Only by virtue of a continual and constant negation of self via a practical ego – albeit one premised on an affirmation (of difference, of life) – will we prevent ourselves from slipping too far in either direction: the micro-facism of the absolute abyss or manageable subject of convenience of the segment. Thus to be authentic is not to find some true sense of self, 'to be oneself', that would bring with it, by necessity, a series of exclusive disjunctions that define and manage the coordinates of identity by which a 'stable' self is plotted. To be authentic is to genuinely and honestly – which means, in good humour and flagrant irony – accept that there is no one true self, no one definitive subject as such, that all is open, and to behave in a manner consistent with that fact; one must not take his/her sense of self too seriously, nor get too enthralled with feelings of guilt and remorse as attached to a 'subject who can promise', nor obscure – in behaviour and thought – our procedural and fluctuating nature. The instant one is proclaimed or self-proclaimed authentic, authenticity is turned into an identity, a static and serious state, and thus a negation of difference in-itself, of life. The irony being, then, that taking life 'seriously', particularly the life of the ego, actually negates it. Sartre compares this attitude to that of the lost boys in *Peter Pan*. They consistently resist the demand to grow up and enter the world of seriousness. Instead they wish to stay as innocent children, playful, joyful and affirming. They understand that 'life is a game', and should be treated as such (Sartre 1984: 327). Indeed, the authentic life is equal to that of a child playing different roles and trying on different costumes throughout his or her playtime (a policewoman, a fireman, a doctor), in which the child takes none of these as absolutes, knowing full well that s/he is *more than* a policewoman, a fireman, a doctor and so on. The authentic life of micropolitical resistance is a mode of joyful multiple becoming and affirmation. Which is also to say that micropolitics, despite claims to the contrary, is an existential affair. It concerns a person's existence in the concrete world, in its very core, in his/her very activities, in his/her very desires. Questions of authenticity, bad faith, the responsibility and requirement for the creation of one's own values and one's own way of life and so forth, are all central to practising a micropolitics.

Bio-social evolution is entirely dependent on this authentic, creative, multiple becoming. This, according to 'pure' immanence, is what life means and what it is. And if changing politics is not for the sake of such a life, taken in its earthliest immanent sense, then for what sake is it? And if we do not change our-multiple-selves – the split 'I' that merely speaks to the occasion of an actualised variant of the multiple and unconscious virtual self, as in the i+i+i+i …, OR = n-I, OR = i^n – how could it be possible to change our politics? Conscious deliberation, as I have argued, is a mere surface effect of this more primordial, unconscious and affective level of transformation. Immanence is critical, then, not only because it concerns the validity of a critique that retains a moment of transcendence or grasps more fundamentally the nature of being itself, but principally because it concerns practical philosophy or an ethico-political domain preceding that of traditional politics and the kinds of politics we are told we must enact. Immanence is the ontological centre of a different type of emancipatory politics, where *to be truly radical is to practice a radicalness of existence.*

Notes

1. In his early work, Deleuze (2004a: 277) refers to the system of difference, or more specifically the disjunctive syntheses of difference, as a 'simulacrum' in which identities emerge as surface effects or simulations created by the simulacrum's multiplicity. As the term itself conjures a deeply Platonic image as that of a 'false difference', it has been subject to misinterpretation (see, for example, Badiou 2000: 25). For this reason, Deleuze and Guattari drop the term in favour of 'multiplicities' and the 'rhizome', as in an underground plant that grow horizontally without a fixed centre. Nevertheless, the point apropos the semblance of the ego and identity (and indeed Oedipal desire) remains intact (see Widder 2012: 54–8).
2. For instance, primitive systems of alliance and filiation; despotic or monarchical lateral alliances and filiations, underpinned by a connection to a deity via divine right; or the political and economic interests of a certain class and pervasive and self-perpetuating libidinal investment.
3. By which I mean 'Westernised', though there is undoubtedly a partial symmetry with 'non-Westernised' states and societies, due in part to rampant globalisation and the universalisation of Western practices.
4. William Connolly (1991), for instance, argues that genealogical agonal pluralism (as opposed to Laclau's antagonistic pluralism, see Tønder and Thomassen (2005)) should be injected into the democratic edifice, institutionalising agonal contests so as to allow for a *politics of disturbance* or an ethic of permanent resistance. Paul Patton (2005: 191) argues that Deleuze and Guattari's concept of 'minoritarian becomings provide one important vector of "becoming-democratic" in contemporary societies'. Simons (1995: 116) argues that 'radical liberal democracy constitutes the appropriate political conditions of possibility for his [Foucault's] aesthetics of existence', for it is 'the presence of liberal regimes which make possible the practice of liberty'. See also Nicholas Tampio (2015). Hardt and Negri (2000), for their part, do not propose embedding micropolitical practices within liberal institutions. Far from it. They propose a radical resistance to and implosion of *Empire*,

or rather the world capitalist and bio-political system in its entirety. Nevertheless, their 'multitude as subject' and three political demands proposed by them as a method of animating micropolitical resistance among the multitude ((1) global citizenship; (2) social wage; and (3) the right to reappropriation) is still a politics of segment and identity. That is, it is still macro, to the extent that it obscures the imperativeness of *active* desiring-machines. How are we to encourage and enact this political programme in a society full of reactive desiring-machines?

5. Now this may raise a broader political question of preliminary causes: what conditions will effectuate the BwO, at least enough to provoke it into engaging with practices of self-effectuation? This would no doubt require a study of its own, although a provisional answer can be suggested: conditions of crises. Haphazard conflicts, the crises that arise from or are related to them, and harsher resistances to the virtual-becoming that typically results, provoke an undeterminable series of counter-movements, becomings and creative explosions. As Rainer Maria Rilke (2002: 38) put it: 'without resistance there would be no movement'. And as said, capitalism even seems to provoke the actual material by which such becomings can be actualised.

Bibliography

Adorno, T. W. (1973) *Negative Dialectics*. Trans. E. B. Ashton. London: Routledge and Kegan Paul.
Agamben, G. (2000) 'Absolute Immanence', in Heller-Roazen, D. (ed.) *Potentialities: Collected Essays in Philosophy*. Stanford: Stanford University Press.
Allen, B. (1998) 'Foucault and Modern Political Philosophy', in Moss, J. (ed.) *The Later Foucault*. London: Sage Publications Ltd, pp. 164–98.
Althusser, L. (2005) *For Marx*. London: Verso.
Althusser, L. (2008) *On Ideology*. London: Verso.
Anderson, P. (1983) *In The Tracks of Historical Materialism: Weekly Library Lectures*. London: Verso.
Anderson, T. C. (1993) *Two Ethics: From Authenticity to Integral Humanity*. Chicago: Open Court.
Ansell-Pearson, K. (1999) *Germinal Life: The Difference and Repetition of Deleuze*. New York: Routledge.
Aronson, R. (1978) *Jean-Paul Sartre: Philosophy in the World*. London: Verso.
Badiou, A. (2000) *Deleuze: The Clamor of Being*. Trans. L. Burchill. London: University of Minnesota Press.
Badiou, A. (2006) *Being and Event*. Trans. O. Feltham. London: Continuum.
Badiou, A. (2012) *The Adventures of French Philosophy*. Trans. B. Bosteels. London: Verso.
Barbaras, R. (2004) *The Being of the Phenomenon: Merleau-Ponty's Ontology*. Trans. T. Toadvine and L. Lawlor. Bloomington and Indianapolis: Indiana University Press.
Barnes, H. E. (1974) *Sartre*. London: Quartet Books.
Barrett, W. (1990) *Irrational Man: A Study in Existential Philosophy*. New York: Anchor Books.
Baugh, B. (2003) *French Hegel: From Surrealism to Postmodernism*. New York: Routledge.

Beauvoir, S. (1976) *The Ethics of Ambiguity*. Trans. B. Frechtman. New York: Kensington Publishing Corp.
Beauvoir, S. (1998) 'Merleau-Ponty and Pseudo-Sartreanism', in Stewart, J. (ed.) *The Debate Between Sartre and Merleau-Ponty*. Evanston: Northwestern University Press, pp. 448–90.
Beistegui, M. (2010) *Immanence: Deleuze and Philosophy*. Edinburgh: Edinburgh University Press.
Bergson, H. (1998) *Creative Evolution*. Trans. A. Mitchell. New York: Dover Publications.
Bergson, H. (2001) *Time and Free Will: An Essay on the Immediate Data of Consciousness*. Trans. F. L. Pogson. New York: Dover Publications.
Berlin, I. (2002) 'Two Concepts of Liberty', in Hardy, H. (ed.) *Liberty*. Oxford: Oxford University Press, pp. 166–217.
Bernauer, J. W. and Mahon, M. (2007) 'Michele Foucault's Ethical Imagination', in Gutting, G. (ed.) *The Cambridge Companion to Foucault*. Cambridge: Cambridge Univeristy Press, pp. 149–75.
Boradori, G. (2001) 'The Temporalization of Difference: Reflections on Deleuze's Interpretation of Bergson', *Continental Philosophy Review*, 34 (1), pp. 1–20.
Boundas, C. V. (1996) 'Deleuze-Bergson: An Ontology of the Virtual', in Patton, P. (ed.) *Deleuze: A Critical Reader*. Oxford: Blackwell Publishers Ltd, pp. 81–106.
Bourriaud, N. (2002) *Relational Aesthetics*. Trans. S. Pleasance and F. Woods. Dijon: Le presses du reel.
Brown, W. (1998) 'Genealogical Politics', in Moss, J. (ed.) *The Later Foucault*. London: Sage Publications, pp. 33–49.
Buchanan, I. (2000) *Deleuzism: A Metacommentary*. Edinburgh: Edinburgh University Press.
Buchanan, I. (2008) 'Power, Theory and Praxis', in Buchanan, I. and Thoburn, N. (eds) *Deleuze and Politics*. Edinburgh: Edinburgh University Press, pp. 13–34.
Buchanan, I. and Thoburn, N. (2008) 'Introduction: Deleuze and Politics', in Buchanan, I. and Thoburn, N. (eds) *Deleuze and Politics*. Edinburgh: Edinburgh University Press, pp. 1–12.
Butler, J. (1989) 'Sexual Ideology and Phenomenological Description: A Feminist Critique of Merleau-Ponty's *Phenomenology of Perception*', in Allen, J. and Young, I. M. (eds) *The Thinking Muse*. Bloomington: Indiana University Press.
Butler, J. (1990) *Gender Trouble: Feminism and the Subversion of Identity*. London: Routledge Classics.
Butler, J. (1997) *The Psychic Life of Power: Theories in Subjection*. Stanford: Stanford University Press.
Butler, J. (2012) *Subjects of Desire: Hegelian Reflections in Twentieth-Century France*. New York: Columbia University Press.

Cannon, B. (1985) 'The Death of the Objective Observer: Sartre's Dialectical Reason as an Epistemology for the Social Sciences', *Man and World*, 18, pp 269–93.
Carbone, M. (2004) *The Thinking of the Sensible: Merleau-Ponty's A-Philosophy*. New York: SUNY Press.
Catalano, J. S. (1985) *A Commentary on Jean-Paul Sartre's 'Being and Nothingness'*. Chicago: University of Chicago Press.
Catalano, J. S. (1996) *Good Faith and Other Essays: Perspectives on a Sartrean Ethics*. London: Rowman & Littlefield Publishers.
Catalano, J. S. (1998) 'The Body and the Book: Reading *Being and Nothingness*', in Stewart, J. (ed) *The Debate Between Sartre and Merleau-Ponty*. Evanston: Northwestern University Press, pp. 154–74.
Catalano, J. S. (2005) 'Sartre's Ontology from *Being and Nothingness* to *The Family Idiot Joseph S. Catalano*', in Hoven, A and Leak, A. (eds) *Sartre Today: A Centenary Celebration*. Oxford: Berghahn Books.
Choat, S. (2010) *Marx Through Post-Structuralism: Lyotard, Derrida, Foucault, Deleuze*. London: Continuum.
Cohn, H. W. (1997) *Existential Thought and Therapeutic Practice: An Introduction to Existential Psychotherapy*. London: Sage Publications.
Colebrook, C. (2005) *Philosophy and Post-Structuralist Theory: From Kant to Deleuze*. Edinburgh: Edinburgh University Press.
Colebrook, C. (2008) 'Bourgeois Thermodynamics', in Buchanan, I. and Thoburn, N. (eds) *Deleuze and Politics*. Edinburgh: Edinburgh University Press, pp. 121–38.
Compton, J. J. (1998) 'Sartre, Merleau-Ponty, and Human Freedom', in Stewart, J. (ed.) *The Debate Between Sartre and Merleau-Ponty*. Evanston: Northwestern University Press, pp. 175–86.
Connolly, W. E. (1991) *Identity\Difference: Democratic Negotiations of Political Paradox*. London: University of Minnesota Press.
Connolly, W. E. (1998) 'Beyond Good and Evil: The Ethical Sensibility of Michel Foucault', in Moss, J. (ed.) *The Later Foucault*. London: Sage Publications, pp. 108–28.
Connolly, W. E. (2002) *Neuropolitics: Thinking, Culture, Speed*. London: University of Minnesota Press.
Connolly, W. E. (2005) 'Immanence, Abundance, Democracy', in Tønder, L. and Thomassen, L (eds) *Radical Democracy: Politics Between Abundance and Lack*. Manchester: Manchester University Press, pp. 239–55.
Connolly, W. E. (2012) *A World of Becoming*. London: Duke University Press.
Coole, D. (2007) *Merleau-Ponty and Modern Politics After Anti-Humanism*. Plymouth: Rowman & Littlefield Publishers.
Cooper, D. (1999) *Existentialism: A Reconstruction* (2nd edn). Victoria: Blackwell.

Craib, I. (1976) *Existentialism and Sociology: A Study of Jean-Paul Sartre*. London: Cambridge University Press.
Crittenden, P. (2009) *Sartre in Search of an Ethics*. Newcastle: Cambridge Scholars Publishing.
Cumming, R. D. (1979) 'This Place of Violence, Obscurity and Witchcraft', *Political Theory*, 7 (2), pp. 181–200.
Danto, C. (1975) *Sartre* (2nd edn). London: Fontana Press.
Davidson, A. (1986) 'Archaeology, Genealogy, Ethics', in Hoy, D. C. (ed.) *Foucault: A Critical Reader*. Oxford: Basil Blackwell, pp. 221–34.
Deleuze, G. (1991) *Bergsonism*. Trans. H. Tomlinson and B. Habberjam. New York: Zone Books.
Deleuze, G. (1992) *Expressionism in Philosophy: Spinoza*. Trans. M. Joughin. New York: Zone Books.
Deleuze, G. (1995) *Negotiations: 1972–1990*. Trans. M. Joughin. New York: Columbia University Press.
Deleuze, G. (1997) *Appendix. Review of Jean Hyppolite, Logique et existence*, in Hyppolite, J., *Logic and Existence*. Trans. L. Lawlor and A. Sen. New York: State University of New York Press.
Deleuze, G. (2001) *Pure Immanence: Essays on A Life*. Trans. A. Boyman. New York: Zone Books.
Deleuze, G. (2002) *Desert Islands and Other Texts: 1953–1974*. Trans. M. Taormina. London: Semiotext(e).
Deleuze, G. (2004a) *Difference and Repetition*. Trans. P. Patton. London: Continuum.
Deleuze, G. (2004b) *The Logic of Sense*. Trans. M. Lester. London: Continuum.
Deleuze, G. (2006a) *Dialogues II*. Trans. H. Tomlison, B. Habberjam and E. Ross Albert. London: Continuum.
Deleuze, G. (2006b) *The Fold: Leibniz and the Baroque*. Trans. T. Conley. London: Continuum.
Deleuze, G. (2006c) *Foucault*. Trans. S. Hand. London: Continuum.
Deleuze, G. (2006d) *Nietzsche and Philosophy*. Trans. H. Thomlinson. London: Continuum.
Deleuze, G. (2007) *Two Regimes of Madness: Texts and Interviews 1975–1995*. New York: Semiotext(e).
Deleuze, G. (2013) *Francis Bacon: The Logic of Sensation*. Trans. D. W. Smith. London: Bloomsbury.
Deleuze, G. and Guattari, F. (1994) *What is Philosophy?* Trans. H. Tomlinson and G. Burchell. New York: Columbia University Press.
Deleuze, G. and Guattari, F. (2004a) *Anti-Oedipus: Capitalism and Schizophrenia*. Trans. R. Hurley, M. Seem and H. R. Lane. London: Continuum.
Deleuze, G. and Guattari, F. (2004b) *A Thousand Plateaus: Capitalism and Schizophrenia*. Trans. B. Massumi. London: Continuum.

Descartes, R. (1969) *Discourse on Method and The Meditations*. Trans. F. E. Sutcliffe. London: Penguin Books.

Detmer, D. (2005) 'Sartre on Freedom and Education', in Hoven, A. van den and Leak, A. (eds) *Sartre Today: A Centenary Celebration*. Oxford: Berghahn Books.

Devenney, M. (2002) 'Critical Theory and Democracy', in Finlayson, A. and Valentine, J. (eds) *Politics and Post-Structuralism*. Edinburgh: Edinburgh University Press, pp. 176–93.

Dews, P. (2007) *Logics of Disintegration: Post-Structuralist Thought and the Claims of Critical Theory*. London: Verso.

Downing, L. (2008) *The Cambridge Introduction to Michele Foucault*. New York: Cambridge University Press.

Dreyfus, L. H. (2002) 'Intelligence without representation: Merleau-Ponty's Critique of Mental Representation', *Phenomenology and the Cognitive Sciences*, 1 (4), pp. 367–83.

Dreyfus. L. H. and Rabinow. P. (1983) *Michel Foucault: Beyond Structuralism and Hermeneutics* (2nd edn). Chicago: University of Chicago Press.

Duncan, J. (2005) 'Sartre and Realism-All-the-Way-Down', in Hoven, A. van den and Leak, A. (eds) *Sartre Today: A Centenary Celebration*. New York: Berghahn Books.

Fell. P. J. (1979) *Heidegger and Sartre: An Essay on Being and Place*. New York: Columbia University Press.

Flynn, T. R. (1997) 'An End to Authority: Epistemology and Politics in the Later Sartre', in McBride, W. L. (ed.) *Existentialist Politics and Political Theory*. London: Garland Publishing, Inc., pp. 50–67.

Flynn, T. R. (2005a) 'Introduction: Sartre at One Hundred – a Man of the Nineteenth Century Addressing the Twenty-First?', in van den Hoven, A. and Leak, A. (eds) *Sartre Today: A Century Celebration*. Oxford: Berghahn Books, pp. 1–14.

Flynn, T. R. (2005b) *Sartre, Foucault, and Historical Reason: Volume Two, A Postructuralist Mapping of History*. London: University of Chicago Press.

Foucault, M. (1980a) 'The Confession of the Flesh', in Gordon, C. (ed.) *Power/Knowledge: Selected Interviews and Other Writings 1972–1977*. New York: Vintage Books, pp. 194–228.

Foucault, M. (1980b) 'Truth and Power', in Gordon, C. (ed.) *Power/Knowledge: Selected Interviews and Other Writings 1972–1977*. New York: Vintage Books, pp. 109–133.

Foucault, M. (1981) 'The Order of Discourse', in Young, R. (ed.) *Untying The Text: A Poststructuralist Reader*. Boston: Routledge & Kegan Paul Ltd, pp. 48–78.

Foucault, M. (1988) 'The Ethic of Care of the Self as a Practice of Freedom', in Bernauer, J. and Rasmussen, D. (eds) *The Final Foucault*. Cambridge, MA: The MIT Press, pp. 1–20.

Foucault, M. (1990) *The Care of The Self: The History of Sexuality Volume 3*. Trans. R. Hurley. London: Penguin.
Foucault, M. (1991a) *Discipline and Punish: the Birth of the Prison*. Trans. A. Sheridan. London: Penguin Books.
Foucault, M. (1991b) 'Nietzsche, Genealogy, History', in Rabinow, P. (ed.) *The Foucault Reader: An Introduction to Foucault's Thought*. London: Penguin Books, pp. 76–100.
Foucault, M. (1991c) 'On the Genealogy of Ethics: An Overview of Work in Progress', in Ranibow, P. (ed.) *The Foucault Reader: An Introduction to Foucault's Thought*. London: Penguin Books, pp. 340–72.
Foucault, M. (1991d) 'Politics and Ethics: An Interview', in Rabinow, P. (ed.) *The Foucault Reader: An Introduction to Foucault's Thought*. London: Penguin Books, pp. 373–80.
Foucault, M. (1991e) 'What is Enlightenment', in Rabinow, P. (ed.) *The Foucault Reader: An Introduction to Foucault's Thought*. London: Penguin Books, pp. 32–50.
Foucault, M. (1992) *The Use of Pleasure: The History of Sexuality Volume 2*. Trans R. Hurley. London: Penguin.
Foucault, M. (1996) 'The Ethics of the Concern for Self', in Lotringer, L. (ed.) *Foucault Live: Michele Foucault: Collected Interviews, 1961–1984*. London: Semiotext(e), pp. 432–49.
Foucault, M. (1998) *The Will to Knowledge: The History of Sexuality: Volume One*. Trans. R. Hurley. London: Penguin.
Foucault, M. (2000a) 'Life: Experience and Science', in Faubion, J. D. (ed.) *Aesthetics, Method, and Epistemology*. Trans R. Hurley and Others. London: Penguin Books, pp. 465–78.
Foucault, M. (2000b) 'Theatrum Philosophicum', in Faubion, J. D. (ed.) *Aesthetics, Method, and Epistemology*. Trans R. Hurley and Others. London: Penguin Books, pp. 343–68.
Foucault, M. (2001a) 'Interview with Michel Foucault', in Faubion, J. D. (ed.) *Michele Foucault: Power: Essential Works of Foucault 1954–1984*. London: Penguin Books, pp. 239–97.
Foucault, M. (2001b) 'Truth and Juridical Forms', in Faubion, J. D. (ed.) *Michele Foucault: Power: Essential Works of Foucault 1954–1984*. London: Penguin Books, pp. 1–89.
Foucault, M. (2001c) 'The Subject and Power', in Faubion, J. D. (ed.) *Michele Foucault: Power: Essential Works of Foucault 1954–1984*. London: Penguin Books, pp. 326–49.
Foucault, M. (2002a) *The Archaeology of Knowledge*. Trans. S. A. M. Smith. London: Penguin.
Foucault, M. (2002b) *The Order of Things: An Archaeology of the Human Sciences*. London: Routledge.
Foucault, M. (2003) *The Birth of the Clinic: An Archaeology of Medical Perception*. Trans. A. M. Sheridan. London: Routledge Classics.

Foucault, M. (2004) 'Preface', in Deleuze, G. and Guattari, F. (eds) *Anti-Oedipus: Capitalism and Schizophrenia*. London: Continuum. pp. xiii–xvi.

Foucault, M. (2008a) *Introduction to Kant's Anthropology from a Pragmatic Perspective*. Cambridge, MA: The MIT Press.

Foucault, M. (2008b) 'Two Lectures', in Roach, S. C. (ed.) *Critical Theory and International Relations*. London: Routledge, pp. 317–25.

Fox, N. F. (2003) *The New Sartre: Explorations in Postmodernism*. London: Continuum.

Fraser, N. (1989) *Unruly Practices: Power, Discourse and Gender in Contemporary Social Theory*. Cambridge: Polity Press.

Freud, S. (1997) *The Interpretation of Dreams*. Trans. A. A. Brill. St Ives: Wordsworth.

Freud, S. (2005) 'On the Pleasure and the Reality Principle', in Freud, A. (2005) *The Essential Freud*. Trans. J. Strachey. London: Vintage, pp. 505–17.

Frie, R. (2012) 'Existential Therapy and Post-Cartesian Psychoanalysis: Historical Perspectives and Confluence', in Barnett, L. and Madison, G. (eds) *Existential Psychotherapy: Legacy, Vibrancy and Dialogue*. London: Routledge, pp. 21–33.

Frosh, S. (1997) *For and Against Psychoanalysis* (2nd edn). London: Routledge.

Gardner, S. (2009) *Sartre's Being and Nothingness: A Reader's Guide*. London: Continuum.

Gatens, M. (1996) 'Through a Spinozist Lens: Ethology, Difference, Power', in Patton, P. (ed.) *Deleuze: A Critical Reader*. Oxford: Blackwell Publishers Ltd, pp. 162–87.

Genosko, G. (2012) 'Deleuze and Guattari: Guattareuze & Co.', in Smith, D. W. and Somers-Hall, H. (eds) *The Cambridge Companion to Deleuze*. Cambridge: Cambridge University Press, pp. 151–69.

Gillan, G. J. (1997) 'A Question of Method: History and Critical Experience', in McBride, W. L. (ed) *Existentialist Politics and Political Theory*. London: Garland Publishing, pp. 193–206.

Gilliam, C. (2013) 'Existential Boredom Re-examined: Boredom as Authenticity and Life-Affirmation', *Existential Analysis*, 24 (2), pp. 250–62.

Grace, W. (2009) 'Faux Amis: Foucault and Deleuze on Sexuality and Desire', *Critical Inquiry*, 36 (1), pp. 52–75.

Grimsley, R. (1955) 'An Aspect of Sartre and the Unconscious', *Philosophy*, 30 (112), pp. 33–44.

Grosz, E. (1999) 'Merleau-Ponty and Irigaray in the Flesh', in Olkowskie, D. and Morley, J. (eds) *Merleau-Ponty, Interiority and Exteriority, Psychic Life and the World*. New York: SUNY Press, pp. 145–66.

Habermas, J. (1987) *The Philosophical Discourses of Modernity*. Trans. F. Lawrence. Cambridge, MA: The MIT Press.
Hacking, I. (1986) 'The Archaeology of Foucault', in Hoy, D. C. (ed.) *Foucault: A Critical Reader*. Oxford: Basil Blackwell Ltd, pp. 27–40.
Hall, R. (1998) 'Freedom: Merleau-Ponty's Critique of Sartre', in Stweart, J. (ed.) *The Debate between Sartre and Merleau-Ponty*. Evanston: Northwestern University Press.
Hardt, M. and Negri, A. (2000) *Empire*. London: Harvard University Press.
Hatzimoysis, A. (2011) *The Philosophy of Sartre*. Durham: Acumen.
Heidegger, M. (1971) 'Building, Dwelling, Thinking', in *Heidegger, Poetry, Language, Thought*. Trans. A. Hofstadter. New York: Harper and Row, pp. 141–60.
Heidegger, M. (2012) *Contributions to Philosophy: Of the Event*. Trans. R. Rojcewicz and D. Vallega-Neu. Indiana: Indiana University Press.
Hendley, S. (1991) *Reason and Relativism: A Sartrean Investigation*. New York: SUNY Press.
Hindes, B. (1998) 'Politics and Liberation', in Moss, J. (ed.) *The Later Foucault*. London: Sage Publications, pp. 50–63.
Holland, E. W. (2008) 'Schizoanalysis, Nomadology, Fascism', in Buchanan, I. and Thoburn, N. (eds) *Deleuze and Politics*. Edinburgh: Edinburgh University Press.
Holland, E. W. (2012) 'Deleuze and Psychoanalysis', in Smith, D. W. and Somers-Hall, H. (eds) *The Cambridge Companion to Deleuze*. Cambridge: Cambridge University Press, pp. 307–36.
Houlgate, S. (1986) *Hegel, Nietzsche and the Criticism of Metaphysics*. Cambridge: Cambridge University Press.
Hoy, D. C. (1986) 'Power, Repression, Progress: Foucault, Lukes, and the Frankfurt School', in Hoy, D. C. (ed.) *Foucault: A Critical Reader*. Oxford: Basil Blackwell, pp. 123–48.
Hoy, D. C. (1998) 'Foucault and Critical Theory', in Moss, J. (ed.) *The Later Foucault*. London: Sage Publications, pp. 18–32.
Husserl, E. (2001) *Logical Investigations: Vol 1*. Trans. J. N. Findlay. London: Routledge.
Husserl, E. (2012) *Ideas: General Introduction to Pure Phenomenology*. Trans. W. R. Boyce Gibson. London: Routledge Classics.
Ingram, D. (2007) 'Foucault and Habermas', in Gutting, G. (ed.) *The Cambridge Companion to Foucault* (2nd edn). Cambridge: Cambridge University Press.
Irigaray, L. (1993) 'The Invisible of the Flesh: A Reading of Merleau-Ponty, *The Visible and the Invisible*, 'The Intertwining—The Chiasm', in *An Ethics of Sexual Difference*. Trans. C. Burke and G. C. Gill. London: Athlone, pp. 151–84.

Jay, M. (1986) 'In the Empire of the Gaze: Foucault and the Denigration of Vision in Twentieth-century French Thought', in Hoy, D. C. (ed.) *Foucault: A Critical Reader*. Oxford: Basil Blackwell, pp. 157–74.

Jung, H. Y. (1971) 'The Political Relevance of Existential Phenomenology', *The Review of Politics*, 33 (4), pp. 538–63, [online] accessed at <http://www.jstor.org/stable/1406378> (last accessed 10 January 2011).

Kazashi, N. (1999) 'Bodily Logos: James, Merleau-Ponty, and Nishida', in Olkowski, D. and Morely, J. (eds) *Merleau-Ponty, Interiority and Exteriority, Psychic Life and the World*. New York: SUNY Press, pp. 107–20.

Kerslake, C. (2009) *Immanence and the Vertigo of Philosophy: From Kant to Deleuze*. Edinburgh: Edinburgh University Press.

Kierkegaard, S. (2000) 'The Concept of Anxiety', in Hong, H. V. and Hong, E. H. (eds) *The Essential Kierkegaard*. Princeton: Princeton University Press, pp. 138–55.

Kline, M. (1990) *Mathematical Thought from Ancient to Modern Times*. Oxford: Oxford University Press.

Kwant, R. C. (1963) *The Phenomenological Philosophy of Merleau-Ponty*. Pittsburgh: Duquesne University Press.

Lacan, J. (2001) *Écrits: A Selection*. Trans. A. Sheridan. London: Routledge Classics.

Laclau, E. (2000) 'Identity and Hegemony: The Role of Universality in the Constitution of Political Logos', in Butler, J. et al (eds) *Contingency, Hegemony, Universality: Contemporary Dialogues on the Left*. London: Verso, pp. 44–89.

Laclau, E. (2001) 'Can Immanence Explain Social Struggles?', *Diacritics*, 31 (4), pp. 3–10.

Laclau, E. (2007) *Emancipation(s)*. London: Verso.

Laclau, E. and Mouffe, C. (2001) *Hegemony and Socialist Strategy: Towards a Radical Democratic Politics* (2nd edn). London: Verso.

Lambert, G. (2008) 'Deleuze and the Political Ontology of Politics in the Work of Gilles Deleuze', in Buchanan, I. and Thoburn, N. (eds) *Deleuze and Politics*. Edinburgh: Edinburgh University Press, pp. 35–53.

Landes, D. A. (2013) *Merleau-Ponty and the Paradoxes of Expression*. London: Bloomsbury.

Langer, M. (1998) 'Sartre and Merleau-Ponty: A Reappraisal', in Stewart, J. (ed.) *The Debate Between Sartre and Merleau-Ponty*. Evanston: Northwestern University Press, pp. 93–120.

Lawlor, L. (2006) *The Implications of Immanence: Toward a New Concept of Life*. New York: Fordham University Press.

Levinas, E. (1990) 'Sensibility', in Johnson, G. and Smith, M. (eds) *Ontology and Alterity in Merleau-Ponty*. Evanston: Northwestern University Press, pp. 47–90.

Lord, B. (2010) *Kant and Spinozism: Transcendental Idealism and Immanence from Jacobi to Deleuze*. Basingstoke: Palgrave Macmillan.
Lukács, G. (1949) 'Existentialism', in Lukács, G. (1973) *Marxism and Human Liberation: Essays on History, Culture and Revolution*. New York: Dell Publishing.
Lukes, S. (2005) *Power: A Radical View* (2nd edn). Basingstoke: Palgrave Macmillan.
McCumber, J. (2011) *Time and Philosophy: A History of Continental Thought*. Durham: Acumen.
Malabou, C. (1996) 'Who's Afraid of Hegelian Wolves', in Patton, P. (ed.) *Deleuze: A Critical Reader*. Oxford: Blackwell Publishers, pp. 114–38.
Mallin, S. (1979) *Merleau-Ponty's Philosophy*. New Haven: Yale University Press.
Marcherey, P. (1996) 'The Encounter with Spinoza', in Patton, P. (ed.) *Deleuze: A Critical Reader*. Oxford: Blackwell Publishers, pp. 139–61.
Marcuse, H. (1948) 'Existentialism: Remarks on Jean-Paul Sartre's *L'Être et le néant*', *Philosophy and Phenomenological Research*, 8 (3), pp. 310–36: New Jersey:Wiley, [online] accessed at <http://www.marcuse.org/herbert/pubs/40spubs/48hmsartre.pdf?sici=0002-8762(194904)54%3A3%3C557%3AEOFAP%3E2.0.CO;2-F> (last accessed 28 June 2012).
Margarit, E. (2012) 'Deleuze Transcendental Empiricism as Exercise of Thought: Hume's Case', *Research in Hermeneutics, Phenomenology, and Practical Philosophy*, 4 (2), pp. 377–403.
Martinot, S. (1993) 'L'Esprit objectif as a Theory of Language', *Man and World*, 26, pp. 45–62.
Marx, K. and Engels, F. (2002) *The Communist Manifesto*. Trans. S. Moore. London: Penguin Classics.
May, T. (1993) *Between Genealogy and Epistemology: Psychology, Politics, and Knowledge in the Thought of Michel Foucault*. Pennsylvania: Pennsylvania State University Press.
May, T. (2003) 'Foucault's Relation to Phenomenology', in Gutting, G. (ed.) *The Cambridge Companion to Foucault* (2nd edn). Cambridge: Cambridge University Press, pp. 284–311.
Mengue, P. (2003) *Deleuze et la question de la démocratie*. Paris: L'Harmattan.
Merleau-Ponty, M. (1964a) *Sense and Non-Sense*. Trans. H. L. Dreyfus and P. A. Dreyfus. Evanston: Northwestern University Press.
Merleau-Ponty, M. (1964b) *Signs*. Trans. R. C. McCleary. Evanston: Northwestern University Press.
Merleau-Ponty, M. (1968) *The Visible and the Invisible*. Trans. A. Lingis. Evanston: Northwestern University Press.
Merleau-Ponty, M. (1998) 'Sartre and Ultrabolshevism', in Setwart,

J. (ed.) *The Debate between Sartre and Merleau-Ponty*. Evanston: Northwestern University Press, pp. 355–447.
Merleau-Ponty, M. (2002) *Phenomenology of Perception*. Trans. C. Smith. London: Routledge Classics.
Merleau-Ponty, M. (2003) *Nature: Course Notes from the Collège de France*. Trans. R. Vallier. Evanston: Northwestern University Press.
Merleau-Ponty, M. (2004a) 'The Crisis of Understanding', in Baldwin, T. (ed.) *Maurice Merleau-Ponty: Basic Writtings*. London: Routledge, pp. 325–45.
Merleau-Ponty, M. (2004b) 'Eye and Mind', in Baldwin, T. (ed.) *Maurice Merleau-Ponty: Basic Writtings*. London: Routledge, pp. 290–324.
Miller, J. (1979) *History and Human Existence: From Marx to Merleau-Ponty*. London: University of California Press.
Miller, J. (1993) *The Passion of Michel Foucault*. London: Flamingo.
Mills, S. (2003) *Michel Foucault*. New York: Routledge.
Molina, F. (1962) *Existentialism as Philosophy*. New Jersey: Prentice Hall.
Moss, J. (1998) 'Foucault, Rawls and Public Reason', in Moss, J. (ed.) *The Later Foucault*. London: Sage Publications, pp. 149–63.
Mouffe, C. (2005) *The Return of the Political*. London: Verso.
Moulard-Leonard, V. (2002) *Bergson-Deleuze Encounters: Transcendental Experience and Thought of the Virtual*. New York: SUNY Press.
Mullhall, S. and Swift, A. (1992) *Liberals and Communitarians: An Introduction*. Oxford: Blackwell Publishers.
Nietzsche, F. W. (1968) *The Will to Power*. Trans. W. Kauffman. New York: Vintage.
Nietzsche, F. W. (2000a) 'Ecce Homo', in Kaufmann, W. (ed.) *Basic Writings of Nietzsche*. Trans. W. Kaufmann. New York: The Modern Library, pp. 655–802.
Nietzsche, F. W. (2000b) 'The Genealogy of Morals', in Kaufmann, W. (ed.) *Basic Writings of Nietzsche*. Trans. W. Kaufmann. New York: The Modern Library, pp. 437–600.
Norris, C. (1993) *The Truth about Postmodernism*. Oxford: Basil Blackwell.
Novack, G. (1972) *Understanding History: Marxist Essays*. New York: Pathfinder Press.
Olssen, M. (2006) *Michel Foucault: Materialism and Education*. London: Paradigm.
Paras, E. (2006) *Foucault 2.0: Beyond Power and Knowledge*. New York: Other Press.
Patton, P. (1998) 'Foucault's Subject of Power', in Moss, J. (ed.) *The Later Foucault*. London: Sage Publications, pp. 64–77.
Patton, P. (2000) *Deleuze and the Political*. London: Routledge.
Patton, P. (2005) 'Deleuze and Democratic Politics', in Tønder L. and

Thomassen, L (eds) *Radical Democracy: Politics between Abundance and Lack*. Manchester: Manchester University Press, pp. 50–67.
Patton, P. (2008) 'Becoming Democratic', in Buchanan, I. and Thoburn, N. (eds) *Deleuze and Politics*. Edinburgh: Edinburgh University Press, pp. 178–95.
Plato (1980) 'Meno', in Thomas, J. E. (ed./trans.) *Musings on the Meno*. London: Martinus Nijhoff Publishers.
Poster, M. (1986) 'Foucault and the Tyranny of Greece', in Hoy, D. C. (ed.) *Foucault: A Critical Reader*. Oxford: Basil Blackwell, pp. 205–20.
Poulantzas, N. (2014) *State, Power, Socialism*. London: Verso.
Protevi, J. (2000) 'A Problem of Pure Matter: Fascist Nihilism in *A Thousand Plateaus*', in Ansell-Pearson, K. and Morgan, D. (eds) *Nihilism Now! Monsters of Energy*. London: Macmillan, pp. 167–88.
Putnam, H. (1983) *Realism and Reason: Philosophical Papers: Volume 3*. Cambridge: Cambridge University Press.
Racevskis, K. (1991) 'Michel Foucault, Rameau's Nephew and the Question of Identity', in Bernauer, J. and Rasmussen, D. (eds) *The Final Foucault*. Cambridge, MA: The MIT Press.
Ransom, J. S. (1997) *Foucault's Discipline: the Politics of Subjectivity*. London: Duke University Press.
Read, J. (1998) 'The Age of Cynicism: Deleuze and Guattari on the Production of Subjectivity in Capitalism', in Buchanan, I. and Thoburn, N. (eds) *Deleuze and Politics*. Edinburgh: Edinburgh University Press, pp. 139–59.
Read, J. (2003) *The Micro-Politics of Capital: Marx and the Prehistory of the Present*. New York: SUNY Press.
Riemann, B. (2007) 'On the Hypotheses that Lie at the Foundations of Geometry', in Peter, P. (ed.) *Beyond Geometry: Classic Papers from Riemann to Einstein*. New York: Dover Publications.
Rilke, R. M. (2002) *Letters on Cézanne*. Trans. J. Agee. New York: North Point Press.
Rorty, R. (1986) 'Foucault and Epistemology', in Hoy, D. C. (ed.) *Foucault: A Critical Reader*. Oxford: Basil Blackwell, pp. 41–50.
Sandel, M. (1998) *Liberalism and the Limits of Justice* (2nd edn). Cambridge: Cambridge University Press.
Sartre, J. P. (1957) *The Transcendence of the Ego: An Existentialist Theory of Consciousness*. Trans. F. Williams and R. Kirkpatrick. New York: The Noonday Press.
Sartre, J. P. (1963a) *Saint Genet: Actor and Martyr*. Trans B. Frechtman. Minneapolis: University of Minnesota Press.
Sartre, J. P. (1963b) *Search For a Method*. Trans. H. E. Barnes. New York: Vintage Books.
Sartre, J. P. (1969). 'Itinerary of Thought', *New Left Review*, 58, pp. 48–66.

Sartre, J. P. (1976a) *Anti-Semite and Jew: An Exploration of the Etiology of Hate*. Trans. G. J. Becker. New York: Schocken Books.
Sartre, J. P. (1976b) *Critique of Dialectical Reason I: Theory of Practical Ensembles*. Trans. A. Sheridan-Smith. Paris: Éditions Gallimard.
Sartre, J. P. (1981) *The Family Idiot*, Volume 1. Trans. C. Cosmon. Chicago: University of Chicago Press.
Sartre, J. P. (1984) *War Diaries: Notes from a Phoney War, November 1939–March 1940*. London: Verso.
Sartre, J. P. (1988) *Life/Situations: Essays Written and Spoken*. New York: Random House.
Sartre, J. P. (1990) *In Camera and Other Plays*. Trans. K. Black and S. Gilbert. London: Penguin.
Sartre, J. P. (1992) *Notebooks for an Ethics*. Trans. D. Pellauer. Chicago: University of Chicago Press.
Sartre, J. P. (2000) *Nausea*. Trans. R. Baldick. London: Penguin.
Sartre, J. P. (2001) *What is Literature?* Trans. B. Frechtman. London: Routledge.
Sartre, J. P. (2002) *Sketch for a Theory of the Emotions*. Trans. P. Mairet. London: Routledge.
Sartre, J. P. (2004) *The Transcendence of the Ego*. London: Routledge Classics.
Sartre, J. P. (2006) *Critique of Dialectical Reason II (Unfinished)*. Trans. Q. Hoare. London: Verso.
Sartre, J. P. (2007) *Existentialism & Humanism*. Trans. P. Mairet. London: Methuen.
Sartre, J. P. (2008a) *Being and Nothingness: An Essay on Phenomenological Ontology*. Trans. H. E. Barnes. London: Routledge.
Sartre, J. P. (2008b) *Between Existentialism and Marxism*. London: Verso.
Sartre, J. P. (2010) *The Imaginary: A Phenomenological Psychology of the Imagination*. Trans. J. Webber. London: Routledge.
Sartre, J. P. (2013) *We Have Only This Life to Live: The Selected Essays of Jean-Paul Sartre 1939–1975*. Ed. R. Aronson and A. Van Den Hoven. New York: New York Review Books.
Silverman, H. J. (1993) 'Cézanne's Mirror Stage', in Johnson, G. A. (ed.) *The Merleau-Ponty Aestehtics Reader*. Evanston: Northwestern University Press, pp. 262–77.
Simons, J. (1995) *Foucault & the Political*. London: Routledge.
Smith, D. (2003) 'Deleuze and Derrida, Immanence and Transcendence: Two Directions in Recent French Thought', in Patton, P. and Protevi, J. (eds) *Between Deleuze and Derrida*. London: Continuum, pp. 46–66.
Smith, M. B (1999) 'Transcendence in Merleau-Ponty', in Olkowskie, D. and Morley, J. (eds) *Merleau-Ponty, Interiority and Exteriority, Psychic Life and the World*. New York: SUNY Press, pp. 35–46.

Somers-Hall, H. (2006) 'Symposium', *Canadian Journal of Continental Philosophy/Revue canadienne de philosophie continentale*, 10 (1), pp. 213–21.
Somers-Hall, H. (2012) *Hegel, Deleuze, and the Critique of Representation: Dialectics of Negation and Difference*. New York: SUNY Press.
Stewart, J. (1998) 'Merleau-Ponty's Criticisms of Sartre', in Stewart, J. (ed.) *The Debate between Sartre and Merleau-Ponty*. Evanston: Northwestern University Press, pp. 197–216.
Tampio, N. (2015) *Deleuze's Political Vision*. New York: Rowman & Littlefield.
Taylor, C. (1976) 'Responsibility for Self', in Rorty, A. O. (ed.) *The Identities of Persons*. Los Angeles: University of California Press, pp. 281–99.
Taylor, C. (1986) 'Foucault on Freedom and Truth', in Hoy, D. C. (ed.) *Foucault: A Critical Reader*. Oxford: Basil Blackwell, pp. 69–102.
Taylor, C. (1989) *Sources of the Self: The Making of the Modern Identity*. Cambridge: Cambridge University Press.
Thoburn, N. (2003) *Deleuze, Marx and Politics*. London: Routledge.
Tiebout, H. M. (1959) 'Tillich, Existentialism and Psychoanalysis', *The Journal of Philosophy*, 56 (14), pp. 605–12.
Tønder, L. and Thomassen, L. (2005) 'Rethinking Radical Democracy between Abundance and Lack', in Tønder, L. and Thomassen, L. (eds) *Radical Democracy: Politics Between Abundance and Lack*. Manchester: Manchester University Press, pp. 1–13.
Vaz, A. (1995) 'Who's Got the Look? Sartre's Gaze and Foucault's Panopticism', *Dalhousie French Studies*, 32, pp. 33–45.
Voss, D. (2013) 'The Philosophical Concept of Meat and Flesh: Deleuze and Merleau-Ponty', *Parrhesia*, 18, pp. 113–24.
Waltzer, M. (1986) 'The Politics of Michel Foucault', in Hoy, D. C. (ed.) *Foucault: A Critical Reader*. Oxford: Basil Blackwell, pp. 51–68.
Wambacq, J. (2011) 'Maurice Merleau-Ponty's Criticism of Bergson's Theory of Time Seen Through the Work of Gilles Deleuze', *Studia Phaenomenologica*, 11 (1), pp. 309–25.
Warnock, M. (1970) *Existentialism*. London: Oxford University Press.
Warren, M. (1988) *Nietzsche and Political Thought*. Cambridge, MA: The MIT Press.
Weiss, G. (1999) 'Body Image Intercourse: A Corporeal Dialogue between Merleau-Ponty and Schilder', in Olkowskie, D. and Morley, J. (eds) *Merleau-Ponty, Interiority and Exteriority, Psychic Life and the World*. New York: SUNY Press, pp. 121–44.
Widder, N. (2002) *Genealogies of Difference*. Chicago: University of Illinois Press.
Widder, N. (2004) 'Foucault and Power Revisited', *European Journal of Political Theory*, 3 (4), pp. 411–32.

Widder, N. (2008) *Reflections on Times and Politics*. Pennsylvania: The Pennsylvania State University Press.
Widder, N. (2012) *Political Theory After Deleuze*. London: Continuum.
Williams, J. (2011) *Gilles Deleuze's Philosophy of Time: A Critical Introduction and Guide*. Edinburgh: Edinburgh University Press.
Wolin, R. (2004) *The Seduction of Unreason: The Intellectual Romance with Fascism, from Nietzsche to Postmodernism*. Oxford: Princeton University Press.
Young, I. (2005) *On Female Body Experience*. Oxford: Oxford University Press.
Yovel, Y. (1991) *Spinoza and Other Heretics: The Adventures of Immanence: The Adventures of Immanence, v. 2*. Princeton: Princeton University Press.
Žižek, S. (1999) *The Ticklish Subject: The Absent Centre of Political Ontology*. London: Verso.
Žižek, S. (2006a) 'Da Capo senza Fine', in Butler, J., Laclau, E. and Žižek, S. (eds) *Contingency, Hegemony, Universality: Contemporary Dialogues on the Left*. London: Verso.
Žižek, S. (2006b) 'Schlagend, aber nicht Treffend!', *Critical Inquiry*, 33 (1), pp. 185–211.
Žižek, S. (2008) *The Sublime Object of Ideology*. London: Verso.
Žižek, S. (2011) *Living in the End Times*. London: Verso.
Žižek, S. (2012a) *Organs without Bodies: On Deleuze and Consequences*. London: Routledge Classics.
Žižek, S. (2012b) *Welcome to the Desert of the Real*. London: Verso.

Index

abundance, x, 5, 8, 11, 133, 149; *see also* lack
active destruction, 51, 149, 150, 165, 184
actual (also actualisation), 8–17, 25, 27, 32, 36, 44–51, 56, 60, 66, 72, 83–88, 99–100, 104, 120, 132–44, 148, 150–1, 154, 158, 162–9, 174–5, 178, 180, 183–7; *see also* virtual
aesthetics, 57, 85–9
affectivity (also affect), 3, 8, 16, 48, 68–9, 73, 87–92, 96, 106, 121–5, 127, 132, 140, 146, 148–50, 161–5, 172, 185
agency, 24, 27, 50, 126, 137
agonism, 20, 127, 177; *see also* antagonism
Althusser, Louis, 3, 6, 16, 129n.9
antagonism, 6, 20n.16, 44, 47, 117, 186n.4; *see also* agonism
anti-humanism, 56, 90; *see also* humanism
anti-representation, 98
Apollo, 12, 183
assemblage, 24, 44–6, 48, 52, 69, 114, 126–7, 132–3, 151, 155, 161–2, 166, 171, 174, 178–9, 184; *see also* dispositif
austerity, 178
authenticity (also authentic), 24, 43, 49–52, 55–7, 69, 91, 93, 124, 130, 164, 166, 177, 184, 185
axiomatic, vii, 11, 49, 132, 155, 156, 162, 164, 174, 175, 179, 181

Bacon, Francis, 91
bad conscience, 126, 157–62, 165, 175, 182
bad faith, 34, 40–3, 51, 184–5
Badiou, Alain, 9, 19n.11, 21, 170
Baroque, 142–4
becoming
   active destruction, 150
   becoming and affirming, 185
   becoming a BwO, 131, 162–5, 172, 183
   Becoming Other, 172, 179, 180
   creative becoming, 148
   preliminary causes, 187

being-in-the-world
   Heidegger, 5, 9
   Merleau-Ponty, 61–74, 79, 82, 85–92
   Sartre, 23–59
Bergson, Henri (also Bergsonian), 32, 33, 72, 79, 83–4, 109, 135–6, 141–2, 171, 172
Berlin, Isaiah, 5
bio-power, vii, 16, 119–22, 173, 180
Body without Organs (also BwO), 16, 131, 144, 153–4, 157, 162
Butler, Judith, 93n.9

capitalism, vii, ix, 10, 11, 17, 54, 75, 116, 131, 133
   overturning capitalism, 1–7
   micropolitics, 169–83
   re-territorialisation, 156–62
care of the self, 124, 165; *see also* becoming a BwO
caress, 42–3, 68
Carnot, Nicolas Léonard Sadi, 141
Cartesian (also Descartes), 5, 60, 63, 76, 79, 81, 91
   anti-Cartesian, 56–7, 77–8, 80, 95, 99
   Cartesian myth, 135
causality, immanent, 86, 106–7, 139, 162–3
choice, 100, 133, 126, 152
   existential, 71
   human, 75
   Nietzschean, 164
   original, 39, 41, 49, 66
   radical, 41, 49, 55n.13
   sexual, 170
   situated, 50
class, 1, 2, 3, 40, 72, 74, 126
   transnational, 183
Cogito, 23, 27, 52, 61
   aborted, 137, 141
   body, 76
   Descartes, 167
   tacit, 78, 99–100, 143
commodification (also commodify), 164, 175, 177

Connolly, William, 11, 17n.3, 19n.14, 20n.16, 186n.4
consciousness, 15, 21, 26, 27–77, 83 92, 98–101, 105, 136–8, 158
  embodied, 85, 97
  field of, 22
  science of, 25
  synthetic, 24
consumerism, 175, 177
contingency, 33, 70, 74–7, 90, 91
contradiction, viii, 5, 151, 171, 181
creativity, 133, 180, 181

dark precursor, 14, 137, 140, 148, 153, 155, 164
death instinct (also death drive), 6, 141, 153, 184
democracy, 5, 76
depth, 48, 64, 65, 79, 84, 90, 132, 140–4, 172
Descartes, Rene, 57, 78, 166, 167n.11
desire, vii, ix, 3–17, 32, 30, 38, 41, 42, 48, 56, 64, 73, 74, 92, 96, 117, 119, 120–7, 132–8, 148, 150, 154, 160–6
desiring-machines, 132, 150–5, 161, 179, 182, 184, 187n.4
desiring-production, 151–5
deterritorialisation, 156, 182; see also territorialisation
detotalised (also detotality and detotalisation), 21, 24, 31, 33, 45–6, 52
dialectic (also dialectical), 3, 4, 9, 46, 47, 53, 100, 102, 121, 137, 159, 166n.7
  of consciousness, 138
  dialectic of self, 97
  dialectical materialism, viii
  of identity, 7
  look, the, 68
  Praxis, of, 21
difference, ix, 7, 9–11, 18–19, 73, 83, 88–9, 136, 138–9, 171–3, 179, 182, 184
  disjunctive, 102, 108, 127, 143, 144
  in-itself, 137, 141, 145, 148–9, 153 164–6, 168, 185
  negative, 12, 86
differenciation, 137, 154; see also differentiation
differential, 8, 9, 12, 13, 20, 81, 135, 138, 139, 143, 145, 151, 156
differentiation, 27, 84, 89, 92, 138, 153, 154, 163; see also differenciation
discourse, 3, 4, 16, 23, 45, 96, 100, 101, 107, 112–20, 129, 137, 160, 173, 174, 178, 192
discursive, 16, 96, 100–20, 113, 125, 127, 129, 131, 139, 156, 165, 166, 172–82
disjunctive synthesis, ix, 11–15, 95, 1–102, 107–37, 139, 140, 142–6, 152, 154, 164–5, 171–81, 186n.1; see also dispersion and fold
dispersion, logic of, 16, 96, 101–8, 123, 130, 138, 173

dispositif, 19n.13, 114, 121, 123; see also assemblage
double-conditioning, 16, 86, 96, 114–18, 123, 129, 133, 166, 171, 174, 180; see also causality, immanent
double-movement, 155
drive, 126, 137, 152–4, 161, 172, 184
dualism, 10, 28, 34, 43, 56, 58, 60–1, 79, 91, 134, 151
duration, 31, 33, 66, 72, 83, 84, 135, 136, 172

ego (also 'I'), 61–2, 66–8, 84, 90–1, 99, 98, 100, 101, 113, 118, 121–2, 135, 137, 141–5, 153–4, 162, 165, 157, 172–3, 179, 186
emancipation, 4, 6–7, 111, 166, 170, 183
emotion, 38, 42, 157
empiricism, 57–60, 149
  transcendental empiricism, 17, 131–3, 146–8, 154
Enlightenment, 107, 121, 128, 147
episteme, 95, 97–100
epoché, 24
essentialism, 127, 139, 176
eternal return, the, 139, 141, 142, 149, 172, 179
ethics, 49, 54, 67, 69, 96, 105–6, 109, 118–29, 132, 146, 148, 151, 162, 165, 182
Euclidean, 79, 81, 86, 89
  non–Euclidean, 12, 57, 84
European Union (EU), the, 161, 177
event, 9, 11, 32, 40, 48, 59, 39, 63, 66, 72, 103, 106, 119, 134, 140
existentialism, viii, 36, 55n.14, 75, 93n.5, 96
extensive, (also extensivity), 16, 32, 41, 42, 45, 72, 83–6, 94, 132, 134–43, 145, 169, 171
exteriority, (also exteriorisation), 47, 89, 92, 112, 119

facticity, 23, 29–32, 36, 41, 65, 69, 71, 78
fascism, 118, 165
fold, ix, 11, 17, 23, 39, 53, 56, 65, 80–92, 95–6, 102, 105–8, 114, 119–29, 132–51, 156, 159, 163–74, 180
for-itself, 7, 12, 15, 29–43, 63, 67, 69–70, 73, 92, 136, 141; see also in-itself
freedom, 16, 36, 41, 49–51, 68–71, 75–6, 109, 120–1, 124, 129, 131, 149, 162, 179
Freud, Sigmund, 38–9, 127, 131, 140, 150, 153, 155, 158, 166, 167n.14

Gauss, Carl Friedrich, 81, 142
Gaze, the, 64–8, 109–10, 116
genealogy, viii, 3, 14, 105–7, 115, 118–20, 125, 128–9, 173
Gestalt, 70–1, 78, 93n.6, 94n.8

God, 7, 145, 147, 159, 160
Gramsci, Antonio, 2, 17, 54, 179

Habermas, Jürgen, 93n.2, 130n.14
habit (also habitual), 40, 64–6, 70, 72, 90, 116, 125, 135, 140–1, 151, 156, 164
Hardt and Negri, 20n.16
Hegel, Georg Wilhelm Friedrich, 5, 7, 10–11, 13, 18, 44, 54, 68, 100, 134, 138, 144, 146, 157, 169
Heidegger, Martin (also Heideggerian), 3, 5, 23, 37, 38, 61, 94n.16, 100, 134, 143
humanism, 56, 90, 91, 118
Husserl, Edmund (also Husserlian), 14, 22–8, 33–6, 49, 54n.5, 61–2, 76, 93, 97, 99, 103–5, 133–6, 143

idealism, 5, 16, 36, 49, 71, 75, 123, 127, 133
identity, 1, 3, 6–7, 13, 15, 23, 24, 27, 31, 50–31, 90, 117, 119, 123, 130, 134–42, 149, 153–4, 165, 173, 175–6, 182–7
ideology (also ideological), 2, 3, 6, 18, 17, 54, 73, 111, 113, 159, 169
impersonal, 24, 44, 48, 72, 152
in-itself, 7, 12, 15, 29–30, 36–7, 41–3, 55, 63, 67, 69–71, 73, 92, 134–5, 137, 141, 144–5, 149, 168, 179, 182, 185; *see also* for-itself
incompossibility (also incompossible), 44, 136–7, 145
individual (also individuality), 1, 6, 12, 26–8, 37, 39–40, 46–8, 61, 74, 90, 102, 114–18, 126, 129, 135–7, 143–4, 152, 173, 178
intensive, 23, 41, 44, 72, 83–4, 87, 91, 91, 102, 106, 129, 138–9, 141–2, 144, 148, 150, 162–9, 171–82
intentionality, 14, 22, 27–8, 35, 61, 66, 92, 97–9
interiority (also interiorisation), 16, 23, 40, 47–8, 52, 54, 58, 84, 86, 89, 93, 96, 109, 119, 122, 123, 128–9, 131–3, 142, 156–7, 164, 173–4, 183

Kant, Immanuel (also Kantian), 4, 5, 6, 13, 25, 26, 34, 36, 53, 62, 71, 84, 95, 98–103, 125, 128–36, 166–7

Lacan, Jacques (also Lacanian), 5, 6, 7, 8, 18
lack, viii, 5–9, 19, 30–1, 49, 55, 91–5, 124–33, 157, 160–1, 167, 170, 177–8, 183
Laclau, Ernesto, ii, 6, 16–17
language, 6, 10–11, 14–15, 45, 53, 56–7, 63–7, 79, 91, 95–9, 144, 121–2, 127, 147, 159, 179
Lebenswelt (also life–world), 56–7, 60–3, 76–9, 95, 100
Leibniz, Gottfried, 142–3

liberation, 75, 101, 117, 120, 121, 176–7, 185
libidinal (also libido), vii, 3–4, 9, 16, 39, 126–7, 150, 152, 156–7, 161, 171, 178, 186
lived-experience, 24, 34, 38–45, 54–5, 64, 69, 79, 89, 97–9
logos, 57, 77, 99, 100
look, the, 36–7
love, x, 11, 18n.7, 38, 91, 126, 128n.5, 152, 165

macro (see micro), vii–viii, 10–11, 13, 16, 19, 24, 45, 47–8, 52, 76, 96, 114, 117, 119, 121–3, 131–3, 143, 151, 154, 160, 162–3, 166, 174, 176, 179, 180
manifold, 79–87, 171
Marx, Karl (also Marxism), ii–ix, 2–5, 21, 22, 44, 74–6, 90, 111, 126, 131, 150, 156, 169, 170
materialism, viii, 17, 44, 75, 107, 129
monad, 142–5, 167n.10
multiplicity, x, 8, 19, 32–3, 41, 45–7, 62, 83–4, 108–9, 113–14, 118, 120, 129, 131–2, 135, 137, 143, 145, 152, 169, 171–2

negativity (also negative), ix, 5, 7, 9, 11–13, 15, 18, 29, 37, 42–3, 49, 52–5, 69, 70, 86, 90–1, 105–6, 120, 126, 131, 144, 150, 159, 161, 165, 166, 169, 170–2
neurosis (also neurotic), 133, 140, 150, 153, 157, 161–2, 177, 183
Nietzsche, Friedrich Wilhelm, (also Nietzschean), viii, 14, 121, 138, 147–50, 154, 160, 167, 181
    eternal return, 137, 142
    force, 16, 92, 108, 138
    genealogy, 3, 129n.7, 100, 146, 173
    will to power, 127, 140, 149–50, 157–60
nihilation, 29, 32–3, 43, 135–6
nihilism, ix, x, 159–60
non-discursive, 104–5
nothingness, 11, 14, 21, 23, 29, 30–9, 41–6, 51, 54, 69, 135, 150

Oedipus complex, 155, 160–1, 178
ontogenesis, 16, 84, 148, 149
Other, the (also Otherness), 6, 9, 13, 15, 22, 23, 27–9, 44, 48, 52, 53, 56, 60, 62–8, 74, 109, 118, 132, 136, 144, 161, 178–9, 181, 184
outside, the, 5, 8, 9–13, 17, 23–8, 34–5, 41, 44, 46, 52, 53, 61–3, 68, 86, 95, 102, 105, 106, 114, 119, 122, 127, 132, 137, 140, 143–144, 147–9, 158, 159, 169, 171, 173–4

panopticism, 109, 116
partial objects, 152, 167n.13
perception, 35, 42, 58, 61, 62, 63–73, 76–9, 85–6, 90, 138, 143, 163

phantasy, 115, 140, 175
phenomenology, 15, 16, 22, 24–7, 36, 53, 56, 60–6, 70, 76–9, 85, 92, 95, 97, 98, 99–100
Plato, 5, 9, 10, 12, 51, 93n.3, 98–99, 104, 111, 134, 186n.1
pleasure, 43, 96, 121–7, 161, 167n.14
poststructuralism, ii, 3, 97
power, vii–ix, 1–4, 6–11, 16, 45, 56, 64, 66, 71, 75, 89, 91, 96, 106–9, 111–13, 114–18, 119, 120–6, 131, 133, 137, 161–6, 173–4, 179–81
power-knowledge, 96, 97, 99, 101, 103, 105, 107, 111–15, 117–19, 121, 164, 173
practico-inert, 47
praxis, 1, 17, 21, 41, 46–7, 52, 75, 78, 110, 124, 170–1
psychoanalysis, 3, 39, 54n.10, 123, 126–7, 150, 166n 2,
psychosis, 153

quality, 139, 142, 144, 159, 165
quantity, 80, 108

rationalism, 57, 59–60, 72, 78
Rawls, John, 4
reaction (also reactive), 11, 19, 20, 109–10, 115, 122, 124, 126–7, 139, 145–8, 150, 158–65, 177, 182, 184
realism, 52, 55
representationalism (also representation), 24, 27, 28, 32, 26, 53, 58, 61, 63, 66, 73, 84, 87, 89, 91, 98, 103, 111, 115, 118, 128, 133, 135
repression, 4, 8, 117–20, 126–9, 131, 133, 139, 150, 152, 155, 161, 165–6, 169, 173, 180, 183
resemblance, 59, 127, 133, 135, 140, 144
resistance, viii–ix, 7, 10, 13–15, 17, 20, 49, 52, 56, 69, 95–6, 105, 109–10, 113–14, 120–8, 131, 133, 164, 169–71, 179–82, 185
ressentiment, ix, 126, 133, 157–9, 161–2, 165, 177–8, 183
rhizome, 151, 186n.1
Riemann, Bernhard, 79–84, 86–7, 94, 142, 171

sedimentation (also sendimentation), 64–6, 72, 78, 93
segmentation (also segment), 8, 48, 107, 113, 155, 163, 173, 175, 183–4, 187n.4
sense, viii, 7, 9, 12, 14–15, 27–8, 37–41, 49, 52, 58–9, 66, 85–90, 101, 109, 111, 119, 124, 134–5, 144–5, 147–8, 157–8, 172, 175, 184–5
sexuality, 104, 113, 117–20, 125–9, 175, 180
simulacra, 15, 19, 41, 172, 186

situatedness (also situation), 3, 15, 21, 23, 34, 36, 39, 52, 44, 46, 50, 61, 65–7, 69, 71–5, 87, 90–1, 99, 119, 136, 176
social–production, 8, 40, 103, 132, 151, 152–7, 160, 164, 166, 174, 175–6, 180
social contract, 15, 22, 49, 50, 91, 178
social Darwinism, 113
social machines, 132, 151–6, 172, 173, 178–81,
space, 12, 14, 32, 41, 63–7, 73, 81–9, 97, 102, 139–43, 156, 175–80, 182, 184
spatium, 141, 145
Spinoza, Baruch, 7, 13, 29, 125, 148–50, 167
state, the, 107, 110–11, 117, 129n.11, 179, 186n.3
structuralism, 9
subject, the (also subjectivity), viii, 3–9, 17–18, 20, 23–4, 27, 36–7, 44–5, 49, 52, 57–8, 61, 67–8, 73–4, 77, 79, 88, 90, 92, 98, 106, 124, 133, 144, 146, 157, 170, 178
superego, 141, 165; *see also* ego

Taylor, Charles, 18n.5, 55n.13, 130n.14
temporality, 29–32, 43, 45–6, 54, 83, 136
territorialisation (*also* re-territorialisation), 126, 155–7, 164, 178, 181, 182
time, 29–35, 43, 50–7, 62–5, 72, 75, 79, 82–5, 94, 98, 100–2, 134–43, 152–3, 158, 172, 179
totalisation, 21, 24, 32, 36, 45–52, 61, 166; *see also* detotalisation
transcendence, 5, 8, 11, 14, 15, 21–6, 32–6, 53, 56–7, 60, 62, 79, 95, 98–9, 111, 146, 147, 182
transcendental, the, 7, 14, 17, 22, 24, 26, 28, 33–6, 49, 61–2, 68, 84, 92, 97, 98, 100–1, 106, 128, 131–7, 146–8, 166–7

unconscious, the (also unconsciousness), ix, 3–4, 7–8, 11, 33, 54, 64, 73, 83, 86, 109, 115, 126–9, 134–5, 137–8, 140, 141, 143, 150–1, 154, 158, 165, 167, 169, 170, 172–5, 182, 185
univocity, 9, 12, 19, 22, 43, 70, 132, 134, 145–6, 151

vice-diction, 45, 108, 138, 141, 171; *see also* contradiction
virtual, ix, 8–11, 16, 23, 30, 32–3, 41, 45–8, 64–7, 83–7, 90–2, 96, 106, 109, 110, 118–19, 131–54, 164–9, 172–4, 179, 182, 185, 187; *see also* actual

Weber, Max, 75–6, 90
Widder, Nathan, 17n.3, 20n.16, 94n.12, 102, 128n.1, 166n.6, 186n.1

Žižek, Slajov, 5–6, 8–9, 16–20, 129, 131, 146, 166, 170

EU representative:
Easy Access System Europe
Mustamäe tee 50, 10621 Tallinn, Estonia
Gpsr.requests@easproject.com

www.ingramcontent.com/pod-product-compliance
Lightning Source LLC
Chambersburg PA
CBHW051117230426
43667CB00014B/2614